EVERY THING IS FINE

EVERY THING IS FINE

— A Memoir —

VINCE GRANATA

ATRIA BOOKS

New York London Toronto Sydney New Delhi

An Imprint of Simon & Schuster, Inc.
1230 Avenue of the Americas
New York, NY 10020

First Atria Books hardcover edition April 2021

ATRIA B O O K S and colophon are trademarks of Simon & Schuster, Inc.

For information about special discounts for bulk purchases, please contact
Simon & Schuster Special Sales at 1-866-506-1949
or business@simonandschuster.com.

The Simon & Schuster Speakers Bureau can bring authors to your live event. For
more information or to book an event, contact the Simon & Schuster Speakers Bureau
at 1-866-248-3049 or visit our website at www.simonspeakers.com.

Interior design by Jill Putorti

Manufactured in the United States of America

1 3 5 7 9 10 8 6 4 2

Library of Congress Cataloging-in-Publication Data

Names: Granata, Vince, author.
Title: Everything is fine : a memoir / Vince Granata.
Description: First edition. | New York, NY : Atria Books, 2021. |
Identifiers: LCCN 2020039378 (print) | LCCN 2020039379 (ebook) |
ISBN 9781982133443 (hardcover) | ISBN 9781982133450 (paperback) |
ISBN 9781982133467 (ebook)
Subjects: LCSH: Parricide—United States. | Schizophrenics—
Family relationships—United States.
Classification: LCC HV6542 .G73 2021 (print) | LCC HV6542 (ebook) |
DDC 364.152/3092 [B]—dc23
LC record available at https://lccn.loc.gov/2020039378
LC ebook record available at https://lccn.loc.gov/2020039379

ISBN 978-1-9821-3344-3
ISBN 978-1-9821-3346-7 (ebook)

For Mom

PROLOGUE

I remember the first time I wrote my brother's name. I was four and a half, standing on our driveway next to where the gutter spilled rainwater off our garage. In chalk, I wrote his whole name, TIMOTHY.

I wrote all of their names, my new siblings, CHRISTOPHER, TIMOTHY, ELIZABETH, triplets, etched in birth order. I was eager to show off, my whole fist around the chalk, scraping my knuckles when I thickened each letter. When I was done with their names, I held a chalk pebble, a handful of red dust. I needed a new piece to finish my message.

WELCOME HOME MOMMY.

They were coming home for the first time, my new siblings, our family now doubled in size. I waited, perched on our suburban driveway in Orange, Connecticut, until I spotted my father's Oldsmobile. He stopped in front of my mural, a bassinette fastened next to him on the passenger side. Through the windshield, I saw my mother, still in her blue-and-white nightgown, between two bassinettes braced in the back seat.

I remember the nested bassinettes, my bundled siblings in their hospital caps, caps too big for their infant faces, covering their ears, grazing their eyelids. I remember how they each blinked, in the sun for the first time.

I don't remember running down the driveway, sticking my head into my father's open window, declaring, *This is the best day of my life.*

I know I must have said it. My parents always included that part of the story, used my words like a punch line, the cornerstone to our foundation myth.

I believe that I said it. I was happy, happy enough to mash my chalk into the driveway, happy for siblings after more than four years of pushing Tonka trunks alone on the family room floor.

Tim's bassinette was the one in the front seat. I've seen him there in our pictures. In those pictures, Tim's black hair sticks out beneath his blue cap, his skin more olive than that of his siblings. In one of those pictures, our mother holds him, standing next to me on the driveway. Tim is a bundle the length of her forearm.

I was twenty-seven when Tim killed our mother. He attacked her while she was sifting through used-jewelry listings on eBay. Tim's demons, electric in his ill mind, convinced him that the woman who had made him peanut butter sandwiches when he was a grass-stained child was the source of his constant pain. These delusions, schizophrenia's unchecked crescendo, raged in his head, a rising tide flooding him in madness. After he killed her, he dialed 911, sitting on our front steps, clutching a white Bible.

I was a thousand miles away. I sat, knees wedged under a class-room table, across from a girl named Yamilet. We were reading a Spanish translation of *Oh, the Places You'll Go!* I helped her blend syllables into words—*por-que, ver-dad, os-cur-as*—while she marveled at Dr. Seuss's neon world. She wore a bracelet around one of her slender wrists, LIBERTAD sewn into the black strands, the name of her Dominican village, a collection of stucco houses pressed up against Autopista Duarte, sixty miles from the Haitian border.

My mother was dead for two hours before I knew. She was dead while I labored in Spanish, tried to answer Yamilet's questions—*¿Que significa "inexplorado"?* While we read, Yamilet and I drank water from little sealed bags—*fundas*—to combat the heat. To open the *fundas*, we used our teeth, gnawing at the corners of the plastic.

My phone was off. It had been off for most of the past three weeks. Jon, my childhood friend who ran this summer program, approached our table as Yamilet and I finished the story.

"It's your dad," he said.

"Momentito," I said to Yamilet. She was still looking at the book, running her hands over its last illustration, a child moving a Technicolor mountain.

Jon handed me his phone, but when I brought it to my ear I couldn't hear my father over the children sounding out words in the classroom.

"Dad?" I reached the sliding door. "Dad?"

Outside, sun-seared, I walked toward a shaded alley. Some of the younger children clustered near the classroom, kicking up dust while they chased each other. They called out, "Bince, Bince," the *B* sound easier for the kids to pronounce. When I ducked into the alley, I heard my father's voice.

"Vince?"

My back felt slick against the metal wall outside the classroom.

"Vince?"

In the alley, I asked him, raising my voice, "Are you okay?"

He only needed four syllables.

"No. Tim killed Mom."

The neighboring house dissolved. My father's voice disappeared. Our connection evaporated between the mountains bounding the Cibao Valley. I still listened, my lips rounding in an O, but the *no no no* stayed in my throat, a strangled airless silence. I fell. The gravel in the alley stuck to the backs of my legs.

Juancito found me, the phone still at my ear. He was in his teens and helped us organize games with the kids. That morning he had helped gather spoons for egg-and-spoon relays.

I formed a sentence. With Spanish, I needed a moment to hear the words in my head. Before it was ever a fully formed English thought, my mother's death was a Spanish phrase, assembled one word at a time. Mother, *madre*, died, *murió*.

"Mi madre murió."

I knew how much *murió* didn't say.

On the ground, my body caught up, responded, first just shivering, chin against my drenched collar. Then in waves, wet skin vibrating—cold somehow—then a bigger shaking, a throbbing—now hot, too hot—then retching, platanos and beans a brown paste on my leg.

Jon found me. He and Juancito each grabbed one of my arms, pulled me toward the classroom. Juancito ordered the kids outside. They bobbed past me, filed out into the sun.

Juancito handed me a *funda*. I bit and tore and forgot to breathe. I tried to squeeze water onto my sticky leg. I held the empty *funda*, a plastic carcass dripping in my hand, while Juancito opened another, squirted at the dirt and vomit caked to my shin.

Jon's phone rang, my father calling back with Chris and Lizzie. We said mostly *I love you*, speaking in a high wheeze.

After ninety minutes on dry, cracked roads, I reached the Santiago airport. In the bathroom with an internet signal, standing over a urinal, I opened Facebook. I saw it without scrolling—*Suggested Video, Timothy Granata Killed Mother Claudia Granata in Orange.* One of my cousins was arguing with online commenters beneath the article. Someone had posted, *Ban white boys with guns and mommy issues.* My cousin responded with a paragraph. I stopped reading at the word *knives.*

This was my first detail.

The plane took off an hour late, flew through a storm. The in-flight entertainment stalled, gray lines freezing in jagged tears across my screen. I watched the lightning instead, the flashes only seconds apart.

My father, Chris, and Lizzie were standing outside of the hotel when I arrived. It would take two days for us to be able to reenter our house, a crime scene. I cried when I saw my sister. She stood between Chris and our father, her head resting on Chris's shoulder, hands gripping his left arm.

The next afternoon, after the police finished their work at our house, five men arrived in two Ford Sprinter vans. AFTERMATH, their company's name, was emblazoned on the van's sliding doors. In hazmat suits, they worked for twelve hours, cleaning through the night, sanitizing wood panels on our family room floor, bleaching the walls next to where we used to stack our photo albums.

In the morning, after they finished, we drove to our house from the hotel. We stopped before the driveway, the gentle slope where I had written my brother's name twenty-three years before. A strand of police tape blocked our path. The yellow tape, strung between our mailbox and a telephone pole, grazed the pavement, sagging like a long finish line.

*   *   *

I started writing about my brother, about my mother, about my family, because I was exhausted from trying to hide. I had been terrified of my pain, a pain I hid in a silo, a secret I feared might detonate.

When I started writing—in fragments, in halting sentences—I began to recognize a piece of what had terrified me. All of my memories felt tainted. My mother's death shrouded the past, even the most innocent moments—Tim, a blanketed infant on our mother's lap, reaching for her glasses, each lens the size of one of his hands. Even that memory, a single image, would catalyze a reactive chain, lead me to their final moments together, to our mother's body on the family room floor.

Now, when I think about the months, the year, after Tim killed our mother, I recognize how I tried to hide, how I avoided my memories so that I could drive to work, cook dinner, mimic smiles with friends. I didn't try to write about the illness that roiled in my brother's head. I didn't try to write about why all my mother's attempts to save him had failed. I stopped myself from looking at my family's story.

But avoidance fractured me further, stripped me away from myself, from all of my memories, until it felt like there was little left of me. Eventually, I had no choice but to look at loss and pain, at all the pieces of my family's story that I didn't think I could ever understand.

It was this process, recognizing the pieces, struggling to put them in order, that almost destroyed me.

It's also what allowed me to live again.

1

I avoided the details of my mother's last day until more than a year
after her death. Though I had wrapped myself in fantasies about
how I could have prevented tragedy, how I could have intervened if
I hadn't been a thousand miles away, I didn't weigh that actual day
until my hand was forced, until facts cascaded at Tim's trial, a narrative of catastrophe rendered in precise courtroom detail.

After the trial, I read copies of the defense reports, the documents
two psychiatrists prepared for the court. The reports—each a dense
fifty pages—evaluated Tim, tried to reconstruct his mind. They began
with tables of contents—"Family and Developmental Narrative," "Days
Leading Up to the Event," "Timothy Granata's Account of the Event."

This was their purpose, to build "the event," to explain "the event."

The psychiatrists assembled many collateral sources—police
reports, interviews with Tim's former doctors, interviews with family. But their most extensive information came from Tim. Through
a dozen interviews, they inventoried his life, his memory of the day
he killed our mother.

During early interviews, Tim's memory was fractured. Psychotic amnesia conspired with trauma to make him forget that day, to forget that he had attacked our mother. During the first interview, Tim sat in a cage, bars separating him from his questioners. When they asked where he was, Tim said, "My college library."

Over months, medication worked to lift schizophrenia's haze. Slowly, his memory returned, first in painful flashes, then in a continuous narrative. During his last interviews, Tim could tolerate three hours of questions, offer his own account of his mind.

But even then, nearly a year after our mother's death, Tim still believed his delusions, saw his persecutors as real demons, not psychotic episodes.

It would be a long time before Tim could start using clinical language to describe his symptoms—delusions, psychosis, schizophrenia. It would be a long time before he realized how thoroughly his illness had mangled his world.

I spoke to him during this period, visited him at the facility where he awaited trial. He was slow to talk about his memories, to show me the pain of remembering. But eventually, he would speak to me, corroborate what he had explained to his evaluators. Eventually, we found our way back to what we both could remember.

But first, I need to show you that day, *the event*. To show you the terror of Tim's disease, I have to show you the horror it wrought.

I know how describing this day might color Tim.

But I need you to see him there, see how unchecked disease swallowed him, so I can show you the boy he was before, so that I can show you how we've lived in the aftermath.

I know how the morning went.

I know my mother, Chris, and Lizzie sat around the kitchen table, ate cups of yogurt over our stained place mats, the ones featuring pictures of the presidents. The three of them sat next to the refrigerator, our family bulletin board, the place we posted the number for Michelangelo's Pizza, pictures of our dogs, a newspaper clipping— Tim winning a wrestling tournament. Name magnets, the kind we'd found in tourist shops during childhood trips, fastened these items to the fridge. Our names were stuck in clusters—Chris, Tim, Lizzie, Vince—beneath plastic Statues of Liberty, Maine lobsters.

Chris and Lizzie had moved home after graduating from college. Just that morning Chris had interviewed with a tutoring company over Skype. I know our mother would have told him to wear a nice shirt.

"They'll be able to see your collar," she would have said.

While the three of them ate breakfast, Tim remained in his bedroom, curtains drawn to blot out the sun. He hadn't seen daylight in weeks.

In the months since his discharge from a psychiatric hospital, Tim had grown entirely nocturnal. He spent his nights lifting weights in the basement, his dumbbells piercing stagnant air. My family grew used to the thuds of his dropped weights. The metallic echoes became the white noise of their sleep.

When Tim finished lifting—his sessions lasting hours—he would hang from his feet on an inversion table to alleviate back pain, lingering aches from injuries sustained as a collegiate heavyweight wrestler. Inverted, motionless, he listened to his audiobook of the Old Testament or to Gregorian chants that pacified the demons vying to control his thoughts.

That morning, Tim didn't fall asleep at dawn. Later, he explained that he felt mounting pressure as the sun rose, a throbbing in his head while he retreated from the basement to his second-floor bedroom.

"I felt doom. Something was breaking."

To combat the breaking, Tim returned to the basement, to his weights, to the ways he tried to quiet his world. I know he stopped for water on his way to the basement, entered the kitchen, where our mother was lingering with Chris.

I don't know what she thought when she saw Tim, this break in his nocturnal rhythm marking the first time in weeks she'd seen him in the morning.

Tim's greasy hair fell in strands over light scars on his forehead. These scars, badges he carried from his wrestling days, were a remnant of a form of the herpes virus he'd contracted from wrestling mats. Open sores on his opponents' bodies had oozed onto these mats, infecting cuts, spreading the skin-borne disease, *Herpes gladiatorum.* This is common among wrestlers, and Tim's sores didn't frequently flare, but his face remained lightly pockmarked, as though the imprint of his opponents' blows had fossilized on his forehead.

When Tim looked at Chris, he felt the mounting doom subside.

"I thought Chris was blocking the evil," Tim remembered later. "If he left, the channel would be open. I would be killed."

As Tim stood in the kitchen, filling a plastic cup at the sink, he told Chris and our mother that he was afraid.

"If it looks like I killed myself," Tim said, "it was the devil that did it."

This pressured speech was not new. Tim's ranting had been relentless in the previous weeks, thoughts rushing from his mouth like he had been holding his breath for a long time.

I won't take the medication, the medication destroys me, takes my mind, takes me away from God from salvation perverts my thoughts lets evil win.

Our mother asked Tim what he meant when he said the devil was going to kill him.

"Something bad is going to happen," Tim said. "They are going to come for me. If something looks like a suicide, just know that I love you."

Tim had spoken about suicide. He had told our mother several times that he planned to drive his car into the wall of a tunnel bisecting a mountain near our house, but didn't mention any specific plans that morning.

With his water, Tim left the kitchen.

My mother and Chris sat in the wake of these words. Though the words had familiar themes—suicide, religion, paranoia—something seemed more urgent. I don't know what my mother feared then— Tim, awake in the sunlight, afraid of the devil.

I know that she called my father at work, that she told him what Tim had said—*kill myself, the devil that did it.* They agreed to call Dr. Robertson, the psychiatrist Tim had seen a handful of times since his hospital discharge.

But when my mother called Dr. Robertson, he wasn't available. She left a message asking him what she should do.

Chris sat with her while she made these calls, delaying his plans, a trip to Maine with friends. He was about to meet his friend Peter at the train station, but told our mother that he'd talk to Tim before he left.

Tim was quiet when Chris descended the basement stairs. Chris could smell him, the sweat-stained T-shirt Tim wore during his nightly lifts. Tim's collar looked wet, limp beneath the hairs darkening his neck. Even in the July heat, Tim wore sweatpants, elastic cuffs stopping before his ankles, revealing patches of hairy skin.

Chris told Tim that he was leaving soon, that he wanted, more than anything, to know that he would see Tim when he returned.

"I love you best," Tim said.

"See you Monday?" Chris asked.

"Yeah." Tim's reply was muffled, his chin tucked toward his chest. Chris hugged him, felt dampness on his brother's broad back.

Our mother was still at the kitchen table when Chris found her and told her what Tim had said.

"I don't have to go," Chris told her. "I can stay with you."

Our mother told Chris to leave.

Lizzie also had plans for the day. Earlier that week, a charter school in Boston had hired her to teach. That morning during breakfast, she had reminded our mother that she needed "grown-up clothes." Lizzie feared that her soft features, clear eyes, the pink in her cheeks, made her look like she was still a kid.

When Lizzie asked our mother to go shopping, our mother told Lizzie that she needed to stay at home with Tim, that she had been talking to our father about some of Tim's thoughts. She didn't elaborate.

I know that she wouldn't have wanted Lizzie to be scared.

She told Lizzie to go shopping without her.

Tim returned to his room after Chris and Lizzie left. I know that he sealed himself behind his locked door, sat at his computer.

"I needed to contact the forces," Tim remembered later. "That was entertainment for them."

To contact "the forces," his demons, Tim typed into the Google search bar like it was a medium. He had a conversation with his madness.

I'm sorry ill stop now
I'll act like a man now
please don't kill me
I know killing me would be a joke for you
I'll stop disrespecting you
Just please don't hurt my family or I

Tim was hearing voices, but not in the classic sense. Auditory hallucination is too simplistic, too Hollywood a conception of schizophrenia to explain what Tim experienced at his computer. To Tim, these messages felt more like discoveries, ideas in his head that he knew he hadn't put there. These found thoughts convinced him that some "other" had infiltrated his mind—the "other," his demons. He felt these demons question him, demean him.

What's wrong with you? What's wrong with you? You're cursed by God.

His Google searches were answers, promises to his demons.

I am going to be mature now
I'll stop supplicating now.
I know I live only because it is your will.
this is good for me
I need to be put in my place
please don't kill me

Tim spoke with his executioner, terrified, alone in his room, next to the desk where he used to paint tiny models of alien elves.

how does the world treat strangers historically

I know he felt this way, like a stranger, unable to recognize himself, inundated with foreign thoughts. Tim typed *how does the world treat strangers historically* fourteen more times.

I don't know what thoughts were Tim's as he hit return those fourteen times. I don't know if he was wondering, *Why am I suffering? Why am I in pain?*

I know that he must have made a connection, that he must have found the thought his demons wanted him to hear. He typed one last search, entered it twice.

domineering women
domineering women

My parents spoke once more that morning while Tim was in his room. My father had reached Dr. Robertson, told him that Tim feared that the devil would kill him, that Chris was scared that he would never see his brother again.

Dr. Robertson told my father that Tim's words might be an unconscious cry for help. Tim might need to return to the hospital. Our mother might need to call the police.

I know that this was one of my mother's greatest fears. She was terrified of what Tim might do, barricaded in his room while police battered his door.

"Tim cannot be left alone," Dr. Robertson told my father.

"Of course," my father said. "Claudia is with him and won't let him out of her sight."

"I couldn't hold back the force. The portal was open."

Tim remembers finding our mother in the kitchen. She asked him if he was hungry.

"She was kind."

Tim remembers peeling a banana.

While he stood at the counter, Tim told our mother that things were going to be fine.

My father still has this text message from our mother, her last.

T said 'things are going to be fine.' He ate fruit?! No mention of what he said b4.

Tim left the kitchen for the family room. He sat at our shared computer to search for some weight-lifting equipment. He called for our mother, and she stood behind him at the computer so he could show her something he wanted to buy.

I know that our mother stood close enough for Tim to smell her, the subtle perfume that she wore. Tim remembered this later, how her perfume overwhelmed him.

"It was then. It was her scent."

Our mother's scent twisted in Tim's nostrils, enveloped him, made him choke. Tim's illness amplified the scent—smell not being immune to schizophrenia's power—transforming it into something sexual, feminine, a veiled threat: *domineering women, domineering women.*

"I felt her voice change," Tim remembered later. "I thought, 'Could she intend to rape me?'"

I know this fear drove Tim to the basement, his sanctuary. He used his weights to strain his muscles, to make them scream louder than the demons in his head. He grabbed some of his heaviest dumbbells, performed lunges, deep knee bends that drew his thighs parallel to the floor. He sank toward the floor, the dumbbells sending tension surging through his forearms, his thighs burning.

While he tried to quiet the demons, his hip cramped. He fell to the carpet. His heartbeat slowed.

"Stretching out the cramp, I had an epiphany."

I don't know why it happened there, on the basement floor, his hip pulsing in pain.

"I remembered a friend from middle school football. He had told me, 'Your mother is very nice, very nice.'"

I know that this is how it started, his illness seizing control—*very nice, very nice.*

"I knew then that my mother had raped him."

Tim felt the boy blur, become him, become Tim, become swept up in the demonic chorus in his brain.

She raped you too.

"I found the duct tape because I didn't want her to get away. She had to confess."

I don't know if my mother heard his heavy feet on the stairs.

When Tim found her, she was browsing used-jewelry listings on eBay.

I don't know what she thought when she saw the duct tape.

Tim stood next to where she sat at the computer, their positions reversed from when he smelled her perfume. Tim shook, veins throbbing in rivulets on his forearms.

"I ordered her to her knees."

I know that he had never laid an angry hand on her. I know that she'd hugged him, recently, and he never shoved her away, never shucked her body from his.

"I told her that she needed to stay, that she needed to be confronted."

Tim made her kneel in front of the crate where one of our dogs slept. She faced him and he needed to walk behind her to pin her wrists to her back. He squeezed her hands together, wrapping the tape around her wrists, pulling each strip taut.

"I remember that she told me, 'Tim it hurts.'"

These are the only words Tim remembers her saying. *Tim, it hurts.*

"I wasn't going to kill her. I wanted her to admit that she raped me."

As he wrapped her hands with tape, Tim believed that he could feel our mother's thoughts, like their heads had become permeable.

You were raped as a child.

"I felt that thought. I heard laughter."

The laughter felt foreign, strange, but then Tim recognized our mother's voice, her laughter flooding the space around *You were raped as a child. You were raped as a child.*

"Then I heard it, 'You have to kill her. She is raping you.'"

I know Tim felt this rape, a full-body shudder, his brain twisting inside his skull. I know he sensed *She's coming for you* first as an implanted thought, then, audibly, *She's coming for you.*

In that moment, Tim felt the entire world enter his head.

I know that Tim pulled a standing lamp to the ground. The bulb shattered. I know he pushed our mother to the floor. Her cheek crashed into the wood, her first bruise.

"I didn't want her to suffer."

I know that Tim went to the kitchen, found two serrated knives. I know he went to the basement, chose two of his sledgehammers. He had used these sledgehammers to build strength in his forearms, lifting them by the base of their handles, his arm a stiff line from shoulder to fingertips.

I don't know how he carried two sledgehammers and two knives at the same time.

While he was out of the room, our mother tried to crawl away. I know that she used the phone.

I don't know how she did this with her hands bound behind her back. I don't know if she knocked the phone off the receiver, or grabbed its handle in her mouth. I don't know if she dialed with her nose, or her tongue, or somehow stood and dialed behind her back.

My father received the call at one forty. He was in a meeting, but when he saw *Home* on his phone, he left the conference room.

"Claudia? Claudia?" he said. "Tim?"

He called back but heard only a droning *beep beep beep.*

I don't know why my mother didn't dial 911—four digits shorter, response guaranteed.

I've imagined her calling 911. I don't know if this would have saved her life, but I know that it hurts to wish that she did something that she didn't do.

I think she knew when she made that call, knew that her life was in danger. I think she knew that Tim was not Tim, that her son had vanished.

I think she knew and wanted to hear my father's voice.

Tim found her by the phone.

"She had tried to wriggle away."

I know that he described it this way, that he used this word with his psychiatrists, *wriggle*.

I know that Tim brought her back to the spot next to the computer, the spot where he had smelled her perfume.

I remember my mother's perfume, how it smelled like citrus, like the lingering scent of orange peel on my fingertips.

I know that Tim turned over a coffee table, snapped one of its legs, spilled a board game Lizzie had left behind.

And I know this—I know all this—because police reports smother with details: lists, details, endless details.

Detailed, but detached.

"Claudia Granata sustained blunt and sharp trauma to the head, neck, torso, and extremities."

Sustained, a long period without interruption.

Sustained, endured without giving way.

Sustained, like my mother absorbed Tim's blows, gathered them to herself.

Coroners also speak in details, in bulleted lists, my mother's wounds like notes taken during a lecture. At Tim's trial, when the coroner read his report, he elaborated, explained—yes, explained—how the burst blood vessels in my mother's eyes were caused by Tim's hands around her neck.

And I can remember how Tim insisted, later, "I didn't want her to suffer." I can remember at his trial, how one of the psychiatrists said, "He wouldn't have wanted her to suffer."

But I remember that she phrased it this way—*wouldn't have wanted her to suffer*—like it was the first half of a thought, a conditional clause leading to a *but*.

But Tim was not in control. I know that Tim was not in control.

This is where I arrive, every time I reconstruct this scene, every time I imagine the spot where he wrapped duct tape around her wrists, the spot where she told him, "Tim, it hurts."

I think this too.

Tim, it hurts.

If I plotted their history on our family room floor, the spot where he left her would hold hundreds of moments the two of them shared. This is where she slipped Velcro shoes onto his feet, unfolded a Monopoly board by his side, slid him a package of candy canes on Christmas mornings.

This is the spot where she watched him take his first steps. Here, he walked for the first time in a cushioned nursery, a playpen she partitioned with Fisher-Price gates, one of the many safe worlds she made for him.

2

When Tim was born, he barely cried. He was quieter than Chris, who had screamed until Tim joined him, like arriving ahead of his siblings was terrifying.

"We knew Chris's vocal cords worked," my mother used to tell me. She told this story often, the one about the day they were born.

"I couldn't hold Chris right away," she would say. "I couldn't hold him because I had more work to do." She laughed when she said this, *work*, the labor of bearing Tim and Lizzie.

She told me how my father held Chris and Tim, how the three of them watched Lizzie's birth.

"So calm," my mother remembered. "Lizzie was silent, didn't make a sound."

"You know, your father and I met at that hospital," she always reminded me.

A bee sting brought my parents together.

In 1983, a police officer directing traffic in Hamden, Connecticut, was stung by a bee. He collapsed in anaphylactic shock and was rushed to the Yale New Haven ER. My father, a doctor at the hospital, saved his life, coaxing his heartbeat to return with a defibrillator. For several days, the officer remained in the hospital, as my mother, an attending physician, monitored his recovery.

Several weeks later, to complete his discharge paperwork, they each went to the medical school library to consult literature on bee sting–induced shock. In search of the same journal, they arrived at the library at the same time.

I never once heard them agree on who spoke first.

At birth, Chris and Tim experienced slight respiratory distress, a condition common in multiples. Tim also had uncomplicated jaundice, his infant liver struggling to filter harmless yellow pigment from his bloodstream.

Because of these minor complications, I met my brothers through a glass pane. I stood outside of the intensive care nursery while my father held each of them in a window, one of his hands as large as each of their torsos.

After three days, Chris and Tim joined Lizzie and our mother. When I visited them, together for the first time, our mother had tilted her bed upright so they could lie against her stomach, three squirming bodies she could tuck into her lap.

During the month before their birth, my mother had stayed in bed, the weight of three too much to support on two feet. Earlier in the pregnancy, my father had installed a chairlift along the left side of our staircase. At four, I looked with awe at this machinery, the chair ascending its metal track as enthralling as a carnival ride.

Even though I was used to seeing my mother in bed, wrapped in a floral comforter, eating Rocky Road ice cream, there was something different when I saw her in the hospital room. She wasn't wearing glasses and I could see all of the flushed skin on her cheeks and around her eyes. I had only seen her without glasses in pictures, in the framed photo from my parents' wedding on a living room window-sill. She didn't look like my mother in that picture—hair too long, lips too red, eyes too dark. I remember her looking that way while she rested with my infant siblings, younger maybe, even though she was wearing a hospital gown.

Born alone, four and a half years earlier, I spent my first years with only my parents for company. I didn't know until later that my parents had wanted a shorter gap between their children, that they had tried, before Chris, Tim, and Lizzie, to ensure that I wasn't an only child.

I learned about their struggle to have more children on a long summer afternoon—I was ten, maybe eleven. My mother knocked on my bedroom door, interrupting me while I devoured a Redwall fantasy novel. For much of that summer I buried myself in the Red-wall series, preferring the medieval combat of woodland creatures to games of sharks and minnows in the local pool.

My mother was also a voracious reader. I can't remember a single childhood beach trip when some novel didn't shade her face. Her stacks of books, teetering beneath the packed bookcase in my par-ents' bedroom, would become my library. As a child, I read till my eyes ached. I read so that someday I would need thick glasses like my mother, glasses I would cradle like a trophy.

That afternoon, she sat on my bed, on top of my comforter fea-turing the caps of all thirty Major League Baseball teams. When she spoke to me, her eyes narrowed behind her glasses like she was aim-ing her pupils directly at mine.

I was still a year or two away from my father's puberty speech, delivered to me in the guest room with a physician's anatomical pre-cision. The only part of his lecture that I remember is his concluding joke, *Now remember, Vince, there's a vas deferens between the male and female genitalia.*

That afternoon, sitting with my mother, I asked her if our family would stay this size. I told her about my fantasy books, how many of the heroes came from sprawling families, had dozens of siblings. I asked her if she and my father had always planned to have four kids.

She told me that two years before Chris, Tim, and Lizzie's birth, she had miscarried twins.

"Why don't I remember that?" I said.

"You were barely two years old."

I cried. Crying, then, wasn't rare for me. In those prepubescent years, shameful tears accompanied moments when I felt that I had failed, when I struck out during a Little League baseball game or lost a new jacket on the recess field. I'm not sure why I was such a tightly wound ten-year-old, why I sometimes felt an uncontrollable welling that I had to bury in my baseball cap.

The crying stopped on the eve of my teens, as though I had learned to steel myself against what had been minor misfortunes. But I remember my tears, how crying made me feel like a wimp, how I felt weak crying in my father's car after missing free throws during an elementary school basketball game.

But those tears, the ones I cried after my mother told me about the miscarried twins, were different. Those tears felt like loss, experienced for the first time, a helpless feeling, an awareness of absence.

"But Vince," my mother said, "it was a blessing. We have three now instead of two."

She called them a miracle. She explained to me, while I looked toward the creased book in my lap, that though I had been conceived "the natural way," my parents had encountered difficulty having more children.

She told me that Chris, Tim, and Lizzie were born because of something called *in vitro fertilization*. She never shied away from exact language, always used the technical terms—*egg, sperm, embryo*. Sperm plus egg equals embryo, I learned that afternoon, though the words had no literal meaning.

During in vitro fertilization, my mother explained, sperm met egg in a laboratory dish, a test tube. My young mind spawned science-fiction scenes, babies sprouting from tubes in dimly lit laboratories.

"But how did they come *from* you?" I asked.

She smiled. "They implanted the embryos into my uterus to grow."

I heard *plant* and *grow* like my siblings were the basil plants my father watered behind our house.

"Did you choose to have three?" I had stopped sniffling. Too much had changed about my world.

"They implanted three," she said, "and we were lucky that they all stayed healthy."

"If they had been twins, which two would they have been?" I thought of it this way, as if any embryo implanted in my mother had to come out as Chris, Tim, or Lizzie.

She laughed and took the Kleenex from my lap, crumpled and damp with my tears.

I didn't know, at ten, that IVF is difficult, uncertain, rife with heartache. The miscarriage of the twins, also conceived through IVF, must have devastated my parents, left them uncertain about whether they could have more children.

While she was pregnant with Chris, Tim, and Lizzie, my mother must have been terrified. She must have been afraid while I watched her ride that chairlift, afraid that this pregnancy might also fail.

But they were born. They survived.

I think about the miscarried twins now, when I'm alone, when all

I have for company is *what if what if what if.* What would have happened if there had been only two blanketed infants against my mother's stomach? Would illness lie dormant in one? Would one be born with a long coiled fuse, a fuse that would wait twenty years to ignite?

I hate these thoughts, their winding paths, the way this alternate reality eliminates three people I love.

But Tim's birth also means her death. It means her pain, my pain, his pain.

And when Tim was born, when he was handed to my father, a slick six pounds of flesh, my mother smiled at the tiny feet of her third son, at the life she had fought so hard to give him.

Chris, Tim, and Lizzie were intrepid crawlers, their curiosity quickly outgrowing the playpen my mother lined with blankets in the family room. They needed a bigger world, so my mother declared that the living room—a space for assembling visiting grandparents—would be transformed. My father sheathed the furniture in plastic, storing the chairs and varnished end tables in the basement.

The piano was too unwieldy to move, but its sharp corners were treacherous, wooden edges the perfect height to gash toddler foreheads. A few years earlier, I had collided with a changing table while running at a canter like a disoriented drunk.

To prevent future stitches, my father wrapped the piano in pink foam board. The foam was the same pink color as the insulation cushioning the metal ducts in our attic, the secret space my father showed me through a loft ladder he conjured on the ceiling of my mother's closet.

Sealing the piano was a sacrifice for my father. To my young ear, he was a virtuoso, a musical magician. When he played, I stood behind him, my chin just above his shoulder. I remember thinking that the keys looked like a long, smiling mouth, so much cleaner than their worn wooden frame. Before he'd start playing, I would look down toward his feet, hovering over pedals that looked to me like tarnished blown-up pennies.

My favorite song, the one I always asked him to play, was "Malagueña." I couldn't pronounce the ñ or much of the title, so whenever I requested the song, I always said *Mal-uh-gain-yuh*.

The piece starts with a deliberate rhythm, almost like a march. To mimic its pace, I would shuffle my feet like I was a soldier my father was calling to muster. The music grew beneath his hands, his fingers touching the piano and bouncing away like the keys were hot from sitting in the sun. Soon, his hands were far apart—the right dancing over the high notes, the left powering the song's driving momentum.

Later, when I heard other versions of this song, I realized that my father built speed faster than the music called for, accelerating from allegro to presto as I bounced behind him. It was as if my watching, my responding to each note, fueled his fingers while they flew across the keys.

My mother played the piano too. Later, when we were much older, she took lessons from a woman she found on Craigslist. For almost an entire year, her last year, she worked to perfect a Chopin nocturne, Nocturne in E-flat Major op. 9, no. 2.

My mother was no virtuoso. She didn't have my father's dexterity or flair for performance, and she moved through the Chopin nocturne more slowly than the music directed. But her novice pace gave the notes more time to breathe, to soothe, the melody becoming a lullaby. She practiced that piece over and over until her mistakes vanished, notes floating in phrases.

It wasn't until after her death that I realized how often she had filled the house with Chopin. In the silence I remembered the piece, my memory a phantom sense heightened through absence.

In her last month, when Tim had grown impossibly ill, my mother would play the piano for him while he slept. She would play that Chopin piece directly below his room, trying to lift the nocturnal rhythm of his madness.

Sometimes I listen to that nocturne now. The most beautiful version I've found is on YouTube, played by Lithuanian pianist Vadim Chaimovich. The video features a single still image, Vincent van Gogh's *The Starry Night*.

When I listen to the song, I let Van Gogh's swirling sky fill my screen. I imagine Van Gogh, mental illness haunting his life, and see psychosis as the whirlpools churning the sky around his stars.

I imagine Tim's psychosis, his nocturnal madness, and remember all the hours my mother spent at the piano trying to soothe the raging nightscape that howled in his head.

When I visit my father at home, I excavate Tim's room, a space largely untouched since he killed our mother. There, I've found artifacts—old homework assignments, drawers stuffed with XXXL sweatshirts, Christmas cards from Lizzie signed *Love, your best and only sister*.

I take things from his room that I need, things I've lost. I've taken a stapler, an extension cord, nail clippers. I've taken an abandoned glasses case, one that has his name written on the inside. The writing is not his own—the rounded *a*'s of *Granata* identify our mother's hand. Every night after I remove my dry contacts, I see Tim's name as our mother wrote it when I reach for my glasses.

In his room, I've found a child's journal, a first-grade assignment. In the journal, when he writes his best and only sister's name, the *L*

towers over the other letters. In one entry, he lists his first words—
Mama, Dada, Wince. Wince, because it took him years to pronounce
the *V* starting my name. I look at that entry, at my name next to
Mama, Dada, at his child's mind placing me on the same plane—
older brother, caregiver.

As my siblings got older, they became the playmates I had wanted.
Eventually, the three of them grew tall enough to clamber over the
gates my parents used to partition the house. When they became
capable walkers, my mother decided that it was time for more ambi-
tious outings. They had, of course, left the house before, but these
expeditions only worked if my father was there, or if my mother
pushed the triplet stroller around the cul-de-sacs of our suburban
neighborhood. That stroller—three canopied seats in a straight
line—was as long as a hospital stretcher, difficult to maneuver on
the rolling hills of Wild Rose Drive. Too large to fit in the car, the
stroller offered no help if our mother wanted to move beyond our
quiet streets. She had one more toddler than hand.

Her solution involved a harness system, a way of tethering her
children to one of her hands.

"This is your tail," my mother said, showing the new apparatus to
Chris, Tim, and Lizzie. Because the harnesses attached to the waist,
the three of them took to this game, imagining a tail had sprouted
at the base of each of their backs. With this system, my mother could
hold on to all three at once, allowing us to travel as a blob through
the mall, trundling past window-shoppers and fountains.

On these trips, I was deputized as my mother's second in com-
mand, nudging my siblings back into line when one tested the
bounds of the tether.

My mother must have been conscious of how this operation
looked, holding the knotted end of her children's leashes. She

wouldn't have wanted passersby to see her tugging at one of her kids, yanking their yellow line taut.

I never felt what it was like to walk with one of these harnesses around my waist. Having entered the world alone, I never needed my mother to pin a tail to me.

I don't remember much of my life before Chris, Tim, and Lizzie were born; my memories only sharpened once they entered. Life before them exists only in fragments—an afternoon sitting next to my mother under a circus tent near New Haven Harbor. That afternoon is my first memory, though it feels more like a dream—the arching red-and-white tent, the smell of animals, my feet hovering over crushed peanut shells. I see her too, sitting with her hand over mine, her glasses moving when she smiles, when she laughs, when she points at something in the ring far below.

My mother never needed to hold me by a harness, but I watched her hang on to Chris, Tim, and Lizzie, how she kept them close, a short line away.

At her funeral, I told this story, how my mother held a cluster of knots to lead my siblings through the mall. A nice anecdote, I had thought, a way to bring levity, balance the eulogy against tragedy. Here, mourners could picture my mother—a mother with her hands full—corralling her children, shepherding them logically, lovingly.

But I had another motive, another reason for including this story. I wanted everyone to imagine a time when my siblings had been small enough for her to hang on to. I wanted them to see Tim, a boy in Velcro shoes, slack tail an arm's length from our mother. They needed to see, I thought, an innocent child toddling alongside his mother in the mall.

*   *   *

My parents unwrapped the piano when Chris, Tim, and Lizzie were in second grade. The rug vanished and the fancy furniture returned, shifting our venue for play to the basement.

Until then, our basement had been an untamed cement space, a jungle of metal support posts orange with flaking rust. There, in the dusty dark, I designed haunted houses, hoarded tubes of fake blood, synthetic cobwebs, and mutilated zombie masks. I remember the insides of those masks, how my condensed breath glued the rubber to my cheeks and chin.

My haunted houses were a year-round affair, creations I showcased to my friends through guided tours. Chris, Tim, and Lizzie took part, venturing into the semidark with me. They hid behind old furniture or the furnace, under the space beneath the stairs, in a long narrow corridor extending away from the house's foundation. Had my parents been different people, this cement sliver could have been a wine cellar, the corridor like a catacomb, subterranean space out of a Poe story.

When my parents decided to finish part of the basement, they cut a rectangular hole into what had been my dungeon, sealing the space with Sheetrock and green carpet. This new room became our arena, the scene of the battles I would have with my siblings when they grew from teetering toddlers to sturdy children.

Our basement battles pitted my three younger siblings against me, their strength in numbers compensating for my size. We wielded whatever weaponry was available—discarded foam booster seats, deflated exercise balls, oversize stuffed animals, a bruised beanbag chair.

Despite the effectiveness of some of our makeshift weapons, I don't remember any tears during these brawls. But there was an intensity to those struggles, Chris staggering to his feet after I knocked him down with a booster seat, Lizzie pulling the back of my T-shirt while trying to strike me with her exercise ball, Tim swinging the beanbag chair, his back pressed up against a white wall.

Our childhood was filled with routines, repeated family ventures that grew into traditions, memories. Throughout childhood—for thirteen consecutive years starting when my siblings were five—our family rented the same cottage in West Yarmouth, Cape Cod. We made this trip for a week every August.

The cottage sits on an estuary that spills into Lewis Bay, a broad cove shielded from the naked Atlantic by a long isthmus. I still remember how the inlet stank, its tidal waters flowing over crab carcasses, seagull droppings, abandoned lobster pots. We loved that smell. As children, that smell meant hours of muckraking, digging for fiddler crabs, jabbing at shallow-water dwellers with ragged nets.

We paddled old canoes on that estuary, green boats with faded maple leaves on the bows. We wore sea-bleached life jackets, speckled like ripening peaches.

Our mother had two rules for canoeing. We had to wear the crusty life jackets, which, slippery with seawater, sweat, and sunscreen, chafed our shoulders. We were also not to cross the bay, the cove opening at the mouth of our inlet.

We set out to cross the bay when I was twelve. Chris, Tim, and Lizzie were eight. Tim sat in the bow and I commanded him from the stern while Lizzie sat folded between us on an extra life jacket. Chris—sick, I think—stayed home.

As we left the estuary, we passed a number of boats moored in West Yarmouth harbor. On one boat with a name like *Seas the Day* or *Sea la Vie*, a woman stalked the bow, opening compartments, slamming them shut.

"SHIT! BRIAN!" she yelled back toward the tiller, perhaps at the invisible captain.

At eight, Tim and Lizzie were no strangers to swearing. As their big brother, I had taught them a few words so that no one would mistake them for naïve on the second-grade recess field.

After hearing "SHIT! BRIAN!" projected across the bay, Tim and Lizzie mimicked the harried lady. They yelled, back and forth in a sort of call-and-response, "SHIT, BRIAN, SHIT, BRIAN," and I turned the phrase into a chant, a cadence for paddling.

When the bow of our canoe hit the beach on the far side of the bay, Tim hopped over the side, wincing when his bare feet crunched shells thick as gravel on the sand.

"We're alone," Lizzie said.

Not knowing what else to do, I ordered Lizzie to turn around, unknotted my bathing suit, and peed onto the broken seashells. Tim, cackling like a banshee, pulled down his trunks and did the same.

Paddling back took a bit longer. The wind, which had shortened the first leg of our trip, slowed us down. Lizzie, noticing that we weren't making much progress, cajoled us, splashing her hands in the water to make us paddle harder. Without speaking, Tim and I stopped paddling. He swiveled his hips to face her from the bow, brandished his paddle, and began slicing the water, dousing Lizzie. As she covered her face, I joined in, soaking her.

"Stop. Okay. Stop," Lizzie pleaded. Eventually, she started laughing, yelling, "SHIT BRIAN SHIT BRIAN." We slapped our paddles against the water and in the process of attacking Lizzie, Tim and I soaked each other.

When we started paddling again, the extra water in the boat weighed us down.

"Start bailing," I commanded Lizzie, "or we'll throw you overboard."

Cupping her hands, she bailed in ounces, making little progress.

We had been gone for some time and I was beginning to fear that our absence had grown conspicuous.

When we approached home, our mother sat on one of her reading chairs. No novel shaded her face.

"How far did you go?" She didn't wait for us to tie up.

"Across the bay," I confessed.

"Alone?" she said. "With Tim and Lizzie?"

"They were with me," I said, looking away from her, toward the book she had discarded in the grass.

"We were fine," I said.

I can remember this now, visit that afternoon without fearing that the future will trespass. For a long time, pain worked like subtraction, erased the memories I have alongside my brother. For a long time, when I saw Tim in his childhood life jacket, I would also see him in a white jumpsuit, crying during his arraignment for our mother's murder.

At first, I fought back, tried to separate my life into *before* and *after*, as though memories were photographs to sort into albums.

But our brains don't work this way, don't hold memories in discrete banks. There's no brain librarian scurrying through our archived experiences, pinpointing specific volumes.

In reality, memories are more feeling than fact. Though we want to think of our memories as one long record, the reel of our greatest hits, a memory is a constellation of infinitesimal changes, electrical signals and hormones that elicit feelings—*We felt good paddling our canoe, happy in each other's company, joyful in the sun.*

Feeling drives memory, populates the moving pictures we see.

During the year after my mother's death, all my memories seemed treacherous, only signposts to tragedy.

So I used my memories like ballast, cast them overboard, believed this would counter trauma's weight.

3

You never could have seen this coming.

This phrase—a common refrain, often repeated by friends with good intentions—followed me in the weeks after Tim killed our mother.

You never could have seen this coming.

Psychiatrists have a term for mental illness's prelude—*prodrome*, from the Greek *prodromos*, "precursor." Clinically, the prodrome is a period of decreased cognitive functioning—characterized by unusual thoughts, suspiciousness, grandiose ideas—that can precede serious mental illness. These early symptoms are minor, light work, like the mind is limbering up for the rigors of psychosis.

I've heard mental health experts refer to the prodrome as an "aura of illness"—*aura*, an invisible emanation, a lurking spectral presence. We sometimes use this ethereal language to describe mental illness, the invisible onset. No budding tumors precede schizophrenia seizing control.

When I think about who Tim was in high school, I can create an ex post facto prodrome. Something shifted during high school;

something tilted, at first imperceptibly, toward a new kind of Tim, different from the child I had canoed with.

I wasn't at home often when Chris, Tim, and Lizzie were in high school. I left for college at the beginning of their eighth-grade year, and while Yale was only fifteen minutes down the road, I made a point of separating home from school.

Before I left for college, my siblings and I overlapped for one year at Hopkins, an independent school that sits atop a hill overlooking New Haven. Hopkins was small enough that we saw each other on campus. Often, I would pass Chris, Tim, and Lizzie on my way to the cafeteria, seventh-grade lunch finishing as the high school arrived to eat.

Tim joined the football team in seventh grade, competing in team sports for the first time since he was a young child chasing a soccer ball. My mother and I watched him play, at first struggling to distinguish him from the other boys on the field. But my mother recognized him, pointed him out, taller than most, weight in awkward clumps at his hips. She worried that the extra weight would make him ungainly, but during his first game, playing on the offensive and defensive lines, Tim was rarely knocked down. Most of the other boys seemed to bounce off of him when they collided on the muddy field. He hugged our mother after the first game—helmet still on— careful not to let the plastic face mask bruise her cheek.

Tim transformed in high school. His metamorphosis, to me, was at first entirely physical. He was fourteen when he started lifting weights, and over the course of a year, he evolved from hip-heavy pear to broad iron anvil. I could no longer wrestle him on even terms.

He discovered he could dominate me one afternoon during the summer before his sophomore year. I was living at home that summer, at the midway point of college. We were in the basement, a space that had been transformed once more, from playroom to gym.

I was watching him lift that afternoon, marveling at his precise movements, at how dumbbells decelerated as they lowered toward his heaving chest. Every repetition was exact, the weights hovering over the same point on either side of his rib cage. After a dozen pulses, he let the bulbous weights drop to the floor.

"You're getting strong," I said.

My compliment launched him from his bench and he shrugged his shoulders like he was shedding the lactic acid pooling in his muscles. He ducked into a wrestler's crouch, approached me—forearm tense, hesitating—just as he had when we battered each other with foam booster seats as kids. He didn't know yet that he was stronger than me, and in our recent grappling I'd been able to trick him into a headlock, neutralize his strength with a few sharp squeezes.

That afternoon, as he approached me on the thin green carpet, I clamped onto his shoulders, feeling new mounds of muscle sprouting from the base of his neck. With a shrug, he freed himself of my hands, pressed my body away. In that moment, he grew bolder than he had ever been before. He took the offensive, and when I tried to duck his lunging tackle, he latched one arm to my waist, wrapped me up, pinned me to the ground. With his forearm on the back of my neck, his knees grinding me into the floor, the balance of physical power shifted.

After he pinned me, we stopped grappling. It felt wrong, like the natural order had been upset, the rigid hierarchy of brothers inverted.

He used this new strength to excel in wrestling, his evolving body the perfect instrument with which to batter opponents, to make them submit. He spent winter afternoons in the musty air of our high school's wrestling room perfecting his double-leg takedown, his arm bar, his hip throw.

The first time I witnessed this power, I was sitting in the bleachers with my mother. Tim had just graduated from the 220-

pound division to the heavyweight division, a category capped at 285 pounds.

Hopkins's opponent that day was the American School for the Deaf. The wrestlers from ASD warmed up in orange-and-black singlets, tiger striped to match their mascot. Their coach guided them through quick drills with physical prompts, tapping the shoulders of his wrestlers before they dove at each other's legs.

I spotted Tim's opponent, the largest wrestler in an orange-and-black singlet. While Tim's mass clustered in tense knots beneath his maroon spandex, his opponent's weight sank into the folds of his uniform, sagging from his stomach and hips. He lumbered around the mat during warm-ups, pausing to catch his breath after each drill.

The heavyweights wrestled first, and I watched Tim pull his plastic headgear over his ears. In his corner, his coach—stout, rounded like a cannonball—slapped him twice on either shoulder, then ripped Tim's hands up and down like he was trying to start an engine. Primed, Tim ran to the center of the ring, arriving well before his opponent. They each extended a hand, Tim's opponent's hanging limp, a preemptive surrender.

Within seconds of the start of the match, Tim had ensnared his opponent. He forced him upright, hooked an arm under his shoulder, and used the muscles in his thighs to pry him into the air. When Tim tossed his opponent, I saw my mother's hands grip the metal slab where she sat on the bleachers.

When the boy landed, he was a balloon deflating, air rushing from an open mouth. He wheezed like an injured animal, his wails so high-pitched that everyone on the bleachers winced. It seemed almost merciful that the boy couldn't hear his own cries of pain.

I should have pitied Tim's opponent, this pudgy boy who wriggled beneath my brother, helpless as a squashed bug on a countertop. Yes, I should have pitied this boy as Tim pushed his face into. the mat, drowning him in his own sweat.

But all I felt was pride. All I saw was my little brother, a prime physical specimen, dominating an opponent who'd dared enter his ring. I was proud then, smiling in the bleachers as Tim rolled off the crumpled boy, victorious.

I wonder what my mother thought, if she marveled at how strong her son had become. For the next three years, she would travel to watch him win. On each set of bleachers, she sat on her folded jacket, a cushion against the hard metal.

Every year Tim got stronger. No one trained the way he did. When I came home to visit, I loved watching him lift. He would slide metal plates onto his barbell until it subtly curved, its alloy shuddering like a slender bow. He never grunted, never yelled, never needed the stereotypical machismo to groan his weights into submission. Though he was quiet, his lifting was controlled violence. When squatting, he lowered himself by inches before springing upright like a loaded coil.

"Force equals mass times acceleration," Tim would say, and Tim's mass was accelerating. Tim was accelerating. The weights accelerated. As he curled, lunged, and pressed, as he pushed, pulled, and pried, the bundles of muscle expanded at his shoulders, on his back, in his thighs.

His names—given to him by high school teammates—evolved with his growing body. He was a house, a brick wall, a horse. He was stud, beast, monster.

Yet in high school, he was also Timmy. His classmates called him Timmy, his coaches too. Off the wrestling mat, people wanted a teddy bear. They wanted the gentle giant who loved nerdy video games, Isaac Asimov novels. They wanted the goof, the kid who danced to pop songs in the locker room, the kid who spoke in funny accents in class. They wanted Timmy, the responsible one, team captain senior year, the one mothers trusted to drive their sons to team dinners. They wanted the Timmy who carried Chris off of the football field when Chris twisted his ankle; they wanted the Timmy who passed out donuts after school assemblies; they wanted the Timmy who performed in jazz ensembles, playing a flute that looked thin as a toothpick in his hands.

And he was that Timmy. I remember him then.

But even then, Tim was accelerating. Somewhere, in ways mostly invisible, Tim was accelerating. Somehow it started, on an atomic level, a single cell, something misfiring, an electron hitting the wrong synapse, a chemical imbalance slowly putrefying his brain. Even in high school, that reaction must have been building, accelerating, mounting some type of dysfunctional momentum, a force too big for him to control, too unwieldy for him to lift over his head, too heavy for him to set down among his weights on the basement floor.

In college, years before Tim became sick, I had my first peripheral brushes with serious mental illness.

During college, much of my life revolved around rowing, a sport I had stumbled into after it became clear that my basketball skills were not commensurate with my dreams of playing in college. Rowing, a sport that requires endless hours of monotonous training, matched the physical gifts I had—endurance, a high tolerance for repetitive exercise. Though I was far from one of the key members of the team, I spent four years prioritizing rowing over many other obligations. To that end, I adopted a pragmatic approach to academics. One of my four classes every semester needed to be easy, the type of course

we called a *gut*. Each year an intrepid group of slackers would pub-
lish a list of these courses—safe havens for overworked athletes, fra-
ternity aficionados, or students looking for a painless GPA boost.

Among the classic gut courses was Computers and the Law, a
class you could pass if you had ever operated a computer or watched
an episode of *Law & Order*. When I was a sophomore, I took Life
in the Universe, a course that considered the potential for extrater-
restrial life and offered only a scientific *maybe* as hypothesis. During
my senior year, I took Topics in Reproductive Biology, which was
more commonly referred to as Porn in the Morn due to its salacious
PowerPoint slides.

While I also took courses that required honest effort, rowing
dominated my time. Our thirty-minute commute to and from the
boathouse inflated this commitment—a daily trip down Route 34
past the intersection with Orange Center Road, a crossroads two
minutes from where I grew up.

During my senior year, I shared a dilapidated house with nine of
my teammates and a possum. When we descended into the basement to do laundry, we were wary of our four-legged roommate's
gleaming eyes. We lived across the street from a late-night pizza
shop, Alpha Delta, purveyors of a transcendent Buffalo chicken
sandwich—the Wenzel. The Wenzel drew the masses, students and
New Haven denizens alike, flocking to Alpha Delta's glowing sign.
Our stoop became a resting spot for some of these visitors.

A frequent presence was a balding man with jet-black eyebrows
who muttered to passersby from our steps. We always greeted him
but walked away while he continued speaking to the empty sidewalk.
We never asked him his name. To us, he was Schizophrenic Bob.

When we encountered him on our stoop, his face would freeze in
a grimace, arms twitching in spasmodic motion. His tics reminded

me of my grandfather, my father's father, who had died while in the late stages of Parkinson's when I was in third grade.

Schizophrenic Bob became part of our scenery, a harmless crazy man shaking on our stoop. I didn't know then that long-term use of some antipsychotics can cause these types of tremors, known as dyskinesia.

Schizophrenic Bob was always smoking, his extinguished butts joining piles of others at the foot of our steps. Years later, when I drowned myself in studies of schizophrenia, I would encounter a number of papers that investigated a link between nicotine and an easing of hypofrontality. Hypofrontality, researchers posit, is a reduced firing of neurons in the prefrontal cortex, diminished brain functioning that may be associated with schizophrenia. Nicotine might coax these neurons back toward normal activity, an improvised kick start to combat the illness's paralytic hold. Schizophrenic Bob may have been self-medicating on our stoop while we shuffled by him to class.

I had another encounter with serious mental illness during my senior year, one that was more personal, more connected to my sheltered life on the rowing team.

A few years prior, when I was a sophomore, a walk-on named Jeremy joined the team. Collegiate rowing, at that time, had been the last intercollegiate sport to prohibit freshmen from competing with upperclassmen, creating a one-year experience when freshmen would race only their peers. This rule created a bit of a divide between freshmen and upperclassmen and I didn't know Jeremy well during his year on the team. When he disappeared after that year, I didn't ask too many questions, but I eventually learned some of the story from a teammate.

My teammate used the word *schizophrenic*. To me, that word was still more colloquial than clinical, an insult mocking inconsistency. *Professor Thompson is so hot and cold with his grading, like he's schizophrenic or something.*

I heard a story about Jeremy, something that sounded like a rumor, nothing like my mild-mannered teammate. In the story, Jeremy was driving down a busy highway with his eyes closed yelling, "Jesus, take the wheel!" while his passengers screamed in terror.

He had to be hospitalized, I learned, though at the time *hospitalized* meant little to me. My stock images for mental health facilities came from Hollywood or literature, the oppressive setting of Ken Kesey's *One Flew Over the Cuckoo's Nest* standing in for reality. I had loved that book in high school.

Years later, when I read it again, the Chief's kaleidoscopic hallucinations would no longer seem beautiful. They would remind me of my brother's hallucinations, his terrifying florid psychosis. When I read the book again, Nurse Ratched became the hero.

Midway through my senior year, Jeremy came back, unannounced, arriving at our house on a Sunday night, clutching a bottle of Sprite on our stoop. He wanted to talk about the illuminati, about where they met on campus, about which old stone building housed their secret chambers. He knew—was positive, had figured it out—*they decide everything.* He also knew that they controlled the campus power plant; in fact, they controlled all power plants. They could black out major cities with the flip of a switch, *wherever they want, whenever they want.*

He spoke in bursts, his thoughts chasing each other. *The illuminati print all the world's currency, they're onto me, they know I'm looking for them, they know that I know.*

When one of us told him that he sounded confused, he stopped talking, nodded slowly and told us—*of course, of course*—he was exaggerating. He chuckled.

We were scared. We looked to each other, uncomfortable in the presence of someone who seemed unhinged, insane, bat-shit crazy. I called my parents.

On the phone with my mother, I described what was happening. I used the word *schizophrenic*.

"He's probably off his medication," my mother said. *Medication*, of course, an easy clinical solution.

"I'll ask him," I said, not knowing how naïve I must have sounded.

"Are you alone with him?" my mother asked. She didn't sound afraid, but her speech was slower than usual, like she wanted me to hear every word.

"Ask him if he'll go with you to the hospital," she said. "Tell him they can help. He came to your house because he trusts you."

I believed her. She was still years away from fearing for the mental health of one of her children. In five years she would also face a hospital ER, Tim psychotic and delusional, refusing to stay with the doctors who claimed they could help.

When we asked Jeremy if he wanted to come with us to the hospital, he laughed.

"I'll just play cards for a few days," he said. "They'll let me out again."

I interpreted this statement as another delusion. Surely this wasn't how his treatment would unfold. Doctors, I assumed, would see how *crazy* he had become and help him go back to being the teammate we had known a year before.

Four of us climbed into my car and we drove the half mile to the Yale ER. I don't remember how long we had to wait until someone at triage called one of the doctors from the psychiatric unit. Jeremy left us with a shrug of his shoulders.

"See you soon," he might have said, before following a man in a white coat.

We left the hospital confused, but with some general sense that we had "done the right thing."

Occasionally, over the next weeks, we would ask each other if anyone had heard from Jeremy. One teammate, the same one who had told us the story about the reckless driving, told us that Jeremy had gone back home. I never saw Jeremy again.

The memory of that evening receded, faded to a minor aberration from the routine pattern of my college life. I wouldn't think of Jeremy again for a long time.

Now I know so many more people who live with schizophrenia, people whose lives have followed paths vastly different from my brother's.

I know an artist whose work plumbs his memories of psychosis, who renders the staggering overload of his senses on stages and canvases and film. He shows an experience that is too often obscured in shadow and fear.

I know a social worker who has dedicated her life to helping people who live with the illness, an illness that had left her hospitalized, an illness she's learned to endure. I know her empathy knows no bounds.

And I've met some of the men and women in the places that have housed Tim, listened to how their untreated diseases led them to the same facilities as my brother.

Schizophrenia contains multitudes, yet we gather so many experiences under this single heading. One day, I believe we'll be shocked at how broadly we categorized, how we used a single diagnosis to classify constellations of different types of neurological disease.

This "one" disease can present and persist—or, in some cases, remit—in myriad paths. Some psychiatrists divide schizophrenia prognoses into quarters.

For patients who have had a psychotic break and been given a diagnosis of schizophrenia, one quarter will recover completely. They will never experience another psychotic break or substantial symptoms regardless of how they are treated—with antipsychotics, herbs, thoughts and prayers.

Another quarter will live largely independent lives, but will need to adhere to a treatment plan involving medication to quiet symptoms.

Another quarter will significantly improve with treatment, but will require much more additional aid—shifts in medication, peer and family support.

The final quarter will have difficulty responding to existing treatment options and will need extensive help to function. Many in this quarter die by suicide.

One disease. Many divergent paths.

Unavoidably, diseases diagnosed based only on symptoms—all psychiatric illnesses—will encompass spectrums of disorder. That said, the diagnostic checklist for schizophrenia is long. Not every box needs to be marked. Symptoms become like amorphous bubbles on a Venn diagram. Where a half dozen happen to intersect, clinicians insert the word *schizophrenia*.

And, quite clearly, these many symptoms will vary *extensively* in terms of severity. What one person experiences as a slight glitch in audio perception—light static—another will experience as strident persecutory voices—*you're a fat bitch*. One might detect a slight shimmering in the sky, while another sees fist-size spiders cascading down a bedroom wall. Yet still, for both ends of this spectrum, we level the same diagnosis.

Is there any other disease we think of similarly? Imagine if we thought of cancer this way, if we couldn't distinguish between different types of malignancy. How absurd would it be if we put basal cell cancer—a barely malignant bump that can be cut out with the use of local anesthesia—on the same plane as stage-four pancreatic cancer?

Thinking that there is "one schizophrenia" mangles our own reality, forces us to paint complex, varied illnesses with one broad brush.

We need scores of schizophrenia stories. We need them to overwhelm how a single diagnosis co-opts complexity, imposes inaccurate absolute narratives.

All schizophrenics deny they are sick.
All schizophrenics had traumatic childhoods.
All schizophrenics are violent.
All schizophrenics can help themselves to recover.

Schizophrenia is not a single enemy. The disease is a legion we do not yet understand.

Tim was seventeen when I graduated from college. He didn't make it to the ceremony. I was too exhausted to care, distracted by a disappointing rowing season that muted pomp and circumstance.

I don't remember my parents punishing him for skipping my graduation. He was reaching the end of his junior year of high school, the year when he started to withdraw. My mother would tell me—later, after his illness arrived in earnest—that it was during this year that she started to notice more distance, distance between his words at the dinner table, distance between his closed bedroom door and where he used to do his homework in the family room.

Then, when Tim was in high school, she was convinced that the distance was normal, a shaking-out of teenage masculinity, a necessary push away from his mother. Then, she was certain she'd get Tim back.

Now, it's easy to cast his absence from my graduation as one of a series of retreats, as part of his prodrome, the slow first act preceding his madness.

Seven years after that graduation, when Tim's evaluators prepared their reports for his trial, they examined Tim's experience as a junior in high school to build a prodrome. They note "a gradual deterioration, first in his academic and social functioning."

Gradual deterioration, like Tim eroded, slowly, over time.

I heard about Tim's early struggles in fragments over the phone. Chris left answers on his calculator for Tim to use during a physics test. An assistant wrestling coach who taught Tim math inflated his grades.

I had assumed that Chris and Tim shared friends, but learned in pieces that Chris was the one who invited people over to play video games in the basement. Chris was the one who brought Tim along, his social chaperone when they ate wings at Archie Moore's.

Tim's grades slipped, and at night, after my parents coaxed him into starting his homework, he would complete his assignments by candlelight. My mother laughed off this idiosyncrasy, this need for a flickering candle, as Tim's way of channeling the ambience of classical writers.

During meetings at school, when Tim had to account for his slipping grades, he would sit across from his teachers, clutching his backpack to his lap, hugging it against his torso like a child's security blanket.

Later, Chris told me about the journal Tim kept, how Tim wrote about girls he was embarrassed to talk to. There were some passages of abject despair. "I have no chance with anyone," one entry reads. "My life is hopeless and I should not exist."

Sure, many high school kids scribble these expressions of despair, their fear of cliques clustering against lockers in school hallways. Sure, because of the illness that eventually seized Tim's brain, it's easy for me to point to these signs as evidence, as prodrome.

When Tim's evaluating psychiatrists questioned him about this period, they asked him to summarize high school in one word.

"Departure," Tim said. "I think that's the best word."

Tim told the psychiatrists that he was talking about me, how I'd left home when he was in eighth grade, how he wouldn't see me on the high school campus. He told the doctors the feeling he remembered.

"I'd feel safe," Tim said, "if I could just see him and know where he was."

I'm not sure if Tim was punishing me for that "departure" when he didn't come to my graduation. At the time, I wanted to make it clear to him that his absence hadn't wounded me, that, in fact, I could understand why he hadn't wanted to spend hours baking on a plastic folding chair.

After my graduation, back home for champagne, cake, and coffee, I went upstairs to Tim's room. I opened his unlocked door.

"Sup," he said, pivoting halfway from his computer screen, one hand remaining on the mouse. This nonchalance might have been to cover his anxiety, his worry that I might have been angry.

"Didn't want to sit in the sun for three hours?" I said.

"Couldn't do it, man." He looked toward his feet, and I read this as remorse. I had needed none from him and felt almost embarrassed by his small gesture.

"It's really fine," I said. "But I'm definitely going to be there when you graduate from college."

This is a promise I still intend to keep.

4

Tim's illness began as a whisper, a sadness in his voice when we spoke during his first year of college. That year, Tim struggled.

At 270 pounds, Tim was used to being the biggest guy in the wrestling room. In high school competition, few approached his strength. Only in championship meets did he face opponents who matched his power. When Tim arrived at Lehigh University, the wrestling roster included a heavyweight who was contending for national championships. In fact, later that year, that teammate would win his first NCAA title. Tim was to be his sparring partner.

"Sparring partner" is not what Tim became. "Punching bag" is closer.

It's difficult for me to imagine anyone physically dominating Tim, but this older wrestler mauled him in a way Tim had never experienced before. Tim would try to minimize how his body degraded over the course of the season, and I believed his understated descriptions of his injuries. It seemed impossible that Tim's body—one of the most powerful bodies I had ever seen—could crumble.

During Tim's freshman year, I was in Boston teaching high school English. I learned about Tim's injuries over the phone—torn cartilage in his hip, disks bulging from his battered spine. He wasn't able to finish the season. Alone, without the camaraderie of the team, he limped through the rest of his freshman year.

When he returned home, defeated, from his first year of college, his descent into illness began.

For me, this descent started on a Saturday with a phone call, my mother's voice changing the world in ways I couldn't yet understand.

"Vince?" she said when I answered. "Are you alone?"

She barely paused for me to respond.

"I need you to listen. Tim has been very down recently," my mother said. "I think you know."

I'm not sure if I did. Of course, I thought then, I knew about his wrestling injuries, about how he had struggled in his classes. I had spoken to him, I thought, the week before, remembered him telling me about a chiropractor who might help him wrestle again.

"He was very upset today." My mother's voice broke on *very*. "He spent most of his time in his room. At dinner, he told us that he has plans to commit suicide."

She used that phrase, *plans to commit suicide*, a phrase that both puzzled and flattened—*plans to* somehow blunting *commit suicide*. I was silent, weighed the calculation of *plans* against the chaos of *suicide*. I couldn't fit the two pieces together.

"What plans?" I asked.

"On the Fourth of July," my mother said, "he plans to drive his car into the wall of the West Rock Tunnel."

And I was caught there, for a moment, in the specificity of Tim's "plans"—the particular date, the particular place, the particular means. I was caught—Fourth of July, West Rock Tunnel—until I recognized that my mind was trying to protect me, distract me.

Tim wanted his life to end.

"Why?" I said.

This was my first *why*. Then, *why?* was a question I thought could be answered.

"It's important that he told us," my mother said. "He wanted us to know. We're going to find someone for him to talk to."

"Should I talk to him now?" I asked, but realized then that I had no idea what I would say.

"I think it would be better if you came home," my mother said, "in the morning."

Then she told me, for the first time, "Vince, we need to save Tim's life."

The next morning, my foot was lighter on the gas than normal. I was buying time, stretching out the drive home.

I needed a strategy, a way to convince Tim not to end his life. I moved through what I thought were concrete factors—his struggles at school, his injuries, living away from his best friend, Chris. I spoke out loud in the car, began rehearsing what I would say.

Tim, I know what you're feeling. Sometimes I feel depressed or hopeless or like there's no point in going on.

I rehearsed clichés in my car.

Tim, it'll get better. Eventually things will turn around.

While I wanted desperately for my conversation with Tim to be more than a naïve pep talk, more than a speech to get him to *SNAP OUT OF IT*, I had no idea what Tim needed me to say.

When I arrived home, I spoke to my parents in the kitchen. We sat in our assigned spots, the only places we ever sat—my father to my right, my mother across from me.

"I'm glad you came home," my mother said. She looked tired, eyes blinking behind her glasses like she was trying to focus.

"Where is he?" I asked.

"Upstairs. He might be asleep."

As I climbed the stairs to Tim's room, I saw bulging duffel bags flanking his door. They were still zipped from when he had packed up his dorm room belongings a week before. Stepping over them, I knocked. I heard his weight shift on the mattress, his heavy feet press the ground.

Tim opened the door like he had been expecting me, shrugging his shoulders in lieu of offering a greeting. His hair was long, covering the tops of his ears. He turned and sat on his bed. The corner sagged toward him so I sank when I sat, sliding closer to his side, falling toward his thick torso. Behind him, medals dangled from trophies—his nested accolades, awards naming him NUTMEG STATE GAMES CHAMPION, SOUTHERN NEW ENGLAND CHAMPION.

When I looked at him, stooped on the bed in front of his triumphs, my practiced lines evaporated.

"Promise to call me first," I said, "before you ever think of doing something."

He nodded, looked toward his knees.

I forced an arm around his shoulders.

Soon, these moments would barely be blips. But before psychosis, before the hospital, before he killed our mother, there was this sagging bed, this pathetic hug, this naïve promise.

I told him I loved him. I thought this would be enough to save his life.

*   *   *

We had time, my mother believed, more than a month until the Fourth of July. During this time, she convinced Tim to see a psychiatrist. After three meetings, Tim had his first diagnosis: "severe depression in connection with suicidal ideation."

This diagnosis, like most, came with a prescription. I can't remember the antidepressant the doctor recommended, but Tim flatly refused.

"I don't want them to mess with my head," Tim said.

My parents pleaded with him. They used their medical backgrounds to make the case.

"You could use a serotonin booster," they would say, naming the specific neurotransmitter. "You take Advil when your back hurts."

But Tim claimed there was something different about this kind of medication, that there was something about pills that "unbalanced" you, that manipulated your chemistry, artificially tilted mood.

Even though Tim resisted medication, he told our parents— weeks before July Fourth—that he no longer planned to kill himself. He even started talking about the future, thinking that maybe someday he would go to law school.

Law school. The future. We were back on track.

But there was still that diagnosis—*severe depression*—something, even then, I understood couldn't be easily cast aside.

I was home with Tim on the weekend of the Fourth of July. On the Fourth, Chris, Tim, and I went to see the third installment of the Transformers series. After the movie, we ate at the diner across the street. Chris and I split an order of mozzarella sticks and Tim ate a chicken Caesar salad.

Except for the diner, I can really only remember two things from that weekend—the painful amount of screen time it took for Michael Bay's robots to destroy Chicago, and Tim laughing after the movie, tossing his 3D glasses into the plastic receptacle.

I don't remember speaking about what we had feared that weekend, about the threats Tim had made just over a month before.

Though we didn't speak about Tim's pain, I know my mother thought that these weekends were important, that simply by being with Tim we could show him that he was supported. She had started reading a great number of sources, tracking online blogs where family members detailed how they helped sons and daughters who suffered from depression. She bought books, began to accumulate what would become an impressive collection of psychology texts, books on treatment, coping strategies, various types of therapy.

This process of "helping" Tim was rarely straightforward. I had started to recognize how his rigid self-reliance—foundational to his success as a wrestler—made him cast his struggle with depression as a one-on-one affair.

In the basement, he hung wrestling posters filled with rugged rhetoric:

PERSEVERANCE: FALL SEVEN TIMES GET UP EIGHT.

In high school, Tim had elaborated on this ethos for an article in the school newspaper. The piece was a profile naming Tim "Athlete of the Issue." In the interview, Tim says, "Intensity isn't for everyone, but neither is success."

This line became something of an inside joke between the two of us, one we would fire back and forth when one of us was complaining.

"Sorry I'm late, Tim. The traffic was intense."

"Intensity isn't for everyone, but neither is success."

"I was sleeping in when you called, Tim. Sorry I missed you."

"Intensity isn't for everyone, but neither is success."

In that same article, Tim describes the motivation that fueled his training.

"I worked hard so that I could earn the love and respect of my older brother."

The article identifies me, the older brother, as "a former Hopkins student and four varsity sport stand out." This is a wildly embellished account of my high school sports career.

But that part of the article—Tim's belief that he needed to earn my respect, my love—undercut everything I thought I had been as an older brother.

Chris had sent me the article, and after I read it, I called Tim.

"'Intensity isn't for everyone,'" I said, "'but neither is success'? Where'd you get that one?"

"It's true," Tim said.

I gave him a hard time for that line, using it as a way to cut tension, laughing to delay the question I needed to ask.

"You know you don't have to do anything to earn my love," I said. "You know that, right?"

"It's just an interview," Tim said.

We didn't speak about this again.

My parents' bedroom has remained fossilized since my mother's death. All of her belongings are frozen in place, the room a mausoleum.

My father sleeps in the guest room now. He has remained at home, living among my mother's possessions, his clothes in adjacent drawers to her clothes in their bedroom.

My parents were just shy of their thirtieth wedding anniversary when my mother died. Sometimes it's difficult for me to think about their marriage, difficult not because their marriage seemed unhappy—it did not—but because for so much of their life I saw them from the vantage point of a child, their partnership in terms of how they cared for me.

I can remember them, when I was young, as practical parents, though they were practical in different ways. My father kept meticulous datebooks, printed spreadsheet schedules for family vacations. My mother had innumerable parenting tricks—the tails, for one—strategies that today people sometimes call "life hacks," like the empty peanut butter jar she kept for bathroom emergencies during long car trips, or the plastic molds she used to freeze juice concoctions into popsicles.

I can think of my parents in this way, in how they cared for me, but struggle when I imagine how they loved each other.

This is childish, I know, almost like I'm jealous that the love they had for each other challenged the love they had for me.

My mother told me, many times, *Dad is the smartest person I've ever met.*

As a child, my father skipped two years of primary school, won a four-year college scholarship from the helicopter plant where his father worked, finished his undergrad at Yale in three years, then used the last year of his scholarship to cover his first year of medical school. At twenty-three, he was a doctor in residence at Stanford University Medical Center.

This accelerated early life was something my parents shared.

My mother was a high school dropout. During her junior year at Central High School in Bridgeport, she decided that she wasn't learning anything in her overcrowded classes, that she was sick of dodging fights in the hallways, that she wasn't going to stick around for her senior year. She convinced Smith College to admit her, and enrolled as a sixteen-year-old freshman without a high school diploma.

This shared experience, their precocious early lives, must have drawn them together, and not only because they were both stunningly intelligent. The experience of being young, of being ahead of schedule, must have made friendships challenging, social settings intimidating. Though my father can be gregarious, can stand in a crowded room, he can also withdraw, grow quiet in conversation. Though my mother always appeared warm to others, she rarely sought out social gatherings, described our house like a castle, a place where we could pull up the drawbridge, be together, just us.

In this way, my parents may have offered each other the perfect company. I have no idea how it feels to lose a partner of that kind.

I don't know my father's specific pain, the pain of losing the love of his life at the hands of his son. I will never tell him to get rid of my mother's things, to leave the house, to move, to *move on*.

I know he finds comfort at home, comfort in seeing where her nightgowns still hang, where her books still spill from the shelves next to their bed.

"Vince," he says, "I have more good memories here than bad."

I know he is nostalgic. He's saved the model rockets he built as a space race–obsessed kid. He's shown me his high school yearbook, smiled when I laughed at his sideburns, patches of hair that look almost cartoonish on his young cheeks.

In a way, I'm grateful he's kept my mother's things. I've looked through them to find my memories again. At home, I've searched through these possessions when I've missed her most.

One night, on her bedside table, next to loose earring backs, I found a phone. When I pressed my thumb on the power button, I felt like I had enacted a séance.

This was her old phone, not the phone she had when she died, but one she kept—charged, ready—because she used it to listen to music when she circled the town walking track. She had never asked one of us to show her how to transfer her music onto her new phone.

On this phone are all the text messages she sent and received from the summer of 2011—when Tim made his first suicide threat—to the end of 2012. Of all the evidence I've gathered—doctors reports, court documents, journals, emails—this phone, these messages between Tim and our mother, are some of the most difficult for me to read. Here are her responses to his accusations, his mounting delusions. In these messages, she starts to lose her son.

And here too, are her messages to me:

Hi Vince, finally found the title of the movie I was telling you about. "How to Kill Your Neighbors Dog." Don't be put off by the title.

Hohoho—Santa wants to know if your neck size is 15½ or 16?

Hi, Vince, tried calling u but no answer. Just wondering if u reached Tim. I do appreciate ur help & I am sorry to ask for it. Call me if u can.

I keep that phone close to me now, in the left-hand drawer of my writing desk.

Hi Vince, just calling to say hi.

*   *   *

Tim returned to school in the fall. On one of his first nights back on campus, a Saturday, Tim called me while I was out celebrating a friend's birthday.

He would call during many Saturday nights, the time he felt most alone, sequestered in his dorm while the campus reveled around him.

When I answered that first Saturday-night call, I left the restaurant where I was sitting with my friends for the relative quiet of an alley. I stood next to a dumpster while I spoke to Tim.

"Why do Mom and Dad think I'm stupid?" Tim said.

"Of course they don't think you're stupid," my denial a reflex.

Tim reminded me how his grades had slipped in high school, how our father used to pester him about getting his homework done.

"They didn't trust me," Tim said.

"Just because you didn't get straight A's doesn't mean you're stupid," I said, avoiding his indictment of our parents.

Tim told me about his courses that fall, the philosophy classes he was taking after abandoning his original major, economics. I saw this switch as crucial in lifting his spirits, though that phrase—*lifting his spirits*—shows how naïve I was, how I underestimated his desperation that still simmered from the summer.

"There's a lot of writing in these philosophy classes," Tim said. "I don't think I can do it."

I couldn't remember his voice ever sounding so soft.

"Tim, I'm not sure if I know anyone who reads as much as you," I said. "You couldn't dig into those philosophy books if you were dumb." That summer I had seen thick Kierkegaard texts with cracked spines littered among his weights in the basement.

"It just seems impossible."

Tim started to sob, and between his gasps he returned to the topic of our parents.

"They didn't believe in me," he wailed.

While he cried, I tried to think of something tangible I could do.

"Let me read your papers," I said. "I grade essays for a living."

He agreed to send me what he was working on, and I took this as a sign that we could move forward together, overcome what I saw as only a crisis in confidence.

But he kept talking, crying into the phone, lonely, at that point still enough of my little brother—Tim before the demons arrived—to want to hear someone's voice, my voice, on a Saturday night.

Before Tim returned to Lehigh, our mother called the school's counseling service to refer Tim for treatment. He followed through, meeting with a therapist once a week for most of the fall semester. On the phone, he was terse when I asked him about his therapy.

"I'm seeing some dude counselor."

"A young guy?" I asked.

"He's forty, maybe."

"What do you talk about with him?"

"Depravity. How other people live, how they all seem worthless and just go around getting drunk and moving away from God."

This is the first memory I have of the scorn Tim built for his peers. He cast them in this light to explain why he felt so alone, so unable to connect.

His illness had begun its work, separating Tim from the world. His brain began bending reality, making social situations intolerable.

During some of these conversations with Tim, I started to recognize what would become one of his disease's signatures—malleable religious language, ways to shape a world he struggled to recognize. We had not been raised with this specific type of religion, but religion, for Tim, had become the arena for schizophrenia's coup. Religiosity, a smoldering brand of fire and brimstone, endowed his delusions with cosmic significance, gave him a language for his psychosis—the demons, Tim would say, the demons in my head.

Religion was an important part of my father's life, Catholicism a presence ever since he was an altar boy. He can remember when Latin was the priestly norm, how he traveled with his parents to Naples to make his first communion among family in Italy. When I was growing up, he convinced our local church to let him teach me the catechism himself, promising that I'd pass whatever test they required before my confirmation. I remember that test—*Please name the four Gospels*—and how the questions seemed so different from the conversations I'd had with my father, like the afternoon when he had explained to me how scientists carbon-dated the Shroud of Turin.

For a time—childhood, when I was a young adult—I felt what I believe was real faith. My father was the smartest man I knew. If he believed, who was I not to?

I don't feel this way anymore. I don't resent the religion my father nurtured in me, and do occasionally feel peace when surrounded by stained glass, wooden pews, organ music. But I suspect this comfort stems from familiar ritual more than lingering faith.

Tim's spiritual devotion didn't arrive until college, a late-developing belief that surprised me as my own faith diminished. His illness adopted religious language, a spiritual vocabulary that would animate his delusions.

Years later, I accessed some of the notes from Tim's early therapy sessions at Lehigh, excerpts contained in the evaluations his doctors prepared for his trial. Through these notes, I constructed a time line of his frayed treatment, learned the dimensions of his suffering.

In his sessions with his first Lehigh therapist, Dr. Joseph, Tim described himself as "heinous, deserving of death." He immersed this self-loathing in religious language—he couldn't contain his sexual urges, lusted in a way the Bible forbade.

"This whole campus seems like an orgy, like people just go to these parties and fuck whoever they want and no one cares about anything."

Sometimes, Tim told Dr. Joseph, he felt like he was multiple people and all he could do to hold the versions of himself together was sit alone in his room and listen to an audiobook of the Old Testament.

"This can't be me," Tim said. "These thoughts can't be me."

Suicide remained on Tim's mind. He fantasized daily about shooting or hanging himself, but told Dr. Joseph that he didn't plan to end his own life.

"He would not kill himself primarily out of love for his family," Dr. Joseph notes, "especially for his mother."

That fall, our mother's texts to Tim often went unanswered. Most of her messages were innocuous—any excuse to reach him.

Hi Tim just left LA fitness! My trainer is tough. How's it going with you? Love Mom.

Hi Tim, snowing here. Love u mom

Sometimes, when Tim responded, his words unwound in exasperated strings.

Good morning to you too. But seriously you need to relax. I can feel your anxiety from over a hundred miles away.

This projected anxiety—though, yes, our mother was also nervous—announced a growing agitation, Tim's fear of an asphyxiating world. In November, Dr. Joseph drew some conclusions, named some of these accelerating symptoms, leveled a diagnosis that echoed Tim's first, *severe depression.*

"Severely depressed mood, anxiety, inability to experience pleasure in any social or educational pursuits, hopelessness."

Hopelessness. I had heard this in Tim's voice during some of our phone calls. I had heard his loneliness, the way he tried to extend a conversation, keep me on the phone by talking about a passage from Viktor Frankl, something he had read about existential neurosis, the gulf of meaninglessness, a way to name the emptiness he felt.

Later, I learned that Tim would pull hairs from his knuckles and groin to cope with this pain. Sometimes, I wonder if while we spoke on the phone, he was ripping these hairs from his body, feeling the brief sting, a needle's point piercing his skin.

But Tim also experienced moments of frenetic mental energy, bursts Dr. Joseph described as "sudden emerging feelings of well-being, increased energy, and abundance of ideas."

I remember some of these moments. Once, Tim called me on a Sunday afternoon, surprising me. He hadn't called the night before and few of our recent conversations had happened during the day. I answered the phone and walked out onto my apartment's small balcony, a narrow platform exposed like a diving board.

Tim's words built on each other, each arriving a little bit faster, as though his sentences were sliding down a steep hill.

"I met this couple at church this morning, and they're grad students in the engineering school who are from Germany, or maybe only one of them is from Germany and they're married."

"What were their names?"

"Otto and Rose. Reverend Parker introduced us afterward when I was having coffee in the basement and I was about to leave but they came up to me and started talking."

"Otto," I said. "German indeed." I could hear Tim gulp a breath before he continued.

"And then we had lunch together, and we spoke about all sorts of interesting shit. Like imagine if someday people started storing their genetic material so that they could have kids after they're dead, like posthumous future kids they could write into their wills, but who even controls someone's genetic material after they're dead? Otto is in some kind of bioethics class, but I argued that humans shouldn't interfere with natural reproduction and that artificial creation of life can be seen as a sin. . . ."

Tim continued, rambling—human cloning, eugenics, the morality of sperm banks. He seemed happy to track the paths of his ideas, of a conversation he had enjoyed.

As far as I was concerned, he could have been talking about baseball or the moon. His tone lifted me up, his focus on the future giving me hope. In fact, I was ecstatic. Tim's conversation over lunch might have meant he was making friends.

I couldn't see these instances—moments of exuberance—as anything more than a welcome break from melancholy. I didn't see how these bursts were feints, his disease covering its mobilization with normal gestures, a lunch with friends.

Dr. Joseph put Tim's experiences into a different context. Charting his volatile moods, Dr. Joseph introduced a new clinical suspect:

bipolar disorder. After November, he began talking to Tim about mood-stabilizing medications. It was after one of these sessions that Tim stopped seeing Dr. Joseph.

We didn't know that Tim had terminated therapy until after he got home for Christmas break. Chris would mention how in the weeks before he would receive increasingly bizarre and ranting phone calls from Tim. In the calls, Tim ripped verses from Matthew 23, spun rambling apocalyptic declarations.

Woe to you, you hypocrites, you are like whitewashed tombs which look beautiful on the outside, but on the inside are full of the bones of the dead.

5

Triplets are rare, roughly one in a thousand. For years, I used Chris, Tim, and Lizzie as a fun fact, my triplet siblings the perfect introductory tidbit for getting to know me.

People always follow up when they learn I have triplet siblings, always ask some version of *what's that like?*

I have two stock responses.

"It was like we went from zero to sixty when they arrived, four and a half years as an only child then *boom*, I'm one of four."

I can describe the morning they came home, the nested bassinettes, my chalk mural, the family's founding myth.

The other thing I'll say has to do with their number, three.

"Three can make for an awkward dynamic," I say. "Two of them were often closer to each other than with the third, which meant the third would become closer to me."

While the pairings shifted throughout childhood, in high school, Chris and Tim turned more exclusively toward each other, leaving Lizzie the odd one out. This, their teenage boy alliance, felt natural, a normal function of age, but the onset of Tim's illness meant that he and Lizzie never had a chance to revive their relationship.

And during those years when Tim grew increasingly ill, I know that communication frayed between Tim and Lizzie, that Lizzie feared what was happening with her brother but didn't know how to bridge the gulf expanding between them.

I know this caused Lizzie pain.

Lizzie is the greatest gift giver I have ever known. From a young age, she marked our birthdays with collages, colorful cards, poems.

When I graduated from college, Lizzie gave me a photo album, a gift she had worked on for nearly a month. For some time, she had appointed herself keeper of family history. She curated all of our photo albums, organizing them by year in bound volumes we stored in the family room. When I graduated from college, she siphoned off images from our archive and made an album of my life. She added captions. She decorated every page.

She wrote me a letter on the first page of the album.

Congratulations! I'm very proud of you. You're obviously not as stupid as I expected you to be.

There are more jokes.

I hope you remember your education, or something sappy like that. I'm sure with all that fancy school you'll make an excellent male model.

In closing, Lizzie wrote:

Whatever you do with your life, whatever you experience, whatever, whatever, you're a really good big brother and I love you. Love, your little sister, the best sister, Lizzie

Beneath her name, she pasted a photo, my favorite photo of Lizzie. She's posing with her hands at her shoulders, tongue out, eyebrows raised. She's sitting in the family room, hair in a ponytail, next to a half-finished bowl of ice cream. She's eight, maybe nine years old.

I love that picture because it's Lizzie—unquestionably—the totem of her I hold. Everything is in that frame: the smile curling around her stuck-out tongue, her eyes narrowing to raise her eyebrows, her palms dance-waving toward the camera.

As a child, Lizzie went to one ballet class before attaching herself to a softball glove. The two of us spent sunburned afternoons in our backyard, Lizzie fielding the ground balls I rifled at her shuffling feet.

She was faster on her bike than both of her triplet brothers, the hardest for me to chase on our neighborhood hills. One summer, we tied a long rope to a sturdy branch on a tree in our front yard. In the afternoons, Lizzie would scale the bark, pulling herself onto the highest limbs.

Lizzie joined in our gladiatorial combat in the basement, swinging foam car seats with the same ferocity as her bigger brothers. Sometimes she wielded a large exercise ball to mitigate our size, bumping the ball into us, our blows bouncing off her inflated shield. She would lunge with abandon while we tussled, popping up from the green carpet whenever one of us knocked her down.

By this, I don't mean to say that she was simply a tomboy growing up among brothers.

I mean to say that, even then, she was the most fearless person I knew.

When I was fifteen, Lizzie's dog died. Her dog, a black-and-tan dachshund named Candy Cane, had been her devoted follower, licking Lizzie's ankles as she walked through the house.

On the morning Candy Cane died, my father told me that I had to dig a hole to bury her. It was the day after Christmas; a platter slick with glazed yams still waited in the kitchen sink. On that morning, Candy Cane had struggled to wake up. She made low gurgling noises, curled in her space next to where Lizzie slept. We drove to the vet's office, the six of us, Candy Cane wrapped in a blanket on Lizzie's lap. There, we learned that a tumor had silently grown, strangling Candy Cane's tiny organs.

When we got back from the vet's office, our mother sat next to Lizzie while Lizzie painted CANDY CANE on a flat rock, newspaper shielding the kitchen table from purple paint.

When my father asked me to dig the hole, he pulled down a dent-dimpled shovel from behind our nest of bikes. He told me that the hole had to be deep. I'd rolled my eyes while my father reached for the shovel, but when he passed me the wooden handle I noticed that his head seemed to bow toward where I stood, a small gesture endowing the moment with solemnity.

This was something I needed to do for my sister. This was the first time I'd help her grieve.

Standing in the backyard on that day after Christmas, unaided by either of my brothers, I dug a hole in the frost-sealed ground—it was one of the smallest things I would ever do for Lizzie. The aching in my gloved hands, the vibration of the handle striking the ground, the heaving of packed dirt would later seem minor, almost meaningless in the context of the history we had yet to write. But after I dug the hole and watched Lizzie cry over the grave, I decided that I never wanted to see her sad again.

I know that this wish—impossible as it was, impossible as it is—grew out of what I'd been conditioned to believe. A big brother is a caregiver, a protector, a deputy for parents whose hands were full with three. I know that this role—*big brother*—felt central to me, a core characteristic, one of the ways, from a young age, I constructed my identity.

New fears persecuted Tim in the spring of 2012. Shadows chased him from his college campus to a forest outside town. There, he stripped naked, hid among the trees, hid from the shadows that followed.

Later that spring, Tim felt hives sprout on his forearms and climb his thick neck. At 2 a.m., he staggered to campus security and asked to be taken to the hospital. These hives were real.

At St. Luke's University Hospital, he was given Benadryl, then released. Tim didn't tell the doctor what he was thinking, the particular fear that had begun winding through his brain.

Five hours later, restless, pacing around his dorm, Tim decided to return to campus security. The hives hadn't gone away, he told them when he arrived. Elevated splotches still blistered his hairy arms. He pulled up the legs of his sweatpants to show the rash lingering at his ankles and shins.

But he wasn't having trouble breathing, so the security officer told him to calm down. But Tim couldn't calm down. His fears began to uncoil.

"Someone poisoned me," Tim said. "Someone wants me dead."

Tim came home in May after spring classes ended. In spite of his mounting fears, he had maintained strong grades, his best class that semester, Topics in the Philosophy of Religion: God and Evil.

Our mother cooked for him that summer. I remember her on the porch, her Birkenstocks on the splintered wood, grilling thick steaks for Tim. When he woke up in the morning, she'd be waiting, ready to crack eggs, sprinkle them with crumbled feta.

She seemed happier, like there were pieces of Tim she could recognize—his massive appetite, the way he abandoned a crumpled napkin on his clean plate.

Communication between Tim and our mother felt lighter. When I read the text messages between them, I see some of the goofiness, the playfulness, the quirky manners of speech Tim used when he was younger.

Mom: Hi Tim, just got home. Where abouts r u and when would you like dinner?

Tim: 620ish me thinks Claudius maximus the great.

Mom: Hi Tim, let me know when you know your plans and if I can help in any way.

Tim: Thanks santa claude! 1 min away lolz

We got glimpses that summer, moments that reminded us of Tim. One weekend, I came home with a friend to run a half marathon in nearby Fairfield. The race was on a Sunday morning at the end of July. The course, an oppressive sequence of sun-drenched hills, passed the house my grandmother had lived in, one with a steep backyard slope we had slid down during childhood winters. During the last three miles of the race, kids stood poised with hoses, spraying runners as they went by. I welcomed the cold water at every turn.

My friend Katie, a former Idaho state cross-country champion, had proven time and again to be impervious to extreme heat and physical pain. She beat me by a substantial margin. At the finish line, waiting in the sun, Katie handed me water and followed me to a nearby tree. I wilted in the shade and dumped water over salty streaks on my face.

Before the race, I had told my parents that we would be home in time to join them at a barbecue. My godfather's daughter had just graduated from high school.

I called my mother after the race, told her we would have to drive ourselves, that we were running a little bit late.

"Perfect," she said. "You can stop at home and pick up Tim."

I'm not certain what Katie knew about Tim. She, like many of my friends, had noticed that on weekend nights I tended to disappear with my phone for thirty minutes at a time. When I returned to my friends after those conversations, I would mutter something about how Tim was "having a hard time." Sometimes I mentioned his wrestling injuries, his academic struggles, the difficulty he had making friends.

I didn't talk about his suicidal thoughts, about the extent of his hopelessness, about the disordered ranting when he careened, breathless, on the hypocrisy of the Pharisees, the sin-laced culture of college fraternities, Jeremy Bentham's panopticon. Earlier that summer, he had explained this panopticon to me, social theory I wasn't familiar with.

"It's a design for a prison," Tim said. "There's only one guard, but he's perched so he can see into each of the cells. The prisoners can't tell when he's looking, but they feel like they're always being watched."

I was nervous about this car ride with Tim and Katie, about the path Tim's bizarre tangents might take. With Sunday beach traffic, the trip could be a long one.

Tim rode in the back seat of my Camry, sitting in the middle so that he could splay his thick thighs to either side. He leaned forward for most of the ride. His face filled my rearview mirror.

Katie asked him about what he was studying and we started talking about one of the courses he had taken the year before, Christian Origins: New Testament and the Beginnings of Christianity. Tim rolled up his right sleeve to show Katie one of his tattoos.

"This is the Chi-Rho," Tim said, "the first two Greek letters in *Christos*." The tattoo, in bold black ink, stretched on Tim's tense deltoid.

I had always liked that tattoo. The design was simple, stark, the Greek characters superimposed over each other—an *X* bisecting an extended *P*. Many years later, on a trip to Ireland, I would see the most famous rendering of the Chi-Rho, a massive illuminated monogram sprawling across a page of the Book of Kells. As tourists strained to marvel at the twelve-hundred-year-old script, I froze, remembering my brother's powerful shoulder.

Tim explained the Chi-Rho to Katie. "It's the symbol Emperor Constantine's army put on their shields," he said. "Constantine saw it in a dream when Jesus came to him."

"It's hard to be religious in college," Katie said. I could see Tim nodding in the rearview mirror.

I was nervous about where this conversation would lead, but Katie seemed comfortable, interested even, turning in the seat next to me to look toward Tim.

"Tim's a thoughtful guy," Katie would tell me later. "It must be tough being that thoughtful, that introspective."

That summer, Tim kept appointments with Dr. Briggs, a highly recommended psychiatrist our mother found. Tim hoped to return to campus in July to catch up on missed credits, but our mother, encouraged by Tim's regular appointments with Dr. Briggs, wanted him to stay home.

Tim's sessions with Dr. Briggs were mostly a mystery to me. Later, her notes would challenge how I remembered that summer, how the illness I chose not to see began tightening its grip, a slowly closing vise on Tim's brain.

That summer, Tim told Dr. Briggs that he felt "too permeable," like he was in danger of coming under the influence of other people. He felt that sometimes others could sense his thoughts, like his mind broadcasted his secrets.

A piece of Tim's brain, his interpreter, was beginning to malfunction, leading him to question the origin of everything that entered his mind. He started to question what thoughts belonged to him, what thoughts were visible for all to see.

It didn't take long for Dr. Briggs to quantify Tim's pain. "Not only is he aware that his mind is not working well," she wrote, "he is feeling very alone and isolated. He is suffering tremendously."

When Tim returned for his fall semester, he started to believe he could see into people's minds.

Once, during a Sunday phone call, he told me about a presentation he gave on Kant. After his presentation, his professor had told him, "You addressed exactly the questions I was going to ask."

"Sounds like you made a good presentation," I said to Tim over the phone.

"I could foretell his thoughts," Tim said. "I knew his history."

"Or you were just well prepared," I said, still hoping he was exaggerating, playing around.

"It's different," Tim said. "It's like he knows I have the gift, but I don't know what side he's on yet. I don't know if he's good or evil." Tim laughed.

But it wasn't a happy laugh, not belly-shaking mirth. The noise he made was more of a crackling cackle, three bursts, *ha-ha-HAA*, the last note an octave up, the *ah* sound held as his voice frayed.

I would hear this laugh often in the next two years. Tim would use that cackle to punctuate a rant, or, as in this case, to show that he didn't trust me. This was the noise he made when he felt that I couldn't understand his world.

Many of Tim's delusions began to tilt toward paranoia. These persecutory delusions built, one fear leading to another until his world became a terrifying confluence of forces conspiring against him.

When he was on campus that September, he believed that our parents had paid people to spy on him. It was this belief that eventually made it difficult for him to attend classes. Every classmate became suspect.

When he had moved back to campus, he had found a group of engineering students who went to his church and asked them if he could live in a room in their house. A chance to make friends, I'd hoped, still believing Tim could find friends, that friends could slow the sickness battering his brain.

But these housemates were spies too. Eventually, Tim no longer felt safe sleeping in his house, began spending nights in his car, limbs contorting to fit in his back seat. With class and his living space compromised, there was nowhere for him to go.

On September 24, the day before his twenty-first birthday, Tim called our mother.

"I'm going to be forced to kill myself," he said.

She convinced him to drive home instead. I don't know how she achieved this, how she coaxed him to drive safely away from campus, how she quieted her own fears about what Tim had said he would do with his car one year before.

But he listened to her then, listened when our mother asked him to come home.

When Tim returned home, his illness got a new name.

In order for Tim to be granted a medical leave from Lehigh, he needed a diagnosis. Tim reunited with Dr. Briggs, who—for the first time—used the word *psychosis*.

Psychosis, the presence of delusions (fixed false beliefs) and/or hallucinations (seeing or hearing things that others do not hear or see) that a person believes are real.

Psychosis, a way to lose contact with reality.

Dr. Briggs told Tim that he was suffering with psychosis she couldn't yet name as schizophrenia, but on the required form, the one granting Tim medical leave from Lehigh, she entered a diagnosis, *Psychosis NOS*.

NOS, "not otherwise specified."

Dr. Briggs dispensed this diagnosis based on the *DSM-IV*, the diagnostic bible psychiatrists use to name disorders through observed symptoms. The newest version of the text, the *DSM-5*, has replaced *Psychosis NOS* with *Other Specified Schizophrenia Spectrum and Other Psychotic Disorder*. The gist of the diagnosis remains the same. Though there are observable psychotic symptoms—delusions, hallucinations, disorganized speech—these symptoms alone do not yet fulfill specific disease criteria.

This diagnosis is a hedge. A way of saying, yes, something is wrong here, but it's not all the way wrong yet.

Dr. Briggs had a theory about Tim, about how he masked his emerging "psychosis NOS." Tim, she believed, had been able to hide much of his disorganized thought process through immersion in philosophy and religion. He intellectualized the cacophony in his head, normalized the disturbances as part of a spiritual and philosophical struggle. "Patient is preoccupied with themes of good and evil," Dr. Briggs observed.

Dr. Briggs also suggested medication, a tactic Tim continued to refuse.

I had no idea how to convince Tim to try medication. I remember telling him that getting better can require some collateral pain, just as building his body for wrestling had meant enduring pain while training. I was naïve enough to think that this analogy—*no pain, no gain*—could work.

For a long time, I believed that Tim was in denial. Denial made sense to me. We all want to believe that we are well. I could recognize that it would be difficult to admit that your brain was under attack, that the thoughts populating your mind were not to be trusted, misinformation spread by an enemy.

And the realities of a disease like schizophrenia are doubly difficult to bear. For most, the disease requires medication for an indefinite period and these medications have a range of side effects. The disease carries substantial stigma. One in twenty die by suicide.

Even though the majority of people in this country understand that schizophrenia is a disease of the brain, the connotation of words like *mad*, *insane*, *crazy* still suggest an earlier mode of thinking that views these people as wild and unhinged, as having some agency in their madness.

Of course, I thought then, Tim didn't want these labels and was in denial that he was sick.

Denial is something a person can get over, can snap out of. Denial is a stage in grieving, an eyes closed, fists clenched *this isn't happening this isn't happening*. It's what comes before acceptance, half of a flowchart: denial → acceptance.

I hadn't yet heard the word *anosognosia*.

Anosognosia is a Greek construction, an amalgamation: *a*, "without"; *nosos*, "disease"; *gnosis*, "awareness"—"without disease awareness."

Anosognosia is more than just denial. The ailment is a neurological defect, damage to the brain that prohibits a person from recognizing his illness. This phenomenon, first named in the beginning of the twentieth century, occurs most commonly in people who have suffered strokes. Neurologist and author Oliver Sacks describes anosognosia in *The Man Who Mistook His Wife for a Hat*. "It is not only difficult, it is impossible for patients with certain right-hemisphere syndromes to know their own problems—a peculiar and specific 'anosognosia.'"

People with anosognosia employ confabulations, illogical explanations for the symptoms their diseases spawn. A stroke patient claims that he can't move a paralyzed arm because he's stiff, it's cold, his shirt is too constrictive.

During the last twenty-five years, researchers have examined anosognosia's potential role in schizophrenia. Through examinations of neurological dysfunction, scientists have explored how anosognosia can cripple some psychiatric patients' awareness of their diseases.

But I knew none of this then. Then, all I could do when I saw Tim's resistance was think, *Denial, denial, denial.*

One of the greatest tricks Tim's schizophrenia would ever play was convincing him that it didn't exist.

6

When Tim returned to campus after his medical leave, Lehigh mandated weekly counseling. Tim kept his end of the bargain, an uneasy peace maintained until a few weeks before the end of the term.

That April, the counseling center fielded a call from an anonymous woman. She reported that she had received a number of messages from Tim, messages she interpreted as suicide threats. I have no idea what these messages said.

Lehigh contacted my parents. My mother called me while she and my father drove to see Tim.

My mother knew that I answered her calls with apprehension, that I answered expecting to hear that Tim had deteriorated. To combat this anxiety, she employed a standard opening line.

Hi, Vince. Everything is fine.

The phrase was how we deescalated, kept launch codes in their locked box.

Sometimes, like on this call, my mother would add a "but" to the end of the phrase.

"Hi, Vince, everything is fine, but Dad and I are going to Lehigh for a meeting with counseling services."

"Why is *this* happening again?" I asked her.

"This"—Tim planning suicide, Tim's disease accelerating.

My mother tried to pacify my concerns, convince me that it was good news that Lehigh had called this meeting, a sign that the school cared about Tim.

"Everything is fine," my mother said, "but we are going to be vigilant."

I said nothing. Resolution seemed impossible. Nothing seemed to change. We were suspended above the runway, circling, ready to assume crash positions, losing hope that we might find some way to land.

But at that meeting, Tim seemed to revive. He made promises. He was determined to graduate on time even though he had missed the previous fall. He had a plan, he explained, to stay on campus that summer, to make up the credits he had missed.

We believed him. For his part, he had enrolled in a full slate of courses. Miraculously, he would attend every class.

I visited Tim that summer, on my way home from a trip to DC to see friends. I arrived at his apartment in time for dinner. The apartment, half of a one-story home, sat a few blocks from campus.

He lived in the back portion of the house, and his entrance led into an alley off of the street. The apartment looked clean. Or, if not pristine, empty. The three rooms comprising the unit—bedroom, living room, kitchen—held only his bed, a folding table he used as a desk, and a gray sectional couch. His laundry spilled from a bag in the corner of his bedroom. An unopened case of beer rested against a kitchen wall.

"Why the beer?" I said. "You're certainly not drinking it."

"In case anyone drops by," Tim said.

"Might be more appealing if you kept it in the fridge."

Tim hadn't drunk since his freshman year of college. He had other ways of self-medicating, ways that never involved booze or drugs. Caffeine, weight lifting, and the Bible were his vices, the three places he turned to evade the forces in his head.

For dinner, we drove across the river to the center of Bethlehem, a cluster of shops and restaurants huddled beneath Lehigh's hilltop campus. He had chosen Mama Nina, a small Italian bistro where families and older couples were tucked into a dozen tables and booths.

He was on an egg-whites-and-Caesar-salad diet, his way of eating healthy. He augmented these meals with scoops of protein powder. When I ordered a plate of bruschetta, he balked.

"Okay, man, but you're taking the lion's share," Tim said. "I'm not looking for a binge. No fat-kid food."

But when the appetizer came, soaked in oil and balsamic vinegar, he slid his portion onto his plate.

"I'll turn this into fuel later," he said, "when I lift."

After dinner, we drove to the mall to see if there was a movie playing, but arrived forty-five minutes after the start of *White House Down*. Seeing no other options, we went next door to the Starbucks in a Barnes & Noble. Tim needed to "caff up." He used that phrase often, his way of saying that it was time to gulp a large coffee, replenish his energy, avoid slipping into a patch of lethargy. He told me that he had a paper to finish that night, an essay for his philosophy course Knowledge, Truth and Fiction.

"I don't have to stick around," I told him, looking for an out.

"I'll be up all night no matter what," Tim said. "It doesn't matter."

After grabbing coffees, we poked around in Barnes & Noble.

"I want to read more poetry," Tim said. We walked down the poetry aisle and I plucked a Billy Collins collection, *Ballistics*.

"You might like this," I said, though I was only grasping for something I was familiar with. I opened the book to one of the poems I remembered, "Brightly Colored Boats Upturned on the Banks of the Charles." I liked the honesty of the first two lines.

What is there to say about them / that has not been said in the title?

"Did you just pick this because of the rowing?" Tim asked.

I told him I'd buy him the book. At the checkout counter, Tim spoke to the clerk.

"Do people still buy books anymore? What kind of people buy books on a Sunday night?"

She looked puzzled. "We do okay business."

"But this is all going out of business soon though? Right? Books and all that aren't really what the masses are going for in the future. In a couple of months this place might be done."

"I'm just here for the summer," she said.

"I can't help but be apocalyptic in my worldview, you know, just always looking for the end, the end is nigh and all that. *Ha-ha-HAA*."

I handed Tim the book and nodded at the clerk, my first time apologizing for him in public.

That exchange convinced me not to sleep on his gray couch. I was uncomfortable, had no idea what we would talk about while he typed on his laptop, had no idea if I would go with him when he left to lift weights at his twenty-four-hour gym.

It was after nine o'clock when we got back to his apartment, but I figured that my four-hour drive to Boston was doable. I still felt guilty. Sure, he had acted somewhat erratically during the evening, and my discomfort was part of the reason I felt I had to leave, but my staying might have meant something to him.

When I told him I had to go, he said he didn't mind, telling me again that he would be working all night. Before I left he inserted a pod into his Keurig coffee maker. Somehow, he already needed another cup.

Early the next morning, I received a text from Tim.

It was nice spending time with you last night big boy . . . thanks for the book. I had a very psychotic evening . . . anyways I military pressed 310lbs for 12 reps so all that bruschetta went to good use lol . . . Haven't bragged about my lifting in awhile lol . . . anyways have a great 4th of july man. I love you

I had a very psychotic evening.

Tim never used language like that, *psychotic.* This message could have been an opening, something I could have responded to.

Psychotic, how? When you say psychotic what do you mean? Do you like feeling that way? Do you want to feel that way?

I asked none of those questions.

Instead, I told him that I was impressed with his lifting.

I've seen Tim's transcript from that fall, the full semester he completed after summer classes to catch up on the credits he had missed.

Among his courses was Philosophy of Psychology, a course in which he earned an A.

When we talked over the phone during those months, our calls were still similar to the conversations we had shared on previous Saturday nights.

"What's the point of living another year," Tim told me, after I'd called to wish him a happy birthday.

"Do you think I'm a sociopath?" he asked during another call.

"Maybe you feel things *too much*," I said. "Maybe you're too smart for your own good."

"What does *that* even mean?" Tim said. "You're talking nonsense now, big guy. *Ha-ha-HAA*."

Tim was right. I had no idea what to say.

Tim came home after his semester ended, joining us a few days before Christmas. We went to the mall together to buy some final gifts. Shoppers flocked between winter coat displays and perfume kiosks while Tim blended into their maelstrom, my 270-pound brother wading through the merry crowd.

He bought gifts for us, for me, T. S. Eliot's *The Waste Land*.

"Poetry for poetry," Tim had written on the card, returning the favor of my Billy Collins.

I will show you fear in a handful of dust.

That Christmas we put out the same stockings, laid them flat by the fireplace for our mother to fill with chocolate, candy canes, cherry jellybeans. We divided the space around the Christmas tree for presents—counterclockwise from oldest to youngest.

For the twenty-seventh consecutive time, our mother cooked Christmas dinner. She insisted every year that the family rally here, where she would prepare popovers, creamed spinach, prime rib.

For a long time, I couldn't remember that Christmas, our last to-gether. I strained to remember my mother, sitting at her end of the dining room table, across from my father, Chris, Tim, and Lizzie to her left, me to her right. I couldn't remember her red cheeks, flushed from standing in front of the oven, from bending over simmering pans. I couldn't remember her handing me a crescent roll, asking me—a repeated joke—"Looking for a roll in life?"

When I went home, I struggled in this way. I would see where my mother used to sit at the piano, where she tucked her knitting bag beneath a family room window. I would see the mudroom hook where she hung her maroon jacket, the empty hallway leading from my parents' abandoned bedroom. I would see the fridge, the idle magnets she had used to post reminders about doctors' appointments or Chris's swim schedule, her bulletin board, blank now, blank like her bathroom mirror.

On that mirror, months after she died, I'd found a to-do list, my mother's to-do list, frozen from her last day.

Thurs
Chris interview
Chris gas money
Shopping with Lizzie

I snatched the list from the mirror, the empty space easier to see.

But I kept the note, sequestered it in a desk drawer. Now, when I read that note I can remember her, remember how she thought in lists, ordered her life around the reminders she posted to the refrigerator or the steering wheel of her car.

But this took time, more than a year, more than a year until I could see her and not just the empty spaces she left to fill.

First, I had to find a way to remember Tim that Christmas. I had to remember the muffled thuds of his weights on Christmas morning and not move directly to our family room floor.

I had to remember how he had given us gifts, even that Christmas, even then. I had to see how pieces of him were still there, still Tim.

Now, I can remember our Christmases again, see my mother there.

When I was in high school she gave me a thesaurus—a Christmas gift I had asked for. She laughed when I opened the card.

For Vince, a gift, present, largesse, award. Love, Mom.

After Christmas, Tim's delusions multiplied. His hallucinations sharpened, refracting vividly through the prism of his ill brain. When he turned the key in his car's ignition, he felt light explode onto his face, like his headlights pointed inward, washed over his body, a burning evil emanation.

His illness, his anosognosia, concocted an alibi—childhood trauma—to explain the pain the sickness caused. He started texting our mother about stories of invented child abuse.

Tim called me on a Sunday in February, the day before President's Day, in the waning hours of a long weekend. I was flat on a friend's bed in Ithaca, New York, hiding from the subzero temperature of the windswept college town. The previous day had been my first on cross-country skis, my many falls the cause of my Sunday paralysis.

On the phone, Tim's words stuck together when he tried to speak. I could hear him struggle to breathe.

An assassin had planted a tracking device in his car. A classmate's bracelet, one that glinted in the sunlight, was the devil's amulet. A man sent by his landlord to fix the furnace had poisoned his food.

"He has cameras in the apartment," Tim said. "He wants to kidnap me. All of my stuff is in the car. I need to leave."

I imagined him, huddled in his car, in the shadow of the abandoned coal plants that still ringed the town.

Before I could respond, Tim started sobbing.

"Why didn't you teach me how to make friends?" he wailed. "Why didn't you tell me how to like other people?"

Why didn't you. Why didn't you.

He had never accused me like this before, never told me exactly what I had failed to do.

I don't remember what I said. He was alone then, more alone than I had ever heard him before—*why didn't you, why didn't you*—and I had no idea how to comfort him.

I remember that he hung up. I know that he called our mother.

He told her, "I'm going to blow my brains out in the library."

When our mother called campus security, they asked if she thought Tim had a gun.

Tim's threat led to an emergency meeting, a request that he withdraw to seek treatment. Tim left immediately, drove home through the night.

I know that when he arrived he asked our mother to take him to the hospital, the only time Tim would ask for treatment. I don't know why he wanted the hospital, why for a moment he could see the sickness in his brain.

When I remember his voice that day—*why didn't you, why didn't you*—I don't hear his illness. At least at that moment, when he sobbed, accused me of failing to help, I hear a scared boy, a younger Tim, not his mounting delusions.

And I think it was that Tim, the bit that was still there, who asked our mother to drive him to the hospital, the same one where he had been born.

But his illness recovered, quickly, overwhelmed the frightened boy who wanted his mother, who wanted help.

At the triage desk, standing next to our mother, he said it for the first time.

"I'll kill you if you leave me here."

Soon he was flailing, disappearing down a hallway in the grip of men in blue scrubs.

He called back toward her.

"It's your fault. You're lying to make them keep me here.

"You're lying. You're lying. You're lying."

7

Tim's two-week hospitalization generated five hundred pages of records. I read this ream for the first time a year after he killed our mother.

This—Tim's clinical file—was the first place I looked for answers, though at the time what I was really looking for was a smoking gun.

I started with his hospital records spread in front of me, my pen flying, filling the margins with exclamations—*Really?? Are you fucking kidding me!!* During this first read I was a flailing child. I was punching a pillow to muffle a tantrum. I wrote down the names of all of Tim's social workers and doctors, double underlining them when I felt they had failed.

But naming names, building a case against the people who treated Tim, was a poor attempt at catharsis. Anger was easier then, easier than the quiet that mourning demands.

I had no context for Tim's hospitalization, didn't understand the challenges complicating his treatment. I looked at Tim's doctors like auto mechanics who'd failed to fix the brakes on a car. I saw my mother's death, my brother's descent into madness, as a unique tragedy—my family's alone—not part of a greater crisis I didn't yet understand.

My limited perspective prevented me from extending empathy to the people—the only people except for my parents—who had cared for my brother.

In the hospital, a piece of paper challenged Tim's claims of sanity. In Connecticut, a physician's emergency certificate permits a hospital to hold a person deemed dangerous to himself or others for up to fifteen days. The dangerousness standard is the most common way that an adult with a serious mental illness can be admitted to the hospital against his will.

This physician's emergency certificate—PEC—marks the beginning of Tim's hospital paper trail.

"It was felt that the patient was in danger to hurt himself or others and given safety concerns and need for further stabilization he has been placed on a PEC."

It was felt. This feeling grew from Tim's threats to our mother, his claim, *I'm going to blow my brains out in the library.* Without these kinds of threats, it is unlikely that Tim could have been admitted to the hospital involuntarily.

Even after the PEC, Tim protested. "I'm going home today," he told a doctor. "I'm going home."

During Tim's intake, a social worker observed him. "Patient claims parents made up stories to get him into the hospital," she wrote. "He has trauma from childhood sexual abuse."

The social worker's handwriting—clipped, efficient—mutes the volatility of Tim's delusions.

When I imagine Tim's hospital admission—the first time he mentioned sexual abuse—I remember an image of our mother wrapping Tim in a beach towel. He was skinny as a child, always shivering when he left the water in his shark-shaped goggles.

"Patient claims he almost starved to death as a child," the social worker continued, "but his parents attributed this to his having had dental braces."

I remember those braces, their red tinge, the Waterpik he used to clean their wiring, the hot dogs we ate at Glenwood after the orthodontist pried them from his teeth.

This transference—shifting the source of his pain from illness to invented trauma—was his disease's defense mechanism. The source of this defense, anosognosia, did double duty. It rejected the sickness in his brain and convinced him that he was a victim.

Tim spoke like a victim. He convinced himself that he was suffering from PTSD. "I need to rest up and do intensive therapy," Tim told his social worker. "I need to heal from trauma."

While the PEC ensured that Tim could be held for up to fifteen days, he needed to undergo an additional hearing to be medicated against his will. From the first day of his hospitalization, Tim had been adamant that he would not take medication.

"Patient made threats that he was going to 'kill myself' if he was made to take medications on the unit," one doctor noted.

The only way doctors would get him to take medication was through forceful intervention, a probate court hearing to authorize the administration of pills against his will. In Connecticut, doctors can file for this authorization if a patient is incapable of giving informed consent.

By the letter of the law, Tim was capable of giving informed consent. He wasn't impaired in the sense that he was in a coma. He could ask questions and challenge what his doctors said. But this particular definition of informed consent belies how compromised Tim's brain had become.

For cases such as Tim's, a second standard for involuntary medication exists. If a judge agrees that a patient's refusal of medication places the patient or others in danger of harm, doctors can medicate without consent.

Here's how these medication hearings unfold: Patients are assigned attorneys who represent their right to refuse pills, to remain ill. There's a turgid history of these types of cases, a history that spans decades. When a patient challenges his treatment, an attorney need only prove that the patient won't be putting himself or others in life-threatening danger by rejecting care. There are more infamous examples than I can recount here, but consider a Wisconsin patient who chronically ate his feces. When challenging his treatment, the patient's attorney convinced a judge that his client could not be medicated against his will, because, strictly speaking, his eating his own feces wasn't a substantial threat to his life.

But Tim's threats against his own life, against our mother's life, were still a recent echo. The head of the psychiatric unit convinced a judge that without medication Tim would remain a direct threat to himself or others. Tim "lost" his hearing.

The morning after the hearing, Tim pulled a fire alarm and tried to escape the ward.

"After he learned that he would be medicated against his will," one doctor observed, "patient tried to elope from the unit."

Elope, like Tim was headed for a secret rendezvous, a forbidden marriage.

*   *   *

After Tim's hearing, a nurse sat with him when he took his pills. She made him stick out his tongue, move it up and down, side to side, then pull the corners of his mouth to reveal the crevices next to his molars.

My reports on Tim's progress came from my parents. I remember the conversation we had when he started medication.

My parents had called me five minutes into a run. It was a chilly night, and I held my phone in a gloved hand while my parents' voices came through the headphones tucked underneath my hat.

"They're making sure he takes his medication," my mother said.

They. This group—the arbiters of Tim's health, the team fighting his illness—was a faceless conglomerate to me. I could see white coats, clipboards, notes taken while brows furrowed.

I tried not to picture Tim, imagine what he looked like when he sealed his lips to the pills, to a nurse's gloved hand.

"How long is he going to stay in the hospital?" I asked.

"He'll stay through the week," my mother said. "After that, we aren't sure."

I didn't know how hard my mother and father were lobbying to keep Tim in the hospital.

"Parents expressed much concern about patient being released too early," Tim's social worker noted. "Parents pleaded with treatment team not to discharge him prematurely."

Pleaded. My parents begged for Tim to remain hospitalized. They feared that without the power of the court order, without doctors making sure the pills went down his throat, Tim would never swallow his medication. Our mother feared that once he was home, any strategies to convince him to take his pills would fail.

"Why can't they keep him until he's stabilized on meds?" I asked.

Stabilized, like Tim's illness could be contained, psychosis silenced after a few days of medication.

"Their goal is to discharge him when he's ready to take medication," my mother said.

Discharge is a common word in Tim's hospital notes, the goal mentioned in every assessment. While my mother pleaded for patience, there were real constraints that limited Tim's hospital stay, flaws in mental health care I didn't yet understand.

Many conspiring issues truncated Tim's care—the reliance on perceived dangerousness as the standard for permitting involuntary treatment, the nationwide shortage of psychiatric hospital beds, the looming insurance denials for inpatient psychiatric treatment. These factors, a few of the many cogs on a dysfunctional wheel, create psychiatric units with revolving doors. A cycle persists, one in which doctors stabilize critically ill patients and then discharge them to accommodate the next round of severely ill. These reprieves are temporary life rafts, a moment for a drowning victim to catch his breath before submerging again to thrash and flail.

Tim's rejection of treatment is the sharp end of anosognosia's spear. For the patient, like my brother, who is neurologically blocked from being aware of his illness, this battle—the pleas to *just take your pills*—is often the hill that mental health professionals and family members die on.

Yes, I mean this figuratively, but also, but also.

Tim's anosognosia should have been part of the rationale for his "involuntary" treatment. Yes, I balk at the word *involuntary*, the legal language lobbed at patients who push away pills. This distinction—voluntary, involuntary—implies that a patient with a crippling brain disease remains the governor of his mind. This distinction ignores schizophrenia's coup, does not consider where the will of the patient ends and the will of the disease begins.

I know this concept is slippery. Any argument that appears to denigrate the inviolable human will elicits cries of *Tyranny, oppression, Big Brother mobilizing the thought police.* Many will frame this conversation as a challenge of our civil liberties, as an attack on our American DNA—*Give me liberty or give me death.*

But these illnesses are oppressors, a fact that legal language could more thoroughly recognize. In 1999, Justice Anthony Kennedy acknowledged this—the tyranny of serious mental illness—in *Olmstead v. L.C.*, a case concerning state discrimination against people with mental disabilities.

> *It must be remembered that for the person with severe mental illness who has no treatment the most dreaded of confinements can be the imprisonment inflicted by his own mind, which shuts reality out and subjects him to the torment of voices and images beyond our own powers to describe.*

Justice Kennedy reminds the court to weigh the imprisonment of involuntary treatment with the daily imprisonment of untreated serious mental illness—*the most dreaded of confinements.* He acknowledges, in ways legal language often fails to, the power of mental illness to stifle the individual's will.

But in spite of this rhetoric, our laws do not match the medical realities of serious mental illness. Our laws regarding diseases that spawn delusions are delusional themselves.

Danger. Tim's "dangerousness" was the legal rationale for admitting him to the hospital against his will.

During the first sixty years of the twentieth century, the standard for committing someone against his or her will was broader, defined more in terms of the extent of a person's disability. This rationale stems from the government's parens patriae powers—from the Latin phrase for "parent of the nation." These powers most commonly protect the safety of abused or neglected children, but also extend to those with substantial disabilities. In this way, the state acts as caretaker, champion of the needs of the most vulnerable.

This broader standard for commitment did have significant pitfalls and facilitated the long-term warehousing of the mentally ill in large state hospitals, the asylums that exist largely in our zeitgeist as haunted hellholes.

There's no shortage of literature detailing how state hospitals shuttered. While many of these institutions were indeed "snake pits," the vacuum left in their wake was never filled.

In the 1960s, the state's police powers began to supersede parens patriae as the guiding principle for commitment laws. Police powers, generally defined, are the state's interest in keeping its citizens safe. This shift meant a move to emphasize the "dangerousness" standard in commitment law, an evolution that first occurred in the District of Columbia in 1964, but was reinforced shortly after by the 1967 passage of the Lanterman-Petris-Short Act in California (LPS). LPS became the model for most of the "dangerousness standard" statutes that followed.

In the most practical terms, the dangerousness standard all but guarantees that many people suffering with chronic diseases will be treated as emergency patients. The emergency room is where these orders—Tim's PEC—are enacted.

In emergency medicine, the goal is stabilization. The goal is to bring patients back from the precipice of death.

When psychiatric patients are held on their perceived dangerousness, the goal is similar. The goal is stabilization. The goal is for a doctor to deem the patient no longer dangerous.

But schizophrenia is not a gunshot wound. Schizophrenia is not a gash that can be stanched and stitched. Yes, the bleeding, the psychosis, might stop with some swallowed pills, but stabilization is fleeting. Without consistent care, the wounds reopen, and tyrannical psychosis returns.

And Tim's psychosis returned. After he was discharged, after he was deemed no longer dangerous, anosognosia quickly convinced him that his doctors had lied.

Yes, we are right to be wary of "involuntary" care. We are right to be wary of locked wards, restraints, straitjackets.

But if these are our only concerns, we forget about how these diseases are *involuntary*, how Tim's disease held him against his will for much longer than his hospital PEC. Would it have been crueler to hold Tim longer, to attempt more patient strategies appropriate for a chronic, entrenched disease, than to release him, still vulnerable, after only a week of pills? If we had a different standard for keeping someone in hospital care, if we assessed a patient's *need for treatment* instead of just their dangerousness, would we in fact be more compassionate, provide people with a real chance to quiet their illnesses?

Now, Tim tells me, "I would do anything to change what happened," when I ask him about the length of his involuntary care. "Anything," Tim says.

But we never gave him this chance.

When Tim was discharged, when he was no longer deemed dangerous, his disease was still in control. To expect him to find his way back to the hospital, to care, on his own, is as delusional as expecting a man with a broken leg to walk to the ER.

8

Chris, Lizzie, our mother, and I visited Tim two days before his discharge. Our father also visited Tim while he was hospitalized, but he wasn't with us that particular morning. On that morning—the only time I saw Tim during his hospital stay—we parked in front of the unit, a building with a façade like an office, like an administrative wing of the hospital. I'm not sure why I felt this way, like the building was camouflaged, hiding among familiar landmarks—a corner Dunkin' Donuts, a parking garage shadowing York Street—on the margins of the medical school campus.

In the lobby we faced a gatekeeper, a man behind a Plexiglas window. We announced our intentions, said our name, Tim's name, Granata.

With a key, the gatekeeper sent our elevator to the third floor, the locked ward. A staff member let us into the unit when he saw our visitor name tags.

The visiting room combined sterile hospital tile with weathered furniture, beige couches that looked like the warehoused items in my grandmother's basement. There was some artwork, imagery I categorized as "hopeful," an expansive landscape hanging on gray walls.

When Tim emerged from a hallway, the four of us formed a sort of receiving line. We stood in a row as Tim shuffled in front of us, head bowed like he was about to receive communion. When he stopped in front of me, heavy arms slack at his hips, I thought that if I hugged him too hard he might disappear.

When we sat, Tim's voice—the quietest I had ever heard it—blended into the din of patients and staff moving through the room. I kept my eyes on Tim. Our mother asked most of the questions.

"How did you sleep last night?"

"Good."

"Did you have your breakfast?"

"Yes."

"Did you have a group meeting today?"

"No."

Chris made a bit more progress. He, like Lizzie, was home for a few days on his college spring break. He told Tim that he had been playing one of their favorite video games, an older installment in a popular fantasy series, games where players embarked on quests across sprawling fantastical worlds.

I watched while Chris gestured next to me on the couch, coaxing Tim into the conversation, trying to reanimate his brother.

But Tim's interest was fleeting. When he was quiet, our mother spoke.

"So it looks like I'll bring you home on Monday," she said. She addressed him like a child she was planning to pick up from summer camp, a child who was homesick, alone.

"Good," Tim said.

I said nothing about the medication nurses watched him swallow, the delusions of childhood trauma, the breathless threats he had flung at our mother. I thought then that his denial had been defeated, that his objection to treatment was something that could be vanquished.

I looked at him, sitting across from us, crumpled like a paper shopping bag. He looked sick, sallow in his pale hospital gown like he had just undergone a course of chemo.

During his fifteen-day hospitalization, Tim recanted the threats to our mother he'd made that first night in the ER. Doctors fitted his disease with a temporary muzzle. By the end of his stay, Tim was no longer dangerous.

And when Tim was no longer dangerous, his "involuntary" treatment had to stop. His disease helped him promise his doctors he would stay on his medication. His disease helped him lie.

Yes, I'll take my medicine.

Yes, I'll attend the outpatient clinic.

On his discharge form, Tim's doctors gave him a reminder: "Call your doctor if you begin to hear voices when there is no one physically present or if you see things that other people do not see."

Call your doctor if, like the end of every drug commercial.

Call your doctor if you experience dizziness or shortness of breath.

Call your doctor if demons convince you that your mother secretly abused you as a child.

Tim was discharged on a Monday, in the morning. While he left the hospital, driving away with our mother in her minivan, I was probably taking attendance during ninth-grade homeroom at the high school where I taught English.

Tim was supposed to enter outpatient treatment that same afternoon. He never went. When he got home he told our mother that he wasn't going back. In fact, he was never going back, he said. Then, he retreated to his room and collapsed on his bed, exhausted.

Tim did agree to a few appointments with a psychiatrist he had seen while he was in the hospital. This psychiatrist, Dr. Robertson, was the one my parents would call on the day my mother died.

During an appointment, days after Tim's discharge from the hospital, Dr. Robertson noted his impressions of Tim. "Pleasant and not pressured," Dr. Robertson wrote, "but his thinking is tangential, hyper abstract. He is sicker than he looks."

In his meetings with Dr. Robertson, Tim tried to explain away his hospitalization. He believed the psychiatric ward had been an arena for his mind, a trial he needed to overcome to grow closer to God. He didn't tell Dr. Robertson what he planned to do if our parents tried to bring him back to the hospital. I don't know if my parents relayed these threats to Dr. Robertson.

"I'll kill myself," Tim told them, days after his discharge. "I'll kill myself before ever going back."

Tim flushed his pills down the toilet on his first day home, immediately after my mother gave him his prescriptions. Suddenly without medication, Tim felt his forehead burn, his fever spiking near 103 degrees, withdrawal from the antipsychotics. It was almost like his body built a fire, a last-ditch effort to smoke out the disease. The fever broke a day later.

I hadn't told my friends about Tim's hospitalization. I kept his struggle to myself, a quiet secret I held until a few days after his discharge.

On a Thursday night, I told my friend Pat, my roommate of three years. I remember my preamble, my first attempt to make some sense out of an illness I didn't understand.

There was a narrative I could build for Pat, of Tim's gradual combustion, his resulting hospitalization. I could mention specific events—*he threatened to blow his brains out in the library, he threatened my parents when they left him at the hospital, a probate judge forced him to take medication, his doctors discharged him from the hospital, he flushed his pills down the toilet.*

While Pat listened, I plotted these points on an unfinished time line, beginning to realize that I had no idea what would happen next.

During this time, my mother also wondered what was next.

"Tim might just pick up and try to drive to California," she told me once. "We won't know until he's gone."

This scenario, a road trip that sounded almost picaresque, was the worst possible outcome she would share with me.

When we spoke on the phone, she tried to make our conversations about more than Tim. She worked hard at this tactic, tried to focus on my life, on what I was teaching.

"How are your students liking *Jane Eyre*?" she used to ask.

Jane Eyre was my mother's favorite book. She had read it annually, her hardcover copy braced against her knees on a beach chair. Though it had been her favorite, I hadn't read *Jane Eyre* until I started teaching, scrambling to prepare in the week before my classes began the book.

But I fell for *Jane Eyre* immediately. I remember, after my first read, calling my mother to tell her, *I get it now,* before gushing about the language, the gothic setting, the shadowy fog that hangs off every page. She pointed me to some of her favorite lines, passages that have become my favorite too, like Rochester's description of the pain of parting with Jane.

I have a strange feeling with regard to you. As if I had a string somewhere under my left ribs, tightly knotted to a similar string in you. And if you were to leave I'm afraid that cord of communion would snap. And I have a notion that I'd take to bleeding inwardly.

Jane Eyre became a cord between us, a shared love, something to return to when everything else seemed in flux. *Jane Eyre* became a way for us to have conversations that didn't circle Tim locked behind his bedroom door.

I don't know if these conversations were my mother's way of protecting me. When I asked her about Tim, she would answer, briefly, trying to find some sliver of positive news.

Tim mentioned that he wanted to finish his last credits and graduate.

Tim had dinner with us last night.

Tim met with Dr. Robertson this week.

Sometimes, when we spoke, she would remember stories, memories from when she and I were together, years ago.

You were seventeen, Vince, the end of the summer before your last year of high school. We went on that college tour together. I printed out all the directions from MapQuest, and you held them while we drove around New England. You didn't get behind the wheel until the end of the trip, when we were in Providence.

Remember, in Providence, how we circled the blocks, how when we finally found a spot, I couldn't get into it? I tried twice, blocking traffic, wedging the minivan's back tires into the curb. Then you said, "Mom, let me do it." When you got behind the wheel, you had to tilt the rearview mirror, slide the seat away from the pedals.

You did it in one try, tires flush with the curb.

It's silly, a small thing, I know, but that was one of those moments. I knew you were going to be fine. You were going to leave home, but you were going to be fine.

These were the stories my mother told me while she tried not to talk about Tim, about his accelerating delusions, about how he was growing increasingly nocturnal. I don't think my mother wanted me to know how worried she was.

Toward the end of Tim's hospital record, Tim's social worker comments on a meeting she had with my mother.

"Patient's mother states that she would never bar patient from coming home but that she is afraid of him and his potential to harm her."

My mother never told me that she was afraid.

I should have known that she was afraid. *Of course* she was afraid. Tim had threatened suicide many times, threatened her life too. But when I asked my mother about these threats, about how Tim invented secret abuse in the basement, she explained them away.

She said, "He just wants us to know he's angry."

She said, "He wants us to know that he's in pain."

One night, more than a year after her death, on another survey of my parents' bedroom, I stubbed my toes against the spines of books hidden under her side of the bed. On my hands and knees, crawling on the patch of carpet next to where she had slept, I found a hidden cache, books clustered in stacks. I yanked them into the light, my mother's doomsday stash hiding under a year of quiet dust.

There were nearly twenty books, her arsenal to combat Tim's illness. She must have been afraid that he would find them, that he would know she believed in his disease, the one that he couldn't name.

The first book I opened was in the stack closest to her nightstand, *Surviving Schizophrenia: A Family Manual.*

Surviving Schizophrenia. She understood the gravity—*surviving*, life or death—but saw the struggle as Tim's, as Tim fighting a disease that conspired to end his life. So she read the manual—*A Family Manual*—a way to follow instructions, to help Tim survive.

But did she know that both of their lives were in danger? Did she know that surviving was something they wouldn't do together?

Though I won't know her fears, I know this: my mother wanted Tim to survive. She wanted him to survive in the weeks before her death when she slid notes under his locked door.

Stay strong Tim.
I know you're hurting.
I believe in you.

I found these notes in a pile on his desk, days after he killed her. The last note says *I love you,* in the same curved handwriting that used to mark my name on the tags of childhood jackets.

9

Tim joined us when our family traveled for Lizzie's and Chris's college graduations. To Lizzie's graduation, he wore what looked like a disguise—gray suit, maroon turtleneck. His thick neck stretched his sweater, prevented the fabric from reaching his chin. He was clean-shaven, the first time I'd seen his olive cheeks in months. His hair—plastered down with a part on the left side of his scalp—told me that he cared about his appearance.

But for all his effort, he looked menacing. His bulk, the suit and turtleneck, his slick hair, made him look like hired muscle.

The following weekend, at Chris's graduation, Tim arrived in another costume—blazer, T-shirt, track pants. The T-shirt featured a demonic rabbit, a character from the movie *Donnie Darko*. That movie, a cult classic, features a teenager who is visited by a deranged rabbit who warns him about the coming apocalypse. During one of these visits, the protagonist—a boy diagnosed with schizophrenia—asks the messianic rabbit, "Why are you wearing that stupid bunny suit?"

"Why are you wearing that stupid man suit," the rabbit replies. The rabbit's words were printed on the back of Tim's T-shirt.

Yes, in a way this is almost too much to believe—Tim's shirt the talisman of a cinematic hallucination. Later that night, Tim would give me the clearest picture of his own hallucinations, details I had yet to hear.

In spite of his strange dress, Tim drew little attention when he joined us—Chris, Lizzie, me—at a party the night before Chris's graduation. Most at the party were drunk and nostalgia-ridden, too distracted to notice Tim.

After Tim met some of Chris's friends, I brought him downstairs to a quiet basement—a place to talk, a place to hide Tim from the party. We sat on an abandoned couch behind a coffee table. With Tim, alone, I put a foot on the table, my shoe landing among ringed outlines of long-abandoned cans.

Here, Tim gave me a vivid picture of his madness.

"Last night," Tim said, "I saw something in the basement." He was rigid, at a right angle against one of the arms on the couch.

"When you were lifting?" I said.

"I was just sitting," he said. "I had just finished watching *No Country for Old Men.*"

"Again," I said, trying to laugh. This movie had become an obsession for Tim, a frequent pastime between lifting bouts. Whenever I asked Tim why he repeatedly watched that movie, he would describe the movie's world, one without morality, without God.

"It's terrifying," Tim would say.

That night, next to me on the college couch, Tim held a beer, his hairy knuckles buckling around the can. He didn't take a single sip. I was staring at his hand when I asked him what he'd seen in our basement.

"A coin," Tim said. "A coin floating." He told me like he was describing a frightening scene, a scary movie, a lurching monster.

He told me the coin was a Susan B. Anthony dollar, one he or Chris must have found years before and brought to the basement for safekeeping.

"It was there," Tim said, "a few feet from my face."

I said nothing, seeing for the first time the dark heart of Tim's disease, the power it wielded over him, this floating coin a new kind of nightmare.

I think he could tell that I was scared.

"It's the key to a portal," Tim said, raising his voice like he'd figured it out, "to where the demons are." His mind molded the coin to fit a specific purpose, a purpose he had divined. He named it—portal, doorway to demons—and let that stand as a logical conclusion, like he had found a foreign phrase and translated it into English.

"Were you on the inversion table when you saw it?" I asked, my own mind trying to fit his hallucination into some type of logic, a rush of blood to his head. I stalled, tried to give myself time to process this new insight into Tim's world.

I was still unwilling to believe this picture of his madness, rejected that Tim was hallucinating in the semidarkness of our basement.

But how could I have rejected Tim's reality? How could I have doubted this textbook symptom—though he couldn't use that word, *symptom*—when he had been hospitalized just months before, legally mandated to swallow antipsychotics?

Then, I made another mistake.

"Tim," I said, "you know that wasn't actually there, right?"

Challenging what was real to Tim separated us further, truncated one of the most honest conversations he would have with me about his terrifying world. He cackled, the electric *ha-ha-HAA*, Tim's coda to a conversation, the signal that he didn't trust me.

We were quiet then, the muffled sounds of dance music carrying on above us.

While we sat on that musty couch, I couldn't see how Tim's reality—his floating coin, his demons—was just as solid to him as the coffee table in front of us. And this made me afraid—not of him, not yet—afraid of how convinced Tim seemed that the world conjured forces that were conspiring against him.

Because I was afraid, because I had no idea what to say to him, I took him back upstairs to the party. I let him linger on the periphery, watched as he melted into the dancing bodies. I started talking to Chris, his girlfriend, and her cousin Sarah, a woman I had met at dinner.

I had been attracted to Sarah immediately. When I met her, she stood next to her uncle, a barrel-chested man with a booming voice, but didn't disappear in his shadow. I had learned she was a teacher, and while we spoke, Sarah rocked onto the balls of her feet, leaning forward so I could hear her over our families speaking around us. There was something about her posture, the way she tried to hold herself still, like she was tense with potential energy, a loaded spring. The more we spoke, the more I wanted her to focus all of her coiled energy on me.

At the party, I remember glancing over Sarah's head to look for Tim. I saw him pause in a doorway. I knew that our parents had a rollaway bed for him at their hotel. I knew that Tim's car was nearby and that he could drive to the hotel without my help.

I also knew that I wanted to sleep with Sarah, that our talk was accelerating, that I had told her that I planned on staying in Chris's room because Chris spent his nights with his girlfriend. I told her this like it was a convenient offer—*if you want to stay on campus, I'm happy to share my brother's empty bed.*

On my way out with Sarah, I turned to find Tim across the party.

I saw him, the two of us tall enough to see eye to eye over the crowd. We nodded. The people who should have been his peers—college seniors on the eve of graduation—surrounded him. But Tim was alone.

I left him there. I left him alone after he'd showed me a terrifying picture of his madness. I left him alone and took a woman I had just met to Chris's dorm.

I learned the next morning that Tim never went to our parents' hotel. Instead, he drove the five hours home, tucking himself into bed when the sun rose over our house.

The next night, after Tim woke from his daylight sleep, he texted me.

Tim: *Did u bang the cousin?*

Me: *(yeah)*

Tim: *Why do you put that in parentheses? Why do you wanna keep that shit on the DL? Is she married or some shit?*

Me: *Oh I don't care.*

Tim: *Is she?*

Tim: *Married?*

Me: *No*

Tim: *You're insane.*

One morning, weeks after Chris's graduation, Tim entered our parents' room with fistfuls of salt. He threw the salt across the bed while they slept, waking them when the coarse crystals struck their cheeks.

"Demons are everywhere," Tim said, while my father wiped salt from his eyes.

Tim became a vehement protector of his physical space. He started carrying a cup of water when he walked around the house, sloshing the water when people came too close. Once, after Tim accused our father of searching his car, Tim threw the water.

"Violence is the only language you'll understand," Tim said.

Then, "violence" was spilled water, Tim tossing a plastic cup.

I returned home a few weeks later, toward the end of June, preparing to leave for the Dominican Republic, where I would volunteer at my friend's summer camp. By the time I arrived home, Tim had rejected the sun. It was work to see him.

On nights when I forced myself to stay awake, I would catch him in the kitchen when he emerged to eat. He ate ravenously—pan-size egg-white omelets, serving bowls of Caesar salad. He drank coffee by the pint glass, but never with ice. Steam would escape from the top, his hand obscuring the glass.

Our late-night kitchen rendezvous were the only times I spoke to him. In these brief conversations—garbled through his delusions, my exhaustion—Tim spoke about the demons, the ones he had first described to me in the basement during Chris's graduation party. He told me that they'd convinced him to burn some of his books and to sprinkle salt on the scar they'd left in our backyard.

He spoke about his death—the certainty of his death—a prelude to what he would say on the day he attacked our mother.

"My death is supposed to look like a suicide," Tim said, "but it will be the forces that compel me to die."

On the day before I left for the Dominican Republic, I ate a late breakfast with my mother. We sat at our pockmarked kitchen table, green place mats under bowls of Cracklin' Oat Bran. I remember that she held her favorite mug, the one with the cartoon French dog, Le Chien.

My mother knew that I stayed awake to listen to Tim rant over his midnight breakfasts, but that morning, our conversation didn't start with Tim. Instead, she looked at me, exhausted, bent over a soggy bowl of cereal, and asked me why I had stopped writing.

I was surprised. Tim, hibernating above us, was hallucinating floating coins in the basement, yet she wanted to talk about why I had stopped writing. Our last face-to-face conversation started when she asked me about a passion I had abandoned.

My writing wasn't a new topic of conversation for my mother and me. In the five years since I had graduated college, my mother had occasionally asked me why I had stopped. She knew that writing workshops had been my favorite college courses, that writing stories had been a part of my life since the third grade.

She asked me that morning why I had stopped trying. She was blunt, offering a rare direct challenge.

I tried to deflect. I made oblique references to needing more time, more space away from teaching. I told her that it felt difficult to think creatively, that teaching the same classes for three consecutive years had left me in a rut of indolent mud.

"I don't believe you," she said.

I didn't realize then how desperately she needed me to be happy.

"I don't know!" I shouted, erupting, my fists striking the table. Somehow, my anger found its way to the person who deserved it least.

"You're scared of something." My mother didn't raise her voice.

"There's no point!" I yelled. "I can't get myself to do anything."

"What are you scared of?" Her voice softened, like she was trying to calm me down before my first day of school.

"Of course I'm scared," I said, my voice fraying, a prelude to tears.

"You're worried about your brother."

I remember that she said *your brother*. I remember that she didn't say *Tim*.

"Yes." I looked toward the table. I looked down as if admitting some type of failure, like I was telling her, for the first real time, how powerless I felt in the face of his disease.

"What are you scared of? That he's going to hurt himself?" She put it this way, *hurt himself*, the way we voiced fears about Tim.

Tim had continued to mention suicide. He had mentioned again that he believed he would die on the Fourth of July, echoing his first threat three years earlier.

My mother knew, in that moment, while we sat across from each other at the table, that I was afraid, that Tim's life seemed to be shrinking in front of me.

She hugged me. If she spoke, I don't remember what she said. I remember burying my head into her right arm, my face level with her torso.

This was the last time my mother would see me cry.

Later, the night after that breakfast, I stayed awake hoping to see Tim. He never emerged from his room, so I planned to wake up early and see him before he returned to bed. I went to sleep in my childhood room, surrounded by Michael Jordan, the Boston Red Sox, the posters I had plastered to my walls in middle school. The room remained a time capsule—pictures from Acadia National Park, my complete set of Redwall books—every object pointing to a different time.

When I fell asleep that night, I was not afraid of Tim. I had cried in my mother's arms that morning out of fear of what Tim might do to himself, the fear I had harbored for years, a fear that he might take his own life.

But I had no fear *of* him, only fear *for* him.

That night, Tim woke me with three thundering knocks on my door. The impact shook the entire frame. The knob vibrated, a metallic ringing in my ears.

"What? What?" was all I managed, a half-awake wail. I sat up against my headboard, rigid, sheets tangled around my legs. There was silence, and then heavy shifting on the floorboards, Tim retreating to his room.

He could have come in. My door was unlocked.

I got up when I heard his door close. The noise had also woken my mother, and I saw her as I walked the five steps to Tim's room. I knocked, more gently than he had, "Tim?" There was no response.

I knocked again, "Tim? Did you just knock on my door?" I looked down the hall toward my mother. She watched, squinting without her bifocals.

"That's fucked up, man," Tim said, voice low behind his door. "Go back to sleep." He almost swallowed the last word and I waited to respond.

I looked at my mother. She had taken a few steps down the hallway. The dent of a pillow dimpled her reddened cheek. I raised my hand to tell her to stop.

"Good night," I said into his door.

His fist on my door may seem minor in the context of the violence yet to come. It may seem like a moment I could have folded into my own delusional definition of normal, a definition that my family molded to fit this new Tim.

But when I returned to my room, I locked the door. I lay there for hours, shaking from the violence of his knocking fist. Tim was different now; this pounding had been aimed at me. This violence, violence I hadn't feared when I was alone with him just a day before, had been brought to my door.

Though I had watched him suffer, heard him cry and rant, felt the extent of his delusional anxiety, I had believed that Tim would never be violent. I had believed this in spite of the threats he made at the hospital—*I'll kill you if you leave me here.*

As soon as I became afraid of Tim, I lost him in pieces. Fear stripped him away, piece by piece, until he was only those three thunderous knocks on my door.

Fear drove me away.

I ran the morning after he shook my door. I didn't fold my clothes. I poured coffee into a borrowed travel mug that I promised I would return.

I said goodbye to my mother in the driveway. She was still in the pink nightshirt she'd worn hours before when we stood outside of Tim's door. She had the dog's leash in her hand, and when I hugged her, he jumped toward us, resting a paw on each of our hips.

This was the last time I saw my mother, and all I remember is the dog scratching at our legs.

As I drove down the driveway, I looked back at the heavy curtain darkening Tim's room. I saw the glinting decal on his window, a fireman's helmet, faded after twenty-two years. That silver sticker, placed when Tim was a baby, alerted firefighters: CHILD INSIDE.

I left home wrapped in fear of Tim. My thoughts about Tim, about his violence on my door, fused with the threats I knew he had made toward our mother, the threats we never spoke about.

My route that morning took me through Newtown, Connecticut, thirty minutes from where I grew up. There, my fear metastasized.

A year and a half before, after the school shooting, a local art teacher—a man I knew—had crafted twenty-seven wooden angels, hammered them into a hillside near his Newtown home.

Twenty children. Six teachers. The shooter's mother.

Tim would never, but I realized I couldn't finish that thought. Then, as I drove through Newtown, my stomach seized. I felt my entire body clench, my right foot push through the accelerator like I could hurtle through this fear, speed past it—*it*, the fear, the real fear that Tim might hurt other people.

Nothing about Tim, about his particular delusions, pointed toward mass violence. And now, after interrogating his disease, after listening to Tim talk about his demons, I'm certain that the violence his untreated illness spawned would only ever have targeted the people he was closest to.

But then, in my car, I was terrified. I pulled off the highway. I called my mother and told her that I was afraid.

"It's more now," I said, explaining how everything had changed since when I had sobbed at the kitchen table the day before.

I let my fears build over the phone, fears about Tim's impulsivity, how quickly his moods changed, his visual hallucinations. I ranted about his access to a car, about people sleeping behind unlocked doors, about his refusal to talk to anyone who tried to treat him. His illness had seized control. Little was left of the loving boy we remembered.

When I stopped, I was breathless from ranting. I stopped on the threshold of my greatest fears, the new fears, fears so ugly I could only voice them after emptying myself of all others.

"I think he could be violent," I said.

"What if he gets a gun?" I whispered, afraid to hear the words out loud. "What if he turns on you?"

I said this to my mother. I said this to her three weeks before her death. I said this to her while I was speeding away from home.

Then I was quiet, waited for my mother's voice.

Slowly, she convinced me that I was wrong.

Slowly, with the same soft words she'd used to quiet my childhood nightmares, she comforted me.

I let her voice loosen my grip on the steering wheel. I let her convince me to leave. I let her convince me that she was safe.

"Everything is fine," she said, using the lie we told each other. "Everything is fine."

10

I put a thousand miles between home and me. I left the rest of my family—Chris, Lizzie, our parents—to live with the fear I couldn't bear. They endured far more than Tim's fist on my door.

I arrived in the Dominican Republic and drove with my friend Jon toward the Haitian border, to the village where I would spend the next weeks.

I stumbled through Spanish syntax, grasped at distant vocabulary, read children's novels like *Charlie and the Chocolate Factory* to bolster my rusty language skills. I sweated through my shirts chasing kids in the mornings on a dirt field they called El Play. After lunch, during the hottest part of the day, I plastered my back against a wall of the village community center to read in the shade.

I emailed with my parents. For the first two weeks we exchanged a handful of messages, mostly bulleted accounts of my days and brief summaries of my siblings' lives at home. This is how my mother kept me updated:

*Hi Vince, thanks for the email! Glad you arrived safely and are sleep-
ing well. Stay hydrated, remember your malaria medication! All is
fine here. Lizzie found out that she has a phone interview next week
for a teaching job with Match in Boston. Chris may be working as a
Kaplan SAT tutor in Boston while he continues to look for a full time
job. Tim is in the basement reading all the books he recently ordered,
mostly philosophy and logic stuff. Dad and I are well.*

Love you very much

Mom

Each sibling got a sentence. Lizzie's and Chris's sentences involved job searches. Tim's sentence spins his basement seclusion into
principled study, like he was preparing a survey of philosophy.

I still have these emails, the updates she sent me from home.

I have one saved voicemail from my mother. The message is from
a few months prior, February, while Tim was in the hospital. I'm not
sure why I still had this message when she died, how I'd missed it in
my routine voicemail pruning.

The message is not long, not a deeply meaningful expression of
love or wisdom for me to return to for the rest of my life. It's about
a hotel room. She'd booked me a room so I could travel with her to
watch Chris compete in a swim meet.

There's only one allusion to Tim, to his hospitalization. In her
greeting, she says, *Hi, Vince, there's nothing really new to report here.*

To report, like she was a newscaster at the scene, ready to summarize the day's events.

I hated how this opening phrase made me feel, hated how when
I listened to it later—so many times—I wanted, somehow, for her to
tell me what she had been thinking or feeling or afraid of, anything
more than just this brief report of no news.

*   *   *

While I was in the Dominican Republic, Tim attacked Chris. They fought four days before Tim killed our mother.

On that evening, no one else was in the house. Tim came through Chris's door and accused Chris of snooping in his room. He was certain Chris had trespassed.

"Why were you sneaking into my room what were you looking for why don't you understand."

Of course Chris hadn't gone into Tim's room. Chris understood boundaries. Boundaries were something to be respected, one of the tenets of the tacit truce my family had with Tim, a truce that had, until that moment, never been broken with violence.

When Chris denied that he had gone into Tim's room, Tim moved to different indictments.

"You knew the whole time!" Tim yelled. "You knew the whole time!"

He accused Chris of being a conspirator, a silent observer of the childhood abuse Tim's demons convinced him was real.

Chris was strong, broad shouldered, his powerful upper body built over years of competitive swimming. But none of this strength mattered. Tim threw him like he was tossing a laundry bag.

Chris hit his bureau, falling among duffel bags he had brought home after his college graduation. Tim wrapped his hands around Chris's neck.

For years, Tim had built his grip strength so that he could subdue his wrestling opponents. He trained with Captains of Crush grippers, tools that look like nutcrackers with steel torsion springs. When Tim squeezed this tool in the meat of his palm, his whole forearm would tense, veins popping in jagged lines. I once watched him squeeze a gripper that required 237 pounds of force to close.

This was the power in the hands around Chris's neck. On the floor, Chris was helpless, staring at his childhood best friend.

But Tim stopped. Chris doesn't know why.

After Tim retreated, Chris fled to meet our mother and sister at a nearby Dunkin' Donuts. I'm not sure what they discussed, but I know that Chris must have been afraid.

When the three reentered the house, cautiously, Tim was in the kitchen. He asked Chris if he wanted a cup of coffee. He acted as if nothing had happened.

I have no idea what Chris must have feared during those next days, how he lived with the recent memory of Tim's hands squeezing his neck.

The morning after Tim attacked Chris, my mother called Dr. Robertson, who agreed to a meeting with my family. The four of them—Chris, Lizzie, our parents—visited his office the night before Tim killed our mother.

At the meeting, Chris described to Dr. Robertson how Tim had attacked him.

"That's a little age inappropriate," Dr. Robertson said, "but brothers fight."

Brothers fight. Of course they do. We fought all the time as kids—with playground balls, Wiffle-ball bats, fallen crab apples that left welts on exposed skin. We fought underwater at the town pool, over the hose in the backyard. We fought one-handed while riding bicycles.

Brothers fight.

I didn't learn about the fight or the meeting with Dr. Robertson until after I had returned home.

My mother emailed me twice after the fight, but she didn't mention the attack or the meeting in either message. I know that I have no right to be mad about this, her silence. What would I have done from a thousand miles away?

In the days after my mother died, when I learned about the meeting with Dr. Robertson, I made him—a man I had never met—the arch villain of my family's story. For a year, whenever I thought of him, all I felt was rage. I needed an easy target for the anger I couldn't point at myself, anger I felt for being a thousand miles away, anger Dr. Robertson didn't deserve.

He had seen Tim only a handful of times. Their last appointment had been more than a month before. He had generously stayed in touch with my parents with Tim's safety in mind.

Yes, he said *brothers fight*. Yes, I know how that sounds.

But on the day my mother died, that morning, over the phone with my father, he raised the right alarms—*It might be time to return to the hospital. It might be time to call the police.*

I feel no anger toward him now, this man I had cast as villain.

But when I think about him, about his words to my father that morning, I'm faced with more excruciating thoughts, thoughts that feel like betrayal.

My mother could have called the police. She could have called that morning. She could have called earlier, after Tim attacked Chris.

And I know that another emergency hospital admittance would have only delayed another unraveling, Tim joining the ranks of many who travel through revolving hospital doors.

I know that Tim's anosognosia was persistent, was patient, would wait for discharge to remind him, *You're not sick. You're not sick. You're just a spiritual smear.*

But I also know that my mother is dead. I know that there are ways my mother failed.

I don't know if I can explain how devastated that phrase—*ways my mother failed*—leaves me. It took me three years to write that sentence.

What I mean is this. Yes, my mother could have hospitalized Tim again.

But how could she have gotten him there? His first hospitalization was a near miracle.

My mother would have *had* to call the police, and I know that calling the police was one of her greatest fears.

There's a well-documented and tragic history of police killing people in the grip of psychosis. These deaths are often the result of poor training, of a failure to understand how a psychotic man wielding a knife might not understand commands to drop his weapon, might have delusions that convince him to lash out. To combat this problem, many police departments have invested in crisis intervention training (CIT), a program designed to teach officers how to deescalate situations involving the seriously mentally ill. While far from a solution, some studies suggest that CIT has decreased the number of mentally ill who die at the hands of police. Though it is most commonly practiced in large urban police forces, several states have implemented CIT across all departments.

I don't think my mother knew that Connecticut was one of these states.

I don't know what would have happened if police officers had arrived at our house, if they'd tried to bring Tim to the hospital. Their training might have tempered his resistance, but Tim still might have fought back—fiercely, viciously—in a struggle that might have killed him. I know my mother was thinking about this struggle, about what Tim might do if police battered his bedroom door.

So if my mother failed, her failure grew out of fear for her son's life, out of a love for Tim so fierce it may have blinded her to his untreated disease's capacity for violence.

Or maybe *blinded* is the wrong word. Maybe her eyes were open. Maybe she feared him, knew that her life was in danger.

Maybe her love—her unknowable maternal love—overwhelmed her fear.

But I'll never know this. I never asked her if she was afraid. I didn't ask her if she'd been afraid earlier, when Tim threatened her life in the emergency room. I didn't ask her if she was afraid when I told her, over the phone, that I thought Tim could become violent.

I'll never know if she feared for her life when she didn't call the police on the day she died.

But I know one thing. I know one thing she feared on that day. I know she told my father this fear over the phone, their last conversation.

I know her greatest fear was leaving Tim alone.

11

Tim stood next to our mother's body, alone in the house, after she died.

"The pressure left," Tim remembered later. "It was over."

I don't know how long he waited there, in the family room, facing her.

I know he framed her body with his two sledgehammers, laying one next to each of her arms. I know he tucked a black garbage bag under her head, where blood was beginning to pool. I know he found our bowl of spare change, gathered a fistful of coins, sprinkled them on her body.

Later, Tim remembered that he had needed one more coin, a special coin, the one he had seen floating in the basement.

He retrieved that Susan B. Anthony dollar—it was both a real coin and his demons' talisman—and returned to the family room. He nestled the coin into our mother's auburn hair, hair she had colored, she used to joke, because she wasn't a grandma yet.

After placing the coin, Tim grew worried about our dogs, wondered where they went.

He entered the kitchen and realized that they'd fled to the bathroom by our garage. He closed the doors leading out of the kitchen, sealing the dogs in that quadrant of the house. This is what we used to do when we had company and didn't want the dogs jumping up or begging for scraps.

I know that Tim returned to his room to find a Bible. The one he picked was white.

Tim completed these tasks—placing the coins, trapping the dogs, finding his Bible—before taking the next step. To him, a logical one.

"I called the police. If I had stayed inside I would have killed myself. The demons were too strong in there."

He sat on our front steps while he spoke to the dispatcher.

"My name is Tim Granata. I was raped and abused for years as a child by my parents. I just, I killed my mom. She's in the family room." He paused, then recited our address, slowly, like he was giving instructions for a delivery. "I'm unarmed. I'm sitting on the front steps holding a Bible and the phone. And I'm, I'm calling you to let you know this. And to please take me away."

He told the dispatcher what he was wearing—sweatpants, a white shirt, glasses. He mentioned the blood.

When Tim dialed 911, our father and Lizzie were only minutes from home—our father racing from work, Lizzie returning from the mall.

Somehow, they arrived almost simultaneously. Lizzie saw my father's minivan cut left onto Englewood Drive. She followed him, accelerating, matching his speed as he rushed past the wooded cul-de-sacs in our suburban neighborhood.

Our father saw Tim when he pulled up in front of the house. Tim set the phone aside to speak to our father when he reached the front steps.

"Dad . . . don't go in there, it doesn't look good. Don't go in there. Please don't go in there. She was telling me about how she raped me. And I killed her. She's in the family room. She raped me."

She, she, she, not *Mom, Mom, Mom.*

But Tim didn't stop our father when he moved past him into our house. He didn't attack him too.

I believe that Tim—even in the throes of psychosis—would only have hurt the people in our family he was closest to. He was closest to our mother, his caregiver, the one who had chaperoned his descent into madness. Chris too, the boy who had been his best friend, had been a target for his demons. They had fought only days before.

I know that our father and Lizzie were not in his demons' cross-hairs.

I don't know if Tim would have attacked me.

Tim stayed on the front steps as our father walked across the hallway into the family room.

I know that when my father saw my mother, he knelt, tried to find her pulse.

Later, my father told me that he knew, immediately—*she's gone*—but still dropped to the floor, looked for vital signs.

My father didn't know that Lizzie had parked in front of the house when he left the family room to call 911.

Tim was still on the phone when Lizzie reached him on the front steps.

"Don't go in there," he said. "I killed Mom. She raped me."

Tim grabbed her ankle, but Lizzie pulled away, hard.

I want to believe that some part of Tim wanted to save her from that pain, the pain of seeing. Maybe somehow—for just a moment, a fleeting moment—Tim recognized how seeing would wound Lizzie, indelibly.

My father wishes, in the cruel choreography of that day, that he could have stopped Lizzie from entering the family room.

This is my wish too, my impossible wish.

I would sacrifice anything—*anything, anything*—to pull Lizzie away, away from our house, away from the family room, away from our mother's body.

Later, I would see pictures of my mother's body. I would look at her face, propped for police photography, her slashed throat, her battered blue cheeks.

I would learn how to live with those images, with the knowledge of her wounds.

But Lizzie saw Mom. Our experiences cannot be compared.

I can only imagine what Lizzie feared when she raced behind our father's car, speeding toward home. I haven't asked her what she felt when Tim, slick with blood, grabbed her ankle, held her on the front steps where we'd taken family photos.

I can't describe this, how Lizzie walked into the family room, the place where she'd taken her first steps next to Tim, how this is where she found our mother's body.

I've struggled here, struggled when I remember how my body imploded, sweat-soaked, shaking, after I heard four words from my father.

No. Tim killed Mom.

How can I multiply four words from a thousand miles away to match Tim's hand on her ankle, the blood on the wooden floor, our mother's body facedown next to the photo albums Lizzie had assembled, her chronicle of our family history.

And how can I imagine what it must mean to have almost been

there, to have been shopping minutes from home, to think that a shorter line at a checkout counter, a closer parking spot, might have meant arriving home sooner, arriving home before it was over.

I had made my choice. I had, weeks before, decided to board a plane, to leave, to flee, to put so much more distance between home and me than the quick trip from our cul-de-sac to the mall.

Lizzie and I have never spoken about what she saw when she found our mother's body, about the violence in the room at the center of her childhood memories, about the violence on the body of the woman she loved most in the world. Of course, this trauma could not be explained or quieted with careful words. This was not a nightmare to soothe away.

But I know there was only one person who could have helped Lizzie hold this pain.

When Lizzie was eleven, I listened to our mother explain a way to grieve. Our grandmother, our father's mother, had died.

"It's called a wake," I heard our mother say. "Grandma's body will be in a casket and people will take turns walking past."

I remember that she said *grandma's body*, not *grandma*, not *she*.

"It's a way to say goodbye," our mother said.

I remember watching Lizzie and our mother speak, how they were shorter than me, how I used to think that this helped them trade secrets, their whispers passing beneath me.

Our mother told Lizzie that when we saw grandma's body it might look like grandma, but that it wouldn't be her.

"It won't look like she's asleep," my mother said, "but her body will look peaceful."

There would be no wake for our mother, no peaceful body to display.

But Lizzie had already seen.

Her body, our mother, Mom.

In the weeks after our mother died, I would try to hug Lizzie during bouts of her tears. I tried to help her grieve, be the big brother who could cradle her sadness. I wanted, somehow, for there to be something I could do, something tangible, like the simple grave I'd dug for Candy Cane, her dog, more than a decade before.

But when I hugged Lizzie, when I tried to hold her close, I realized that her billowing sadness was not something I could pull taut.

Once, between sobs, Lizzie told me something that was growing increasingly clear.

"She's the only one who could explain this," Lizzie said. "Mom would know what to say."

12

"Tell me how it happened, just one time."

I said this to my father, sitting next to him in a hotel room, twelve hours after I heard his voice fray over the phone—*No. Tim killed Mom.*

I thought that I needed to hear—*just one time*—how my mother died.

Before I asked my father, I had already started building a story, using scraps of information to shape the terrifying unknown. I started with what was most familiar—our fear of suicide. My mind worked with this—the safer fear—to imagine that my mother died trying to stop Tim from ending his own life.

I imagined Tim holding a knife to his throat, or his wrist, or the meat of his thigh. I had that detail, *knife*, my first, learned from a cousin's Facebook comment while fumbling with my phone over an airport urinal.

Though, even then, I was inventing. *Knives* is what my cousin had written. I substituted *knife*.

I imagined our mother trying to wrestle this knife from Tim. I imagined that the knife slipped, or that Tim lashed out blindly, or that she fell, or that—somehow, somehow—in the throes of suicidal psychosis, Tim had stabbed her instead of himself, an accidental thrust, a tragic mistake.

When I asked my father, "Tell me how it happened, just one time," the four of us—my father, Chris, Lizzie, me—were huddled in a hotel room a mile from our house. Our double beds were close enough so that when we sat across from each other our shins nearly touched.

"No one was home when it happened," my father said. He explained to me, with some help from Chris, where everyone had been. He repeated Tim's morning statement, *If it looks like I killed myself, it was the devil that did it.*

No one knew yet what had happened after Lizzie left to go shopping. The only window my father had was the phantom phone call he'd received at work, the home number flashing on his screen, silence when he answered.

My father described what he saw when he arrived home, how Tim sat on the front steps. My father repeated Tim's words, *Dad . . . don't go in there, it doesn't look good.*

For a long time, these two phrases were all I would have from that day in Tim's voice.

If it looks like I killed myself, it was the devil that did it.

Dad . . . don't go in there, it doesn't look good.

Tim spent his first night without our mother in a cell a half mile from our hotel. That night, Tim ripped a jumpsuit from his body. He stood naked in his cell, sobbing, canvas tattered around his ankles.

I tried to sleep next to Lizzie that night, in the space beside where she had crumpled into a ball. She whimpered into her pillow, making low throaty sounds like the ones our dog used to make to keep himself company in the dark.

At some point, I moved to the floor, stretched out on the green hotel carpet. I stayed awake through Lizzie's crying, lying motionless on the floor, right arm throbbing underneath the pillow I pressed into my ear.

Our father snored in the next room. I could hear him through the adjoining door. He had left it partially open, like we were children whose cries he wanted to monitor.

Hours later, in the early morning, I brewed a single serving of coffee while Chris and Lizzie slept. With my paper cup, I slid into my father's room, closing the door.

My father had already showered. His cane—one he used to steady an ailing hip—rested against the nightstand next to his made bed.

In a few hours, Tim would be arraigned, my father said. Tim would appear in court less than a day after our mother died. My father had arranged for a lawyer, but none of us attended the arraignment.

When I descended to the hotel lobby for bagels, I faced a newspaper box, the *New Haven Register*'s front page on display. First, I saw a familiar intersection—the main image—Blue Ridge Terrace and Wild Rose Drive, five neon cones sealing off the dead-end street where we lived. A police officer stood next to the cones, a sentry in the same yard where I had landed fifteen years before, flying over my handlebars after squeezing the sensitive brakes of a new bike.

My eyes moved quickly from the intersection, jumped to the right, a smaller image, my first look at Tim—this new Tim—his mug shot.

Tim wore white, cloud colored against a blue mug-shot backdrop—almost pastel, a tranquil sky. In the picture, his eyes looked too small for his face. Small, I thought, because he wasn't wearing his glasses. I couldn't distinguish his irises from the tiny points of his pupils. He looked tired.

Tired, I made myself think, tired like he had pulled an all-nighter studying for an exam.

I saw Tim again, later that day, when I searched for news clips reporting his arraignment. On my phone, with my right thumb, I made him appear. I touched the first video, "Orange man in court for mother's murder."

His jumpsuit's sleeves surrendered halfway down his biceps. He wore his dark-rimmed glasses, the frames the same color as his hair.

"This is a case of matricide," a judge says. Then, while the camera remains on Tim, the audio shifts to his attorney speaking off-screen.

"There is a history of psychiatric illness," the attorney says. "There was a hospitalization."

While his attorney speaks, Tim starts crying. He pushes his glasses away from his eyes. His fingernails are long and yellow against his face.

"This has absolutely destroyed this family," Tim's attorney says. "I can't begin to tell you how much it's destroyed this family."

Destroyed, repeated twice, like he was absolutely sure.

I knew he was *saying the right thing*, this man I had never met. But as I listened to him speak about me, about what he was certain I felt, I began to wonder what *destroyed* was supposed to look like. Did it look like Chris and Lizzie?

During those first days, when my father said Tim's name, Chris and Lizzie cursed and cried.

Fuck him. Fuck him. He's dead to me.

I wasn't surprised when I heard how Chris and Lizzie spoke about Tim, their shuddering attempts to make him disappear. Of course anger made sense, rage bundling with sorrow, unwinding in gasps between tears. When Chris and Lizzie exorcised anger—*fuck him, fuck him, he's dead to me*—they fought against trauma's paralytic hold.

I was quiet while Chris and Lizzie cursed. I didn't want to be angry. I didn't want to shout.

If I shouted and sobbed it would confirm that she was gone, that Tim had killed her, that my family was not the family I had held on to all my life.

So I hid, afraid of what it would mean if I let myself be "destroyed," afraid that I'd never be able to build a new me in this new world I couldn't recognize.

But this fear also filled me with shame. And it was this shame that made me hug my siblings every time they sobbed. I hugged them, clutched them to my chest, not because I thought I could ease their pain, but because I didn't want them to see me, my sealed lips, my dry, open eyes.

Late in that first afternoon, the police called my father to tell him that they were finished with the crime scene. The four of us were allowed to enter our house to grab overnight bags, toiletries, clean underwear.

My father didn't elaborate, but it was clear why this had to be a quick trip, an in-and-out to grab essentials. Though the police had "finished" with the crime scene, our family room still looked like one. Their job—taking photographs, bagging evidence, removing my mother's body—cleared the way for the "cleaning service" my father would call to sanitize our tragedy.

We drove from the hotel in Chris's car, my father's minivan still sealed behind police tape in our driveway. Chris's car, littered with empty bags—from CVS, Dunkin' Donuts, Five Guys—smelled like mildew and stale coffee, the scent frozen into the seats with the air conditioner we blasted against the July heat.

On the ride to our house, we passed familiar landmarks—Orange Congregational Church, the rectangular green, the centerpieces of a New England town. We passed Orange Center Convenience, the store at the mouth of our neighborhood, the place where my brothers and I had bought boxes of Tic Tacs, then filled our cheeks with the tiny sweet pills.

At Englewood Drive, the street leading to our network of cul-de-sacs, a familiar sign announced, NO OUTLET, a softer version of DEAD END. As children, we had numbered the four neighborhood cul-de-sacs radiating out from our house. We used this naming system to chart our routes when we pedaled our bikes. *Race you to the third. Wait for me at the second. Let's go all the way to the fourth and back.*

As we approached our street, Wild Rose Drive, our father warned us that we might see a news van.

It was more SUV than van, NEWS8 printed on side paneling. My father accelerated as we passed the truck, sitting in the same spot where Tim had been apprehended. I glanced into the van and saw a slumped figure, head flush against the passenger window, using a balled-up sweatshirt as a pillow.

When we reached the cul-de-sac—the first cul-de-sac, our cul-de-sac—two police cars hugged the curb bounding our yard. An unmarked car guarded the base of our driveway.

"That's Detective Mike," my father said.

Detective Mike was in charge of the crime scene. Later, I would learn that state police specialists had assisted him, partitioning the family room into a grid, tiny numbered quadrants like the pointed coordinates in Battleship, the board game my siblings and I used to play.

My father had rules for how we would reenter the house.

"Only through the back," my father told us. "Grab what you need and come right out."

Detective Mike removed the police tape blocking our path. We walked up the driveway, the four of us together.

I noticed a curtain in one of the family room windows, the one near the phone. All the other curtains were drawn, neatly pinned. That curtain looked jagged, askew.

Askew, I thought, like I was describing lines in a geometry problem.

We entered through the garage to avoid the front of the house, the family room.

In the garage, I saw some of Tim's weight-lifting equipment, heavy ropes and chains piled next to my mother's minivan. In the mudroom, Tim's jackets still hung on plastic hooks. Next to his coat, my mother's red jacket, the one she wore every spring and autumn. Her jacket was draped over abandoned cardboard boxes—the ones that had held the philosophy books Tim had ordered online. After I climbed the back stairs, I saw the door to the laundry closet ajar. I opened the lid of the machine, saw a load of sheets and towels—still damp—wrapped around the washer's plastic pillar. My mother had died in the middle of a load of laundry.

My father didn't follow his own rules for our reentry. While I picked at a few belongings in my room, I heard him talking to Detective Mike beneath me in the front of the house.

My bedroom sits at the top of the front staircase, and from the banister I can see into the front hall, to where the foyer's tile meets the family room's wood. I didn't join my father in the family room, but I walked to the banister, leaned out, looked to the border between the two rooms.

I don't know if what I saw was blood. It looked too dark, like it had scabbed, clotting on the tile closest to the family room. The longer I looked, the more my eyes worked to transform the splotches into mud tracked in from the yard.

But I couldn't transform the smell—a new smell, a different smell. When I try to remember that smell, I feel iron on my tongue, rust in my nose and throat.

Before we left our house, the cleanup crew pulled into our driveway. In thin letters on the sides of the vans, I read the company name, AFTERMATH. The vans had small yellow triangles—the biohazard insignia—above their back bumpers.

I remember the face of the man who led the Aftermath team. He had red cheeks, light eyes. He was thin. When he shook my hand—I don't remember his name—his eyes stayed with mine, softened, sank into gaunt cheeks. He was about to spend twelve hours scrubbing my mother's blood from our family room floor, but in that moment he acted like shaking my hand was his only job.

The four men were magicians. Aftermath made everything disappear. The next morning, when we walked into the family room, they had eliminated every trace. I had to look carefully to find the few differences, notice that a coffee table was gone, that a few stacked board games had vanished. One of the rolling desk chairs had been removed, but my father was quick to explain.

"That chair was broken before," he said. "A wheel had fallen off. I had them take it with the rest."

With the rest. My father remained a practical man.

"I picked up a new router to replace the old one," the Aftermath leader told my father. "The network key is on the back."

He had replaced our router, nothing too small for this physical exorcism.

On the paperwork Aftermath left on the computer desk, I read the company's tagline.

No one should have to deal with the traumatic events that would
require our services, but if you do, we are here to help you on the road
to recovery.

But I wasn't thinking about a "road to recovery." I was thinking
about my mother's red jacket, how it fell over the empty boxes that
Tim had left behind.

After we returned from our first trip home, when I was alone with
my father, I asked about Tim.

"Where is he now?" I asked.

"Bridgeport Correctional," my father said.

I knew my father would focus on knowing details, on figuring out
what there was to do. This was part of the way he lived—to-do lists,
a rigorous datebook, kept by hand—but I know this was also part
of how he coped, part of the way he ordered himself after tragedy,
coordinated arrangements with Aftermath, with the funeral home,
with the lawyer who would represent Tim.

But when my father told me that Tim was at Bridgeport Correctional, I was surprised. I had imagined that Tim would be held in
some type of psychiatric unit, that he would be given the medicine
he had refused for so long, that finally his disease wouldn't have
agency, wouldn't force him to spit out his pills or flush them down
the toilet.

"Is that the right place for him?" It seemed ridiculous to me, naïve
as I was, that Tim would be held with the general prison population. At that time, I had no idea that prisons had become our de
facto asylums—the three facilities holding the largest populations
of the mentally ill being the L.A. County Jail, Cook County Jail,

and Rikers Island. I didn't know that in 2014, an estimated 234,000 inmates—15 percent of the prison population—had serious mental illnesses.

"There's someone I can call," my father said.

My father worked for Community Health Network of Connecticut, the company that administered Medicaid for the state. He had worked with state health care officials, knew their names, had phone numbers. He could call the health services director at the Department of Corrections at 4 p.m. on a summer Friday. She returned his call.

My family's connections—my grandmother was friendly with a respected defense attorney, my father in contact with health care officials—worked in Tim's favor. But these advantages—substantial ones that saved Tim and my family added pain—seemed potent only after tragedy had struck.

Years later, I would listen while someone tried to piece this story together, telling me, "But both your parents were doctors, extremely well educated doctors."

I nodded slowly, anticipated what would come next.

"That it happened to them," he said. "If they couldn't get care for their son . . ."

I think he meant well. I think he was, in a way, trying to support me. His points are valid.

Yes, my parents had networks, knew doctors who could advise them, refer them to the best mental health professionals. Yes, my parents had means, and would have, without hesitating, used all their savings if it meant helping Tim.

But it still happened. We still lost, even though so much was rigged in our favor.

13

It didn't take long for my friends to rally and travel to New Haven. No one told me how they organized, who spread the news. I know that I never had to tell anyone what had happened.

I had spoken to Pat, my roommate and close friend, on the phone earlier that day. He had just finished law school, was about to take the bar exam. He told me he was coming to New Haven, that he could bring me my car, my suit for the funeral, *anything you need.*

Pat told me that a number of people were coming to town. I had some sense of this gathering from the buzzing in my pocket, from the occasional glance at a text—*I love you. I'll see you soon.*

Andy and Karri, my friends from college, lived in New Haven, fifteen minutes from our house. Pat told me that a group of my friends was gathering at Andy and Karri's apartment.

Later that afternoon, Pat picked me up and drove me to meet my friends. In the car, I told Pat a version of the story I was building, my mother's death as a suicide thwarted. I clung to this story, a way to make my mother a martyr for Tim.

"I never thought that he would be violent," I told Pat.

This was a lie.

I didn't tell Pat about the conversation I'd had with my mother over the phone the morning after Tim had banged on my door. I didn't tell Pat what I had told my mother about my fear of Tim's potential for violence. I didn't tell Pat that I had let my mother convince me that I was wrong.

But I had to tell Pat that *I never believed that Tim could be violent.* I had to tell him because that phrase protected me, protected me from the reality that I had left my mother at home, alone, in danger.

"He had made a lot of suicide threats," I told Pat. "He made another threat yesterday morning." I told him the words I knew Tim had spoken—*If it looks like I killed myself, it was the devil that did it.*

I'm not sure how I got to the next part of the story. Maybe I said, *This is what must have happened.* Or maybe, *This is what I think happened.*

Now I know what I meant to say.

This is what I hope happened.

"Tim threatened to kill himself," I said. "She wasn't going to let that happen." I made this sound definitive, defiant. *She wasn't going to let that happen.*

The logic was still absurd. I had created a scenario where a knife got lost in the shuffle. Chaos reigned. A knife entered.

When we pulled into my friends' parking lot, I asked Pat who had come to town.

"A lot of people want to see you," he said.

In the building's elevator, I saw myself for the first time, my reflection in the closing doors. I saw my eyes—red-rimmed, a blood aura hovering around my pupils. They ached when I saw this redness, my squinting intensifying the pain.

Pat had been right. When Andy opened his door, I could see over his shoulder to where my friends stood. Somewhere between fifteen and twenty people had gathered to greet me, to hug me, each person waiting their turn.

I understood what this was. This was the gathering of friends to support someone in the midst of loss, of tragedy. I had seen this before, this rallying around, this holding up, this hugging and affirming and making comfortable. There were Buffalo chicken subs from the greasy pizza shop I loved. There was a case of beer. Here were my closest friends. On any other day, this gathering would have been the best gathering, a reunion, the first time in a long time I had seen all these faces in one room.

When I sat down, when I saw how my friends circled me, perched on sofa arms, sitting on pillows on the floor, I knew their intent was to envelop me, to convince me I wasn't alone.

During much of that first day, I had felt alone. Not literally alone, but isolated, separate from the people around me. I was becoming aware of this new kind of loneliness, one that I still felt then, even when friends surrounded me.

I had received a message the night before, one of the earliest, a message that made me aware of this new state, this alone state, a loneliness that might last longer than I could bear. The message came from the distant past, from a former babysitter. I remembered her well as a curly-haired high school student who wore glasses and played the cello. She was one of the last babysitters we employed. She was probably only three years older than me, but at twelve I was ill-equipped to handle three seven-year-olds.

"I hope you will eventually be able to find some peace and feel whole again," she wrote, "though that might be your life's work."

That phrase—*might be your life's work*—felt honest, accurate, so true that I became terrified. It seemed impossible to think of how this, all this, would ever be over. Then, sitting with the reality of her message, I felt as if I had just surfaced on the other side of a massive gulf, like I had been swimming underwater with my eyes closed, only to emerge and see the bobbing heads of everyone I knew a mile away in the surf.

I was thinking about this new loneliness when I sat among my friends. I still felt like I was bobbing alone, struggling in strange waters that would become my new normal.

But I could tell that they saw me there. Even though they would never be flailing with me, sharing this particular burden, this *life's work*, it was enough to know that they understood that I was in pain. They still knew a big part of me—a part that predated this new pain.

My friend Charlie was the first person to make this clear to me, to show me the way my friends would help me begin to recognize myself again.

I had met Charlie a few days into our freshman year of college during early crew practices. One afternoon at the fitness center, Charlie recognized me from our first team workout. He was sitting on a weight bench and called me over. He said his name was Charlie, then immediately launched into a lengthy bio—he was getting over a knee injury, starting to get strong again after his surgery, had played basketball in high school, had met one of the guys on the crew team at a party over the summer. When he finally took a breath, I told him my name.

I had needed that kind of friend. I showed up at college as a guarded kid, hesitant to reveal myself to others. With Charlie, everything was immediately on the table. There was no posturing, none of the gradual feeling out that happens in stereotypical male friendships. The more time I spent with Charlie, the more I felt myself learn how to be comfortable, how to be at ease with myself.

Charlie was the first person to make me laugh after my mother died.

That night in my friends' apartment, Charlie played music from his phone—songs from the past, from the summer, anything that crossed beneath his finger. At one point I reached over his lap to change the song. As I leaned over, he grabbed my forearm, looked at me.

"Oh. So it's *all* about you now, Vince."

I laughed.

Charlie was the first person who realized that I would still laugh, that I could still laugh. He could see that, sitting next to me on the couch, a can of beer between my legs. I felt alone, unrecognizable, but somehow, long before I could realize it, Charlie knew that I was still there.

My mother received four packages after she died. Three boxes held needlepoint tools—starter kits with thread, thimble, blank canvases—the materials for a new hobby. I left these supplies in the garage, on the wooden shelves with my father's store of canned food and water—an emergency cache languishing since New Year's Eve 1999.

The last package my mother received was a copy of Amy Bloom's *Lucky Us*. Years earlier, I had taken a college writing class with Amy Bloom and had given some of her books to my mother. We loved her story collections, particularly *A Blind Man Can See How Much I Love You*. The novel my mother had ordered, *Lucky Us*, was her most recent book, one I hadn't read, one I was certain my mother would have devoured and then passed on to me.

Lucky Us. I opened the inside jacket and read the first line, "We returned home because my father's wife died suddenly."

When I brought the book inside, Lizzie was sitting alone at our kitchen table, a stack of condolence notes piled to her left. The open envelopes had jagged scars from where her index finger had ripped through. The pile spilled over our mother's space at the table, Lizzie's left hand shaking on the chair where our mother had sat.

I didn't show Lizzie the book. Instead, I nestled it in the box of mismatched gloves sitting by our childhood cubbies. I sat across from Lizzie, silent, *Lucky Us* hidden beneath discarded winter gloves.

In part, I remember those days—the time between my mother's death and funeral—as a parade of food. Everyone brought a tray— eggplant parmigiana, chicken rollatini, lasagna wrapped and ready to freeze for *whenever you need it*.

On one of the nights before the funeral, each of our collective groups of friends came to the house, parking in a ring around our cul-de-sac.

"We're out of beer and wine," my father said, gesturing toward the fridge with his cane.

The nearest liquor store was next to my father's dry cleaner on Orange Center Road. As a child, I'd accompanied him on his Saturday errands, stood at the dry cleaner's counter and watched, enchanted, as racks of pressed slacks whirred by on mechanized hangers.

When I entered the liquor store, I saw one other customer, a woman inspecting wine labels. She smiled as I walked past her to grab two bottles of wine and a case of beer from an adjacent fridge. The cardboard case sagged in my right hand, wine-bottle necks slippery in my left as I turned and approached the counter. The woman was chatting with the clerk.

"It was just down the road," she said. "I can't believe it was her son." She didn't look at me until my bottles clinked on the counter.

I think I'd known that at some point I would stumble into *this* conversation, that my mother's death would be on everyone's mind. In our small suburb, the arrival of Trader Joe's had been big news.

"There's no way you could have known this," I said to the woman, "but she was my mom." I spoke like I was apologizing, like I had interrupted a private conversation about my family's public tragedy.

She turned away from the clerk to face me, her hands clutching the purse she was about to open.

"We weren't gossiping," she said. "We weren't gossiping."

"I know." I nodded while she dabbed her right eye.

But how could I have been upset that they were gossiping? Of course people would talk, shake their heads—*Can you believe? Who would've thought? In this town?*

She apologized—*I'm sorry, I'm sorry*—as she left the store, looking back at me until the door jingled behind her.

The clerk said he was sorry too, then charged me full price.

And somehow that, having to pay the full bill, made me angry as I drove a white-knuckled mile home. My anger finally landed, finding its way to the liquor store cashier, a far easier target than Tim, or schizophrenia, or his doctors, or me.

We buried my mother the next day, a Wednesday. Her funeral was in the same church where she'd married my father.

The casket had six sides, polished wood the same color as our dining room table. It sat on wheels, moved easily in spite of its weight, a single attendant guiding it with one hand.

This was how we referred to her body, *the casket*, an impersonal container for personal remains.

It. The casket. My mother's body. Mom's body.

Father Bob, a friend of my father's, celebrated—*celebrate*, the word Catholics use—my mother's funeral mass. Three other priests and a bishop joined Father Bob on the altar. This support meant a great deal to my father.

While my family assembled in the front foyer, the main entrance to the church, clusters of people squeezed into pews, stood along the walls next to the pictures of the Stations of the Cross. When the church reached capacity, Father Bob siphoned mourners into an adjacent hall. There, he had set up a monitor that would broadcast the service. More than six hundred people watched my mother's casket that Wednesday morning.

While we stood around the casket, waiting for the organ, our cue, it felt almost like we were backstage, waiting for the lights to dim, waiting to meet the gazing audience.

When we started walking behind the casket, I wasn't sure where to look. I was wary of eye contact, not certain how I would respond if I saw a congregation in tears. I kept my eyes on the crucifix on my mother's casket, an old wooden crucifix, a gift from my godmother, one featuring small scenes of brightly painted animals, an homage to St. Francis of Assisi, the perfect crucifix for a child.

I focused on that cross while we walked the aisle, my right hand squeezing Lizzie's shoulder, our father's cane tapping the slate floor.

We had decided, the day after she died, that Lizzie, Chris, and I would eulogize our mother. I can't remember any discussion. I think we just assumed that the three of us would be the ones to remember her.

We began the ceremony with our eulogies, the three of us speaking in reverse birth order. We stood together at the lectern. If Lizzie and Chris were nervous, it didn't show in their delivery, in what they shared about our mother.

Growing up, people would always ask me who my hero was. I would always tell them a celebrity or an author. All those times, I was lying.

A few weeks ago, Mom and I were talking about my future. She asked me if I was happy. I told her that I was and asked her the same thing. She told me that as long as her children were safe, she was happy.

After they finished, I began my eulogy with a story, the story of how my parents met—the bee sting, the medical library. At the end of the story—*I never heard them agree on who spoke first*—I heard one voice in the front pew, my father's, a repeated *oh, oh*.

In my eulogy, I called her a superhuman mother, made sure that everyone knew that we never ate dinner alone, that we never waited for a ride. I told a story from when I was eleven, a reluctant student struggling through violin lessons. One afternoon, exasperated, wanting more time to play sports, I told my mother, "I'm only learning this instrument to make you happy."

When I said that to her, she got quiet, looked at me, pupils narrowing behind her glasses.

"Vince," she said, "promise me that you'll never do something only to make me happy. Promise me you'll never do that again."

I had strained so hard to find these memories, writing alone at our dining room table when we had returned to our house. Holding that handful of memories—the stories I told during her eulogy—incurred tremendous pain, the pain of remembering, the beginning of the chains that led me directly to the violence of her death.

But I needed those memories—the moments when she mothered me—because I didn't want my eulogy to be a wail or a dirge. I needed these tender moments, I told myself, because I needed to show everyone how her love was steadfast, unflinching.

Now, my sentences sound like a defense, like I was trying to convince everyone that she *had not failed, had not failed, had not failed.*

I didn't know much about the history of schizophrenia, how Freudian theories on schizophrenia originally targeted mothers. In the late 1940s, Freud disciple Frieda Fromm-Reichmann coined the term *schizophrenogenic mother*, arguing that a specific kind of mother, one who alternatively smothered and ignored her child, created an emotional volatility that later manifested as schizophrenia. For decades, mothers remained squarely in psychiatry's crosshairs, shouldering the blame for their children's pain.

Few still believe that these factors catalyze schizophrenia. But I think, unconsciously, when I composed my mother's eulogy, I felt that I needed to show people that she was not to blame.

In fact, I needed to canonize her, make her a martyr, her death a sacrifice. And when I spoke of her like a martyr, my voice broke. My voice broke when I got to Tim.

She always took care of us. When no one else could or would take care of Tim, she did. When his illness destroyed the loving boy we grew up with, she took care of him and loved him the same as when he was an infant in her arms. She gave her life so that his illness would never hurt anyone again. She gave her life so that all of her children could be safe.

When I mentioned Tim's name, I felt a crack, an empty sound. My lips shaped his name, but my vocal cords didn't vibrate, put no force behind *Tim*. When Lizzie heard me waver, she put a hand on my shoulder. She kept her hand there until I finished speaking.

When I look at those lines now—*She gave her life so that his illness would never hurt anyone again*—I realize that they aren't true. Of course Tim's illness would continue to cause him pain. Of course Tim's illness would continue to cause us pain too.

But it was easier then to think of her death as sacrificial.

So that all of her children could be safe.

After the funeral, we followed the casket out of the church, watched as some of our friends lifted it into the hearse. Across the street from the hearse, we saw a news van, NEW HAVEN REGISTER on the side panel. A woman stood next to the van, her left shoulder partially obscured. She aimed a camera at us—my siblings and me—as we watched our mother's casket slide into the hearse.

Chris and Lizzie had both started to cry. I don't think they saw the photographer. As they buried their heads against me, I stared directly across the street, directly into her camera. The camera never left her face.

This seemed important then, my staring contest with the photographer. It seemed like some gesture of defiance, some way of shaming her.

Later, I would learn that the *Register* posted a picture of us standing outside the church after the funeral. It accompanied the article "Orange Slaying Victim Laid to Rest." I never saw the picture. The paper removed the image after people complained.

I wish they hadn't. I wish I had seen that image, seen what I looked like, glaring at a camera after my mother's funeral. I'm not sure I would recognize myself, my posturing, my play at strength, at righteous anger.

I know that this photographer didn't choose this assignment. This couldn't have been what she had wanted, to capture the grieving children of a matricide victim. This wasn't the dream beat, wasn't the type of shoot that got her into photojournalism.

I would see this woman again, several times when Tim appeared in court. She never bothered my family, never inserted herself in what was becoming our public grief. She did her job, quietly, perched on courtroom benches, peeling away images of my family's tragedy.

A priest prayed in the parking lot outside of Tim's prison while we eulogized our mother. My father had requested this—a priest to pray with Tim during the funeral. But when the priest had arrived, the prison was in lockdown, no visitors permitted. So the priest sat in his car, read the passages we had selected for the service, prayed for our mother, prayed for Tim.

I have no idea if Tim knew about this priest in the parking lot. I don't know if he knew that during the morning, while his prison was locked down, six hundred people had watched our mother's casket pass in and out of a church.

After the funeral, my family and I tried to reclaim our house. At first, we struggled, moved awkwardly like we were living in a diorama, a curated display—our normal objects in their normal places.

We had friends in town for days after the funeral, friends who gathered with us in the family room in a semicircle on the couch and floor.

A few months prior, as some kind of joke graduation gift, someone had given my sister a copy of *Fifty Shades of Grey*. Somehow, it was one of the books stacked on the end table next to the couch.

One of my friends picked it up, held it for all to see. "Doing some serious reading, Vince?"

We passed the book to David, my friend from college who had been the bass in a famous a cappella group, worked as a singer on a cruise ship, had the timbre of a voice-over actor.

He began reading, scanning for salacious material. We laughed while his booming voice dramatized the protagonist's flustered response to accelerating sexual scenarios. In a book that is, ostensibly, about the nitty-gritty of kinky sex, the protagonist's language is decidedly PG. As she becomes more compromised in her lover's web of fantasies, she exclaims, *Crap! Double crap!* like a Midwestern housewife mourning a casserole gone awry.

Lizzie and some of her friends joined us while David was reading. Her laughs were delayed, a response when she heard everyone laugh around her, an attempt to blend in. I watched her eyes, saw them fix on the corner of the room next to the dogs' crates, the spot where she'd found our mother's body.

But I kept laughing, asked David for more. I laughed harder, gasped in my chair, hoping that Lizzie would look away—like it was that simple—that she could be distracted by David's deep voice, the way he read *Fifty Shades of Grey*.

Guilt shadowed me after my mother's death, building during quiet moments in my childhood room, or when I stood in the backyard next to the skeleton of our old swing set.

For a long time, I thought—believed, even—that somehow, had I been home, I could have stopped Tim.

This guilt sharpened around sentences in newspapers, the stories about my family's tragedy.

"Dr. Claudia Granata was killed by blunt impact and injuries from sharp objects to her head, neck, torso, and extremities."

Head. Neck. Torso. Extremities.

My mother's entire body.

"Police seized various items from the home believed to have been used in the killing."

Various items. Plural, varied, more than what I already knew, more than *knives.*

"The victim's hands were apparently bound behind her back."

Tim had bound our mother's hands.

I started to realize that my first story—of a suicide thwarted—was a delusion, a bulwark to separate me from more guilt and pain.

Yes, guilt was inevitable. When our worlds erupt, it's natural to say, *How did I let this happen?*

But this guilt also gave me cover, let me obscure the full picture, Tim's descent into illness. I focused only on the day he attacked her, on that moment in the family room, the apex of his madness. This guilt saved me from marshaling other memories—how he'd called me, sobbing, before our parents took him to the hospital, or how I'd left him alone after he told me about seeing the floating coin. By thinking only about that last day, I avoided remembering all the moments I'd sat with him, silent, inert in the face of his pain.

My obsession—with that day, with how she died—seized me for the first time during the morning after her funeral. I sat alone in the family room in my mother's chair, the chair where she would read by the window.

From her chair, I stared at the spot. I stared because I knew the spot now. Days before, Lizzie had said—an offhand comment, a brief aside—that she was worried the dogs spent too much time sniffing around the opening of their crates.

I decided to lie there, in the spot where she had died. I didn't know yet which way she'd fallen, if her feet had reached toward the bookshelves or the windows. I lay on my torso, my head beneath the dog crates, legs stretching past the computer toward her chair. I didn't know it then, but I'd laid the right way, my face against the same wood that had touched her cheek.

On the floor, I imagined that I had been in this spot, in the family room, when Tim's illness seized control. I put myself with the two of them, imagined that my knees hadn't been wedged under a distant classroom table.

I imagine, in this fantasy, that I remind him—*Look, look, that's Mom*—that I raise my voice over his demons, that he hears me, stops—just a trance, a trance I stop with a snap.

But I know this is too easy, too easy even for fantasy. Tim wouldn't have heard me—even if I shouted—when his demons governed his mind. So when I lay on the family room floor that first time, the morning after her funeral, I imagined a different way to intercede, a way to fight him, my brother who outweighed me by eighty pounds, my brother who pinned me when he was fifteen.

I imagine him in front of me, weapons not yet in his hands, but our mother is already bound on the floor. His body is in front of me, and I throw my forearms at the muscles in his chest, realize he won't budge, that he's rooted to the floor, legs like pillars I will never topple.

So I try to make a weapon appear in my hands. I think first of our childhood weapons, foam booster seats, exercise balls, our beanbag chair. I think of him as the child from those basement tussles, not my brother in this psychotic body that I'm trying to push away from our mother. And I need a weapon, not a child's weapon, but a baseball bat, or a shovel, or a hammer, or a metal curtain rod I can pull from the window near the phone.

Would I have been able to hit him, bring a metal pole to his skull? Would I have hit him, bludgeoned him like when we were fighting with foam booster seats, kids playing in the basement?

On the floor, obsessing over what I might or might not have done, I imagined my mother's pain. Her pain from the wounds, the *brutal* pain, but also a second pain, the pain I knew she would feel if she could hear me constructing these scenes.

If she could hear me, if she could see what I was imagining on our family room floor, I knew what she would say. I was certain of it.

How could you have stopped him, your muscle-bound little brother? How could you have pried him from the grip of his psychosis? You would be dead next to me. We would be dead together.

Lying on the floor, I thought that maybe that would have been better. Maybe dying next to her would have been better.

I was terrified then, imagining myself dead next to her, terrified because I didn't know if I'd ever make that thought disappear.

14

"I think you should see someone," my father told me, a week after my mother's funeral. "A therapist, Vince. It might be helpful." He mentioned that I was the only one in the family without professional counseling.

A few weeks later, I saw Dr. Franklin for the first time. We met through therapeutic matchmaking. Lizzie had been seeing a psychologist in New Haven who made the connection.

At the time, my feelings about therapy fell into two buckets—the thing that had failed to help Tim, and clichés from books and movies. Aside from my family's experience of therapy, my stock imagery was all Hollywood, the couch, a secular confessional, the therapist coaxing a client's tears with a precise phrase—*It's not your fault. It's not your fault.* I might have started treatment—*treatment*, it took time for me to use this word—with this expectation, that I was something to be unlocked, that Dr. Franklin would position herself around me, observe, collect data, reveal my secret password.

I met Dr. Franklin the morning after I returned to Boston. The night before, when I entered my apartment, a place I hadn't been in nearly two months, a stack of condolence cards waited. Many of the notes were from my colleagues, teachers at my school using the address I listed in our directory.

Among the many cards—thoughts, prayers, *anything I can do to help*—was an audiobook of Bill Bryson's biography of Shakespeare, *The World as Stage*, a gift from the head of the English department. She would, in the months that followed, bring weekly bags of "leftovers" to my office—*I made too much soup last night, we had too much meat sauce for our pasta.* Sometimes there would be a bottle of wine, a bag of cherries, an assortment of cookies. She would remind me, for months, that she hadn't forgotten. Her kindness helped me report to my desk, grade essays, plan lessons on *Oedipus Rex*.

Also among the cards, was a note from a colleague who had joined the faculty with me four years before. In his note, he referenced our conversations about *South! The Story of Shackleton's Last Expedition*. He ended the note with an iconic Shackleton phrase.

By endurance we conquer.

I held those words—*by endurance we conquer*—thinking of a doomed journey across polar ice, trying to make them fit when I drove to school along the Charles River, watching early risers row in the Boston dawn.

I felt immediate tension between this—stoic endurance—and what I thought therapy required—letting go, surrender.

The Shackleton phrase reminded me of a strange compliment—yes, I think it was intended as such—I'd received after my mother's funeral. While we pushed pasta salad around plastic plates, a woman I didn't know approached me, perhaps one of my father's colleagues. She hovered next to me, waited for me to turn, then shook my hand, firmly.

"I just wanted you to know," she said, "that you showed such manly grief." As she held my hand she repeated it: "Such *manly* grief."

I think I know what she meant. I think she meant that I had satisfied a certain image, stood to eulogize my mother, stared into the crowd, set my jaw so my lips wouldn't tremble. This posture—dry eyed, feet rooted, braced to receive a pat on the back—matches the words we use around *manly* grieving, loss as a *hard blow,* a *storm to weather, by endurance we conquer.*

This, an ancient archetype, the opposite of hysterics, elevates stoic strength.

On some level, a desire to live up to this image was working in me. When she said it—*such manly grief*—I felt, for a second, that I had achieved something, like I was *strong, so strong.*

But this conditioning—gruff, manly grieving—asphyxiates all emotion, strangles tears, leaves pain to fester until it oozes to the surface.

By endurance we conquer.

I'm sure I was holding on to this, a posture I practiced unconsciously, when I arrived at Dr. Franklin's door.

To enter her office, I had to follow a protocol. Behind the house, I entered a code in the lockbox guarding the entrance. For months, I had to reference an iPhone note to remember the six-digit pin.

I knew Dr. Franklin was a woman close to my mother's age—the age she had been, fifty-seven. I was ready, I thought, not susceptible to easy transference, any string of association—smart woman around sixty, someone I'll confide in, mother.

But when I first saw Dr. Franklin my mind outflanked me. *This is how Mom would have looked if she hadn't colored her hair.*

I tried to focus on obvious differences—height, eye color, no glasses—but I still felt, right away, like I was reminding myself in a loop *Clearly she's not Mom, clearly she's not Mom.*

This association was inevitable. I don't know if I'd ever spent an hour alone with a woman my mother's age who wasn't my mother.

I don't know if I'd ever confided in a woman my mother's age who wasn't my mother.

Lizzie's psychiatrist had spoken to Dr. Franklin before our meeting. Their conversation had precluded any awkward beginning, *So what seems to be the problem?*

I'm good at taking instructions. I have a deep-seated wish to do things "the right way," to be, as someone close to me once said, a people pleaser. Eventually, Dr. Franklin would chip away at this people pleasing. Her theory, one I initially resisted, is that as a big brother to triplets, I had to "be good" to alleviate strain on my busy parents.

My penchant for following directions had meant that I was pretty good at school. It meant that even if I wasn't a supremely gifted athlete, I was at least coachable, malleable, someone who could be developed.

In a way, some past success may have led to this thought, a belief that therapy was something a person could be good at, was something that could be done *the right way*.

"I'm not quite sure what I'm supposed to do," I told Dr. Franklin. "Do I just start talking?"

With this beginning, I think I revealed my psychic hand.

"Speak whatever floats to the surface," Dr. Franklin told me.

This directive flummoxed me. At first, I think I was expecting her role to be proscriptive, the giver of explicit advice, like she was an orthopedist fixing a ligament in my knee.

I don't remember how we started. I might have described where I was when my mother died. I might have told the family origin story—the arrival of Chris, Tim, and Lizzie, the chalk mural I scratched into our driveway.

I do remember how our first meeting finished.

As the session drew to a close, Dr. Franklin broke in. Here, I assumed she would offer something like an initial diagnosis: *I'm getting the sense that you . . .*

What she said shocked me.

"Really, the first trauma in your life was when they were born."

She hit a pressure point, their birth, the day our family doubled in size, the biggest event on my time line before my mother's death.

But she was right—their birth would also cause me pain. I didn't know yet how to hold these two facts at the same time.

I felt then, at the end of our first session, like Dr. Franklin had drawn psychic blood.

But this pain also convinced me that I would see her again. Pain made sense to me here. Big problems, I thought, needed big solutions. To solve my big problem I would need a difficult solution, one that I assumed would incur pain.

I still hold on to a version of this logic, that choosing a painful process will eventually soothe the big pain I can't seem to control.

I slept normally after my mother died in a way that took me by surprise, a truce between my unconscious and me.

But when that cease-fire lifted, Tim appeared when I slept, in nightmares real and fantastic, dreams I remember—vividly—as if I'd lived them.

I'm frozen on our driveway. I'm in the shadow of our basketball hoop. Through the garage door, I can see my deflated basketballs lining rusted shelves. They look like molded mushroom caps. Tim is in the garage. My dream inertia lifts.

I run to the backyard, press my back against the wall between the porch and cellar door. I crouch, try to slide under the porch like the thin garter snakes we chased as kids. I see my feet in the garden bed where my mother planted sunflowers.

Tim finds me, a serrated kitchen knife in each of his hands. I don't hear him or smell him. I see his greasy hair plastered to his scalp.

I'm stuck. I can't feel my back against the brick. I can't feel my feet sinking into the dirt. There's pressure in my stomach. He's stabbed me.

When I told Dr. Franklin about my first dream, how I had run from Tim to our backyard, she told me that I was imagining what would've happened if I had been home.

I had been mired in these thoughts, my endless *what if*s, the obsession starting when I had lain on the family room floor. Dr. Franklin knew that this dream didn't need deep Freudian analysis.

Dream interpretation puzzled me. At my most skeptical, I saw dream interpretation as a little hokey, as pseudoscience, but I also knew that I wanted my dreams to matter. They were terrifying, arrested my sleep, made me afraid to lie down. I wanted that pain to have a purpose.

My associations with Freud weren't yet burdened by his dismissal of serious mental illness. I didn't know yet how Freud disdained seeing patients in acute pain, patients in the grip of psychosis. I hadn't read his writing about patients like my brother. "I seldom see dements [dementia praecox—a diagnostic precursor to schizophrenia] and hardly ever see other types of psychosis. I feel them to be so far distant from me and from everything human."

Sure, neurology needed to evolve to classify psychotic disorders as diseases of the brain. Sure, pharmacological remedies were still decades from discovery. But Freud rejected patients who suffered the most, and still remained—for far too long—psychiatry's lingering figurehead.

But I didn't have this bias when I first saw Dr. Franklin, and her interpretation of my dreams felt literal, accurate. I listened. My dreams were causing me pain. I wanted them to stop.

Some dreams married real and surreal.

Tim is a terrorist. He has detonated a nuclear bomb. I don't see the bomb go off, but I know he's done it. He is hiding in the basement of our house. I don't want anyone to find him.

Suddenly, I'm standing among police cruisers in our cul-de-sac. No one is going in the house. They can't go in because the house is a crime scene. They can't go in because my mother's body is still on the family room floor.

But this doesn't make sense. They are the police. Why are they standing outside? I'm hiding now too, standing behind the tree that my sister used to scale next to the driveway. I'm afraid that the police will go in. I'm afraid because they might find Tim, who has detonated a nuclear bomb.

"The destruction of the nuclear family," Dr. Franklin said.

At first, I wasn't sure if I was supposed to laugh or read this as serious analysis.

"You're anxious about going back into your house," she said. "You're not sure what's still lurking there."

"Yes," I said. I didn't know what else I could do except agree.

Some dreams were entirely surreal, terrifying in how they distorted reality.

I stand in a dark space, a room I don't recognize. The only object I can see is a wooden chair. Tim appears across from me. He's a blur, broad, dark. His edges are impossible to define, but I know it's him.

He blurs further. A tiger takes his place. Lizzie appears, tied to the lone wooden chair. The tiger lunges toward her. I try to step in front, block the tiger, block Tim. I feel his claws. I hear Lizzie scream.

"Were you scared?"

I described to Dr. Franklin what I had felt when Tim the tiger lunged. It felt like his claws pumped air into my stomach, a bubble rising inside of me, dragging organs from my abdomen, to my chest, my throat, out of my mouth.

"I'd rather not feel that way," I told her.

Even then, even after these nighttime terrors, I still assumed this stoic stance, this play at casual dismissal. *I'd rather not feel that way.*

But, setting aside the psychic pain of running from my brother in dreams, the fact that I was having these dreams—nightly—created very concrete problems for me.

Because I wanted the dreams to stop, I tried tactics that took physical tolls.

I tried the simplest solution first—sleep less, dream less. To avoid sleep I brewed pots of coffee after dinner and watched loops of on-demand television. I almost memorized the entire HBO miniseries on John Adams. I went for night runs along the Charles River, streetlights casting yellow ghosts over the dark water.

Eventually, I had to sleep. Sometimes my dreams would shake me awake on my couch, TV still babbling, lights on over my head.

"You must be tired," Dr. Franklin said. I cradled a large iced coffee between my feet on her floor. I didn't want to press its beading outline onto her end table.

When I started twisting the skin on my thighs to stop myself from collapsing on piles of ungraded papers, I chose a new strategy. I started drinking until I fell asleep, alcohol drowning my unconscious.

But nothing amplified a hangover like clustered ninth-graders chirping while I took attendance. As I moved through homeroom, I had to keep both eyes on my feet to avoid scattered backpack traps.

"Alcohol," Dr. Franklin explained, "inhibits the body's ability to enter deep restorative sleep."

These tactics, my attempts at problem solving—forced insomnia, drinking—had only created more problems. This idea, that problem solving could eradicate the dreams, prevented me from truly addressing their cause.

"If we can make what is unconscious conscious," Dr. Franklin told me, "you won't have to work so hard while you're sleeping."

Speak about what you're afraid of or be tormented when you sleep.

But guilt—I'd been a thousand miles away—also made me cast the nightmares as a sort of punishment, pain by proxy because I wasn't there to stop Tim. I would think this way for a long time, in terms of what pain was deserved, what pain was just for me to suffer. These thoughts created a dizzying loop of guilt—if I deserved the painful dreams, I had no right to want them to disappear.

By endurance we conquer.

Some nights, while I brushed my teeth, I tried to steel my unconscious, like I was preparing for dream combat, the trial that awaited when I closed my eyes.

In some dreams, I fought back.

I'm in a parking lot. It's a dirt lot, the one next to the West Haven beach where we used to swim as kids. I'm with Chris and Lizzie. We're standing behind my Camry. We lean against the trunk.

Lizzie points. She sees Tim, free, walking toward us. He waves. Lizzie starts to run. I don't know where Chris goes. Tim laughs, his familiar cackle, *ha-ha-HAA*. He doesn't speak, but he's smiling. He's definitely smiling. I think he's trying to tell us not to worry.

But I can hear Lizzie screaming. I see a shovel resting against the car. Tim is in front of me and the shovel is in my hands. He stands very still.

I swing the shovel. I hit his face. He takes a step toward me. I step back, swing again, harder this time. He keeps moving forward. I swing again—again, again. Each time the metal strikes his face. Each time he keeps coming.

I keep swinging until I wake up.

It was this way for a long time. For months, I saw Tim in only two ways: in dreams, where he terrorized me, or in my imagination, when I obsessed about what I would have done if I hadn't been so far away.

Fantasy and nightmare became where I lived. The stuff of my days—lesson plans, coaching, dinners with friends—was reduced to a sort of intermission, ambient noise between bouts in my arenas, waking and sleeping, Tim becoming a monster.

In this way, I fled reality, allowed my mind to draw Tim freehand, forming him in the shapes that terrified me most.

In this way, he grew unrecognizable. I lost Tim further.

To find him again, to see more than a monster, I needed a different kind of pain, a real, waking pain, the pain of seeing him—the real Tim—in front of me.

15

Go back to sleep.

Those were Tim's last words to me, spoken from behind his bed-room door three weeks before he killed our mother. I hadn't heard his voice since.

During those months, the state had shuttled Tim between three prisons before sending him to the Whiting Forensic Hospital. He had just turned twenty-three. Whiting, a maximum-security facility, shares a campus with the Connecticut Valley Hospital, one of the state's remaining institutes for the mentally ill.

Tim arrived at Whiting because a judge declared him incompetent to stand trial. Before Tim could face the criminal charges against him, before he could enter a plea of not guilty by reason of insanity, before he could be tried, he needed to clear several hurdles.

To be declared competent for trial, Tim needed to understand the charges against him. To understand the charges against him, Tim needed to repair his memory, combat the illness that blocked his recent history, his crime.

Tim couldn't remember his crime. Tim couldn't remember that he had killed our mother.

Through injected antipsychotics, needles piercing the meat of his shoulder, clinicians tried to lift schizophrenia's haze, to restore his memory, to restore his competency to stand trial, to restore Tim. They always used that word, *restore*, like he was being returned to his factory settings, like he was being wiped clean.

During the process, a panel of psychologists tracked his progress, analyzing his answers to questions—*Can you name the members of your family?*

"I love them all," Tim told his evaluators. "My family understands me well."

Tim would refer to our mother in the present tense, tell his evaluators that she had visited him—just that week—on the day they were served hot dogs in the cafeteria, in the evening after Bible study.

I saw his psychosis as a shroud covering his recent history, concealing the final months when his illness had festered untreated, his madness putrefying his brain. For some time, I thought his memory might return in a single moment. I pictured him, head bent and shaking, remembering every detail, how our mother sat at the computer when he approached, his hands commanded by demons, their strident voices convincing him that she had abused him—emotionally, physically, sexually—that she had to pay for this abuse.

I'm not sure why I imagined that his memory would return in an epiphanic instant. Maybe it was because epiphany is easy—the clichéd light bulb, the sudden moment of recognition. Fiction pivots on these moments, the rush of knowledge to a character mired in denial, depression, disarray.

But I was hoping for epiphany too. In the months since I'd last seen Tim, months when I'd seen him in newsprint, in courtroom video, in nightmares, I'd struggled to figure out when I would visit him, what I would do when I saw him, the real Tim.

To figure this out I decided that I needed to know what my mother would want. Knowing her wishes became desperately important.

But this phrase—*what she would want*—can be a trap, an impossible puzzle, the living left to guess at the wishes of the dead.

I thought I might see her when I slept and waited for the night when she would come instead of Tim.

But she never did, my dreams just another place to feel her absence.

Though I struggled to imagine her, to figure out what she might say to me, I still believed that the way back to Tim was through her. She had been a sentinel, the last person to stand against Tim's mounting illness. She had sheltered him when he was sick, been the guardian who never left him alone.

Eventually, I convinced myself that it was this, how she had refused to leave him alone, how this duty had meant her death, that demanded I visit Tim. Eventually, I made myself believe that I could be her helper, the deputy I had been when she held Chris, Tim, and Lizzie by the tail.

In this way, I convinced myself that I would watch Tim and track his treatment, adopt my mother's duty. I convinced myself that I could help Tim remember, achieve a painful epiphany, a necessary step in his restoration. He would be restored, I believed, thinking that this distinction would be the first step in getting Tim back, back for our mother, the woman who had waited so patiently for him to return.

And I used this goal—helping Tim remember—to focus, to give me what I forced myself to believe was a specific purpose.

I had no idea how long this remembering would take.

*   *   *

It was dark when I drove to Whiting for the first time. Three months had passed since our mother's death.

As I approached that first night, the brick buildings looked hollow, like old warehouses in an abandoned mill town. Whiting had grown out of the state facility for the mentally ill, a compound that opened in 1868. Many of the old structures still line the campus—late-Victorian architecture, broad brick buildings, nineteenth-century boarding school meets asylum. Whiting is on the back side of the campus, on the downslope of a hill near where the Connecticut River bisects Middletown.

After the final turn—Sweet Drive, the road at the entrance of the facility—I saw a rectangular transformer, a steel box flanked by knots of coiled wire. I passed a police cruiser before turning into the parking lot.

I chose a space away from other cars. The lot slopes gradually downward in the direction of the entrance; the decline pulled me toward the building's main door. From street level, I could see only one long wall, the concrete extending away from the parking lot. Once inside, I learned that the compound is an angular parallelogram, each side a long corridor bounding an inner courtyard with grass, a concrete basketball court, a seasonal garden.

At the front entrance, a voice behind a camera asked me questions. *Who are you here for? What is your name?*

I answered, staring back at the circular camera lens, a lidless red eye. The door buzzed, the sound a low hum, like I was being let into a friend's apartment building.

Inside, I stopped to scan the waiting room—chairs, green carpet, framed photographs of former wardens. A glossy copy of *Parenting* magazine sat on an end table.

I stared at a bulletin board that celebrated the clinician of the month. The winner, a freckled woman with full cheeks, looked like a school nurse, one who spent her afternoons comforting kids with upset stomachs.

I let my eyes travel the rest of the room, scan the plaques commemorating distinguished employees, a glass case housing a ceramic Virgin Mary, a series of nesting dolls, a miniature Buddha. I noticed a metal detector, a machine standing like a sentry before a wall-size door. I fixated on these details, let the contours of this broad metal door distract me from the questions I had for Tim.

I had a strategy for this first visit, a strategy that would keep me focused and prevent the details of my mother's death from interfering with my mission—*Help Tim remember, help him be restored.* I crafted a list of innocuous questions, a warm-up I hoped to perform before approaching the business of memory.

As I waited, looking toward the metal door, I heard a voice but couldn't see its source.

"Vincent?" my full name, one I rarely heard, traveled through opaque glass next to the metal detector. Soon a corrections officer appeared.

"Come through the detector," he said.

It beeped when I shuffled through. I moved my hand to my belt buckle like I was explaining myself to airport security. Behind the glass, three uniformed officers scanned a bank of monitors. After I'd handed over my driver's license and emptied the keys, gum, and ChapStick from my pockets, the mechanized door inched open. I cleared a second mechanized door and a voice from behind the glass told me to keep walking until I saw the visiting room on the right.

Along the sterile hallway, open doors revealed offices, a nurse's station, a Xerox machine. I smelled stale coffee, passed a water fountain, a pegboard with key chains, a janitor's closet. I had expected more—patrolling corrections officers, conspicuous cameras, locked doors.

There was no choreography to my reunion with Tim. No one stood at the entrance of the visiting room waiting to point at my brother and say, "There he is," or, "Tim will see you now."

Yet there he was, Tim, on the other side of the door, sitting like he had been waiting for months.

When I'd seen Tim in news clips from his first court appearance, his hands and feet were bound. He shuffled when he walked, head bobbing up and down like he was following music that only he could hear.

I saw him now, completely unfettered.

Without restraints, Tim pushed himself off his chair and stood behind a low table. He waited. The collar of his sweatshirt hung limp below his unshaven neck.

He was in gray sweats, not the standard jumpsuit I'd seen him wear in the news clips. He had dressed this way at home, sweats draped over bulging muscles.

"Hey, man."

After a few steps, I felt his arms wrap around my torso. We hugged, and I remembered how in high school, when he was just starting to realize his strength, he would squeeze me harder and harder until my laughs turned to gasps. Now I felt little pressure, only the weight of his massive hands spread across my back.

The room was spare—cinder-block walls, dark heavy carpet. It felt like an assembly room, one that might be in a church or community center or town hall, a place for coffee in Styrofoam cups. We were alone except for one corrections officer perched on a small platform to our left.

When we sat, our shins pressed into the wooden table separating us. Later, Tim would tell me that the tables were placed this way to prevent one person from lunging at the other.

We laughed during that first visit, almost immediately after we sat down. At first, I wondered what the corrections officer was thinking—two brothers bent over a prison table, one a killer, both laughing. I glanced at the corrections officer and saw his eyes locked on a walkie-talkie in his lap.

"They let you have your own clothes here?" I pointed toward Tim's sweatshirt.

"They gave me these," he said.

"They know your style."

"Pretty much. Pretty much." He laughed, pushing air out of his nose.

When I watched Tim laugh, I realized for the first time that he lived in the same body. When I'd seen him in courtroom video clips and in newsprint pictures, he had looked the part the headlines had cast him in, that of deranged killer. He wore a jumpsuit and hand-cuffs, his glasses falling toward his nose in an image that thousands of people would see. *Psycho*, they would say, and how could I blame them when all they saw were those pictures? How could I blame them when the only Tim I had seen was the monster that visited when I slept?

But sitting across from him in the visiting room, I saw that he had the same olive skin, the same black hair, a shade darker than that of everyone else in our family. He still had the same cauliflower ear, a mass of crushed cartilage above his right ear canal, a common marker among many competitive wrestlers.

And there was something else, a barely perceptible suggestion of who Tim used to be, a softness in his cheeks and on the skin under his eyes. His mouth didn't quiver in agitation, ready to loose a diatribe on original sin, on the immense distance we lived from Christ. There were no sharp head nods, no twitches of response to invisible stimuli.

"How's the food?" I asked, remembering his rigid adherence to chicken breasts and egg whites when he was wrestling.

"It's not that bad," he said.

"How's your back?" This was chronic pain, shooting sciatica, something he had mentioned when he spoke at his arraignment, months before. The judge had asked him if he had any physical problems.

"I have a lot of joint pain and a bad back," Tim said. This line, Tim's response to the judge's question, was printed in several of the newspaper stories, Tim's sober assessment of his physical injuries.

"Not bad," Tim said. "I don't move so much in here." He minimized his pain as he had after high school wrestling matches, bags of ice strapped to his shoulders, his badges of honor. This had been an easy conversation for years, the discussion of his physical aches, the bruises sustained as an athlete. The physical was always easier, easier than when he would tell me that he spent all his time in his room because he was afraid to meet new people.

"Do you have a roommate?" *Roommate* made it sound like college, where the guy in the bunk below him might be from Michigan or Delaware, might have a different major.

"There's one guy. His name is Bill."

Later, I would learn about Bill. During a psychotic episode, Bill had shot and killed a college student at a campus pizza shop. A few visits later, I met Bill's family in the waiting room. They were kind to me, extended easy empathy, a type of understanding that can pass between fractured families, between people trying to find their lost loved ones.

"There's an overhead picture of this place in the waiting room," I said. "I saw a big courtyard. Do you go out there?" I realized *courtyard* sounded like I was talking about a sprawling campus.

"They give us time out there," Tim said. "I usually just walk around."

When I ran out of easy questions, I moved to more intermediate ground. I mined the deep past, memories he might still have, memories recent years hadn't blemished.

"I saw John the other day," I said, mentioning our godfather. "He was in town showing Sean colleges. Do you remember him?"

"Yeah, I think so." Tim squinted like he was trying to see something behind my right shoulder.

During the first times I visited him, those three words—*I think so*—were Tim's most common phrase. They were always paired with some sign of effort—eyes narrowing, drawing a wrinkle on his forehead.

I told Tim about a friend who had gotten engaged. "You remember my friend Andrew, right?"

"I think so."

"He's getting married. It's bizarre, everyone is getting married now." I laughed a bit.

Tim laughed too, lifting from where he sat in the chair. When he settled, his weight sank more conspicuously in folds creasing his gray sweatshirt.

"Do you think you're ever going to get married?" Tim asked.

"Maybe. Someday." I was growing distracted, worried that I was reaching the end of the questions I had prepared. There was only one left.

This last question was different. It involved our mother. Mentioning her to Tim, bringing her between us, terrified me. We had been speaking for thirty minutes, and she had yet to enter, my warm-up questions a strategy purposefully employed, one that would help move us gradually to her, to fraught ground.

But everything was fraught ground. We were speaking for the first time in three months, for the first time since he'd left our mother bound and broken on the family room floor. Could I have asked him then if he remembered when we were kids, clamoring with Chris around the computer in the family room, taking turns with the mouse, standing in a semicircle around the spot where our mother would die? Could I have asked him if he remembered her last words?

This hesitance was why I had my warm-up, this gradual opening I'd thought was for Tim. I'd thought that we could work out some stiffness in his mind, limber him up, before we tested heavier memories.

But the warm-up was also for me. I needed to be able to pretend, if only in a small way, that I wasn't meeting Tim at a psychiatric prison, that I wasn't visiting him months after he'd killed our mother, that I wasn't trying to coax him into a conversation that we would have for the rest of our lives.

Remembering was necessary, the only way, and though I wanted to save him this pain—the pain of remembering—his restoration demanded otherwise. This process could only start when he could stand trial, when he could be acquitted on grounds of insanity, when he could begin what would, in a best-case scenario, be a twenty-year period of incarcerated treatment. At forty-three he could walk out of this building and into my car. We could drive away into the afterward, fully restored. This process was the way I would get him back, the best way to honor our mother, to get him back because she never would.

I hadn't yet realized that this clear-eyed hope for recovery was just the most recent in my own string of delusions, a long string winding through years of naïve hopes. I see the beginning of my delusions, sitting next to Tim in the dent he made in his bed, hugging him the day after he first told our mother that he planned to die on the Fourth of July.

But I still thought that I could reach him, sitting across from him in that visiting room, as close as when we were children paddling a canoe. I thought that I could reach him because our mother no longer could. I thought that because I had hugged him, been close enough to smell his dried sweat, that he would understand why I had to ask my next question, my last question.

When I asked him, I knew that I couldn't use the word *remember*. "Do you miss Mom?"

I had conceived this question as a ploy, a calculated tactic I thought might trigger a rush of memory. But as soon as *Mom* left my mouth, I realized that I wanted an answer.

"I wish I could have gone to her funeral," Tim said, "but I was here."

I looked at his eyes, the dark points of his pupils. The only one having a sudden rush of understanding was me, face-to-face for the first time with the complications of his frayed memory. He could know that she was dead but repress that he had held the knives.

"How was it?" he said, like he was asking about a movie he hadn't seen.

"The music was beautiful," I said, peeling my eyes away from his, letting them settle on the table between us.

That was as far as I went the first time. Soon he was asking me about how long it would take to get back to Boston. Then we stood, hugged, his massive shoulder cradling the bottom of my chin.

I told him that I would be back in a week.

As I walked to my car, I tried to remind myself why I had visited. I tried to remind myself about my mission, the task I had set.

I'm visiting to help him remember, to help him be restored.

I'm visiting for our mother because she never got him back.

I'm sure I wanted these things, for Tim to be restored, for me to act, somehow, as our mother's proxy.

But those reasons alone didn't bring me to the visiting room. I know that now.

I was the one who needed Tim restored to my life. I was the one who wanted Tim back.

I had been looking for him during the entire visit.

16

Chris, Lizzie, my father, and I did not know the same Tim. Individually, we chose what space we wanted to leave for him in our lives.

I don't mean to make this question—who visited Tim—sound simple. During those first years, my father and I visited Tim; Chris and Lizzie did not. But this is not an easy split. Their decision is not one I can question. I didn't share the womb with Tim.

I'm not certain if my father ever considered not visiting Tim. He's told me that Tim is his son, and that this fact means support without condition. He visits Tim, speaks with the clinicians who track his treatment, sends Tim creature comforts—bags of mixed nuts, warm socks, beef jerky sticks. But Tim's relationship with my father had been strained even before his illness took hold.

"They push each other's buttons," my mother used to say, describing Tim's relationship with my father. As Tim got sick, my father couldn't be on the front lines. The two of them spoke a different language. For all of my father's love and patience—love and patience that endure to this day—his tether to Tim was never as strong as our mother's. It can be this way in all families, between all parents and children. Allegiances and bonds are unequal.

For Chris, Tim had been a best friend. Until college, the two had been inseparable. Through childhood, from basement blanket forts to greasy burgers after football practice, they were linked, shadowed each other, until distance and disease intervened. Yes, I grieved losing Tim, my little brother, but Chris lost a best friend. I won't ever understand how that loss feels.

I know you might feel that I haven't shown you Chris. I know that his absence might suggest a greater absence, suggest that he was distant from me after our mother's death.

Nothing could be further from the truth.

Chris, like Lizzie, has always looked young for his age. While Tim's bulk aged him, made him imposing, Chris's face never seemed to match his sturdy physique, a child's smile on a powerful body. As a child, Chris was always in motion, feet fluttering beneath the dinner table while he ate the plain food his picky palate demanded— buttered pasta, a side of apple slices, cinnamon toast.

"Just like my dad," our mother would say. "Steak and a baked potato, every night. Wouldn't even add salt."

Though Chris's diet evolved slightly—I once saw him eat calamari—he's kept his kinetic energy. He has what people call an infectious personality. He is a living yearbook superlative, *Most Likely to Brighten Your Day*.

I know this doesn't capture him, the clichés we throw at people who make us feel good. But I mean this earnestly. No one is ever unhappy to see him.

For so many years, he and Tim moved as a pair. In my memories of them—from childhood through high school—they are often side by side. I remember the morning of their high school graduation,

the two of them standing next to each other in maroon satin gowns. Neither wore formal clothes under his gown, both having convinced our mother that T-shirts and shorts were all they could bear on that humid June day. She didn't object. Chris and Tim would be the only two boys to walk without ties, but their naked necks didn't seem so odd because they marched together.

Our mother and Chris traveled many miles in our mother's minivan. Throughout his years as a swimmer, Chris competed in meets across the state and, as he grew more accomplished, across New England. Chris was easy company on the long rides, even in his teenage years, the time when so many boys retreat behind willful indifference, distance themselves from their mothers.

I can remember my mother describing him this way—open, emotive, a teenager without guile—then laughing about how she'd known this about him since the moment of his birth, the only one of his siblings who sobbed when entering the world.

In the months after our mother's death, Chris processed out loud. He cried—freely, easily—wringing out his pain in a way I envied.

He spoke about our mother often, kept her alive in sentences I couldn't yet form.

Mom would want us to be happy.

Mom would be proud that we're moving forward with our lives.

I'm ashamed of how his grieving made me feel. I'm ashamed that once, on the day before Thanksgiving, I slammed the kitchen table, yelled, *ALL YOU DO IS TALK*, after he described how important it was for the four of us to be together at home.

My outburst startled him. He slowly shook his head, then waited for my fists to unclench on the table before he started speaking again.

This is not to say that Chris had an easier time healing after trag-edy or that Chris's processing was some sort of linear progression, a measured march through stages of grieving.

Chris has faced challenges that far exceed mine. Tim was his partner, his best friend. His memories with Tim are far more com-plex than my own.

And Chris's memory is a wonder. He recalls specific days from his childhood and can, as if by magic, match exact dates with milestones—championship swim meets, graduations. He can do this with mundane moments too—an afternoon fight with water bal-loons, a meal with friends at a diner.

Sometimes he'll use this power as a party trick. He'll ask someone to name a date—any date in the last fifteen years—and he'll provide the day of the week. I've watched as people verify his answers with a Google search. I've never seen him give the wrong day.

This magic is not mathematical prowess. It's the quirks of his mem-ory, Chris claims, a form of synesthesia that literally colors the days of the week, tints all of his memories a certain hue, sharpens his recall. In this way, he can work backward from a date he remembers, note the color, the day, then find a proximal memory, see how it's shaded.

To me, this explanation has always seemed incomplete, like if a figure skater described a triple axel, *I just jump and spin.*

Chris's memory would help me contend with a particular chal-lenge I had started to notice in the months after our mother's death. I began to recognize how my months seemed to build toward each twenty-fourth, the day of the month when my mother died. On every twenty-fourth I woke with a version of the same thought: *It's been two months, five months, seven months since Mom died.*

I told myself that this chronicling meant nothing, that those days, those twenty-fourth days, were no different, were not cause for more

pain. But I would drift on twenty-fourths, lose my place in the middle of lessons, slam on my brakes just feet from a red light I hadn't seen.

I hated how those days—*that* number, twenty-four—seemed to have power over me. That power felt absurd, a gimmick in a horror movie, a supernatural haunting that couldn't be real.

Chris was the first person I told about my twenty-fourths. I was drunk when I told him, at the end of February, seven months after our mother died.

It's so dumb, but every twenty-fourth feels fucking surreal. It's like I'm caught in some kind of loop. Time is moving forward even though I feel the same.

Chris made me a promise. Every twenty-fourth he'd text me a memory, something from an earlier twenty-fourth, a day that he remembered with our mother.

March 24, 2008, was a Monday. Swim season had just ended and I'd shaved my head for championships. I was cold and Mom had knit me a hat. It was small and sort of thin in places. But she loved knitting so much that I wore it around the house. Remember that hat?

June 24, 2011, was a Friday. Mom barbecued and grandma came over because it was a few days before Dad's birthday. I ate three hot dogs.

October 24, 2010, was a Sunday. Mom called me like she did every Sunday and Wednesday. That was my first fall living away from home.

Before I could remember myself next to her, Chris showed me his memories with our mother. He showed me those earlier twenty-fourths, how there were so many more twenty-fourths than the one that had reset my calendar.

He still sends me twenty-fourths every month.

I wasn't sure how to talk to Lizzie about Tim. I couldn't figure out how to explain why I visited. So I cowered, avoided mentioning Tim to Lizzie, rationalized my silence as a way to protect her, to save her from thinking about Tim.

Her fears of Tim had much more fuel than my own. She had lived at home during that entire summer, heard Tim's feet stomping on the stairs in the middle of the night, heard the metallic echoes of his weights hitting the basement floor. She had listened to many more of his vicious rants than I had, felt the fury of his paranoia when he accused our father or Chris of searching his room.

Tim loomed in her memory as the monster his illness had spawned, the monster fuming behind his locked bedroom door, the monster she saw covered in our mother's blood on the front steps.

I feared that discussing Tim with Lizzie would only animate what terrified her most. So with Lizzie, I tried to steer conversations away from the Sundays I spent at Whiting.

But my visits weren't a secret. I knew that Lizzie was aware that I was seeing Tim even though we didn't speak about the visits until weeks after my first. When we spoke, that first time, we sat in a Panera across from my apartment, a place where we would grab quick lunches when Lizzie was in the neighborhood.

Lizzie started the conversation, asking me, "How long is the drive?"

"I can get there in ninety minutes," I said. This wasn't true. I hadn't made the trip in less than two hours, but I started with this lie,

I think, because I was trying to minimize the weight of the visits, like I could make seeing Tim sound like an errand.

"How is he?" Lizzie said.

"His memory is in rough shape." I kept eating, bit my sandwich to the crust. Lizzie didn't press for more details.

Instead, she asked why I was visiting, but not as an accusation, not like my choice to visit had betrayed her trust. I think she was worried about me.

I know that I rambled about *being a big brother*. I told Lizzie that my relationship with Tim was different than her own, that my relationship with Tim had been different ever since I'd helped our mother gather their tails when we walked in the mall. I leaned on this, my internalized role, *big brother*, and hoped this would be enough to answer Lizzie's question.

But when she was quiet, I kept talking, gave the reason I'd constructed for my first visit, how I'd convinced myself that I was visiting Tim as our mother's proxy, that I was visiting Tim because she never got him back.

I should have stopped there, let silence settle between us.

I regret what I said next.

I can remember that moment, my spoon floating in the dregs of tomato soup, crumpled napkin next to scraps of crust. I remember how Lizzie's cheeks looked heavy, how her shoulders melted into the booth, how her entire body looked seconds from inward collapse.

Except for her eyes. Her eyes—narrow, hazel—pointed up, aimed at me.

I know why I can still see this moment, why I remember a Panera booth in lucid detail.

Shame sharpens my memories. So much of what I remember

refracts through a particular pain. Shame grinds my memories to a single point, one that punctures. My memories become like gasps.

"I have to visit him," I said. "It's what Mom would want us to do."

I'm ashamed that I said *us*. I'm ashamed that I projected my impossible twisting of our mother's wishes onto Lizzie. I told my sister, who loved our mother more than anyone in the world, that she wasn't living up to our mother's wishes. I had accused her of letting our mother down.

Lizzie's eyes sank to the table between us.

"Maybe," she said. "But that's not the only reason you visit. You're visiting him because you weren't there when it happened."

I said nothing. I sat across from her, silent, because I knew that what she said was true.

After I visited Tim, I slept.

I would learn, over the next year, that one way to quiet my unconscious was to visit Tim, was to see him as my brother, not the monster I conjured in dreams.

This made sense to me—to Dr. Franklin too. If I could see Tim, recognize some pieces of him, my unconscious wouldn't need to project him, render him only through the horror his illness spawned.

This wasn't a perfect solution—my unconscious doesn't have a simple off switch—but the nightmares thinned, became episodic, were no longer terrors I could count on every time I closed my eyes.

Of course, there was a trade-off. Visiting Tim was never easy. The complications of his frayed memory accosted me during those early visits.

While he seemed to understand that our mother was dead, he struggled when I asked him questions about the months before.

When I asked him if he remembered being in the hospital, he told me that he'd been in the hospital for a long time.

"Not here," I said. "When you were at Yale. I visited you there once, with Mom." I did this, found ways to mention her, ways to bring her into the room to see if Tim might remember.

"It feels like I'm talking about a movie," Tim said. "It feels like it isn't me."

Before I could speak—*What, what doesn't feel like you?*—he leaned into the table, whispered, "Vince, do you think our house is haunted?"

"No," I said; then I went on, told him that I didn't believe that houses could be haunted. But as I spoke, I started to remember all the ways our house must have haunted Tim. I remembered the floating coin, the key to the demons' portal that must have been as real to Tim as the weights he left scattered in the basement.

As we approached the holidays, the visiting room grew more crowded. On Sundays in November and December, Tim and I had to lean forward to hear each other over the ambient noise of everyone else's tragedy.

Tim was lucky to be at Whiting, a place where he received consistent treatment. Nearly a fifth of Whiting's 268 beds are for people who are being restored to competency. This process can take months or years. There is no federally mandated limit on how long a person can be in this competency restoration phase.

Many are less fortunate than my brother. Many flounder without consistent support, are left without the tools to be restored, or achieve competency only to regress when transferred to a prison setting, one ill-equipped to allow them to continue being treated while awaiting trial. There are thousands of these souls, caught in competency limbo, warehoused out of view in forensic units and prisons.

Tim needed to meet two criteria to be declared competent. In addition to needing to understand the charges against him, he also needed to prove able to aid in his legal defense. At Whiting, Tim received "competency restoration services." When I heard this phrase for the first time, it sounded almost like a kitschy spa package, something offered at a meditation retreat where busy professionals could go to *unplug, reset, feel restored.*

For Tim, competency restoration services meant a mix of group therapy, individual evaluation, injected medication. Through these methods, Tim would come to understand the charges against him and learn to aid in his legal defense. Treating his disease seemed a by-product.

I've seen the notes from his restoration. When I read the notes, I created scenes in a sort of montage, a series of jump cuts between Tim in group therapy, Tim responding to questions from a psychologist, Tim waiting in line to receive his injection of Risperdal.

During the first months I visited him, Tim's progress was slow.

"I don't know why I'm at this hospital," he said, when a psychiatrist asked him who had ordered him to Whiting.

In his groups, facilitators observed detachment.

"Timothy sat quiet and did not participate in the discussion," the leader of the emotion-regulation group noted. "He appeared to be paying attention, directing his gaze toward whoever was speaking at the time."

But in December, Tim's third month at Whiting, he showed progress. He began to answer the questions his evaluator posed.

"I'm here because a judge sent me," Tim explained, "for competency restoration."

In the last week of 2014, Tim cleared a major hurdle in his restoration. While he had grown fluent in the elements of his trial, demonstrated that he could aid in his own legal defense, he was slow to convince his evaluators that he understood the charges against him.

But months before he would show me that he was starting to remember, Tim began to reveal the horror his disease had strained to block.

"Do you know what you're being charged with?" Tim's evaluator asked.

"Murder," Tim said.

"How serious is this charge?"

"They say I killed my mom."

17

"Mr. Granata," one of my students said, half raising her hand, "I think you have a crush on Antigone."

Her class, one of my ninth-grade English sections, had just listened to me ramble about Antigone's pleas to bury her brother Polynices, a man authorities believed had betrayed his city.

"You're not wrong," I said, "which is tragic." A handful of students laughed—more than I deserved—and we moved to the next scene in the play, weeks into our unit on Greek tragedy.

I'd taught this class for five years, run through largely the same material, my teacher's copy of *Antigone* coming apart at the binding. This familiarity allowed for a sort of autopilot, a way to teach from muscle memory, to allow myself normal laughs when a student turned in an essay titled "To Antigone and Creon-d."

Working at my high school imposed a comfortable routine. *Lunch at 11:20, third-period announcements, half days on Wednesday.* I could post our weekly vocab on the class bulletin board—*mitigate, circumspect, polarize*—discuss rhetorical appeals: *ethos, pathos, logos.*

This is not to suggest that routine was a sort of antidote, something to numb the days between trips to Whiting, but it was easier to define poetic terms on familiar whiteboards, to smile with familiar faces in the faculty lounge, than it would have been to set out into an entirely new world.

Chris and Lizzie did not have this luxury. Both of their lives were changing while I returned to the same city, same apartment, same job.

Chris moved to Boston in the fall, to an apartment ten minutes from mine. At his first job, he worked in marketing for a growing sports drink company. He drove Patriots tight end Rob Gronkowski to local schools, then dispensed free samples to crowds of kids. After two months of pushing the sports drink, he got a new job at an e-commerce company, a place where he could put his facility with numbers to good use pricing the sites' wares—swing sets, trampolines, pool tables.

Of course, this new life wasn't easy for him. There were times when he struggled.

Once, out for a Sunday breakfast with Lizzie, me, and our father—a frequent visitor that fall—Chris sobbed openly onto a stack of pancakes. The pancakes had been too sharp a reminder, Sunday pancakes one of our mother's practices during childhood. Because we ate them ravenously, our mother used to race to slide them off the griddle, often leaving them undercooked. These were our favorite, the ones with pockets of viscous raw batter. This is what Chris remembered when he stuck his fork into a professionally cooked pancake, and no gooey batter dripped onto his plate. He cried, in gulps, while people ate breakfast at tables around us.

He could do this, grieve our mother in public. He was braver than me.

Lizzie moved to Boston to take a job at a well-known charter school. Weeks after our mother died, she loaded her clothes into duffel bags, wedged plastic drawers and a beanbag chair into the back seat of her car, and drove with Chris to a house in Jamaica Plain, a neighborhood in southwest Boston. She spent her days in middle school classrooms helping students with reading and math, supervising meals in the cafeteria alongside a cohort of twenty new teaching fellows. Lizzie lived with four of her new colleagues, two to a room on the first floor of a triple-decker house.

This new life was difficult for Lizzie. I didn't let myself recognize how every facet of her life was colored by trauma and loss.

The weekend of Halloween, Lizzie and I went to a concert with some of her new coworkers. I can't remember the name of the band. For the concert, Lizzie and I each wore adult-size onesies, mine spotted like a cow, complete with black-and-white ears, Lizzie's striped like a zebra, a pink patch over her torso. We wore beads and sunglasses, called ourselves "party animals."

We didn't live up to our costumes. Not long after the show started, I lost Lizzie's stripes in the crowd. I waited too long—several songs—but eventually started searching, a lanky cow wedging himself between throngs of dancing bodies, asking women if they'd seen a zebra in the bathroom.

Outside, I found her, around the corner, back against an alley wall.

"Relax," she said, when she saw that I was concerned. "I can't fucking deal with this. I just needed some air."

"I know," I said, but I could tell that she had been crying, dark mascara a shadowy scar beneath her sunglasses.

She told me she wanted to go home, that she didn't want to explain to her new coworkers why she had left.

"I'm done with this," she said.

I thought I knew what "this" was. *This*, trying to dance in a zebra costume while trauma and loss howled in her head.

But her desperation, the way *I'm done with this* felt like a waning gasp, made me start to fear a greater *this*, fear how *this* could mean her life.

I felt terrified that I was witnessing a new set of signs, my sister's life spiraling as my brother's life had spiraled, and me—the big brother—standing inert, standing adjacent to her pain, as I had been to his.

I'd done so little to help hold Lizzie's grief in the months after our mother died.

After Lizzie moved to Boston, she and I had fallen into what seemed like a comfortable routine. On most weekdays, I'd drive to her apartment after work. We would walk together to Jamaica Pond and smile at the dogs trotting beside their owners. When the dogs looked friendly, when they tugged on their leashes to sniff my sister's ankles, she would pet them, but only after asking permission.

I don't think anyone ever stopped her. Lizzie's kindness is transparent. Her smile projects *I mean no harm, I mean no harm.*

After our walks, we'd get burritos at the Purple Cactus or make pasta sauce. We'd play board games at her apartment, grow comically competitive over letters in Scrabble.

To an observer, we must have seemed close. We had two decades of inside jokes, a honed brother-sister shtick. Whenever I stumbled into a pun, Lizzie pressed an imaginary button on her palm, produced an exaggerated guffaw, her imitation of a canned sitcom laugh track. If she said, *I didn't have enough snacks for the kids today and I feel badly now*, I'd paw her chair, grope the wall, tell her *I feel badly too.*

I wanted to think that this was enough, that this performance of big brothering could help to hold her up, that wearing matching costumes to a concert was a way to combat traumatic loss. I hoped that simply being around, acting as we had acted before, might offer some comfort. I thought that we could be like two toppled columns, teetering upright only because we'd fallen toward each other.

But when she told me, after the concert, *I'm done with this*, I began to recognize how thoroughly my big brothering failed to help her grieve. I had recently told her that I felt that she was letting our mother down by not visiting Tim. I had avoided further conversation about Tim, but knew that she noticed how often I visited him, the way a trip to Whiting became like a pilgrimage. And I know this caused real pain, pain when Lizzie saw how fervently I'd turned toward Tim.

I tried to pay more attention in the weeks that followed *I'm done with this*. I tried to listen closely when Lizzie spoke, to notice how she held herself when we walked together around Jamaica Pond. I grew so afraid when Lizzie started to struggle with thoughts that threatened her life.

So I tried to be vigilant, vigilant in a way I hadn't been with Tim.

There were few new faces in my life during those months. I surrounded myself with old friends.

Several of those friends—most around my age, twenty-seven— were getting married that year, the beginning of the steady parade of weddings I would attend into my thirties. Among the first were my friends Andrew and Mallory, who got married early that January, in Florida, around the same time Tim's evaluators began to believe he understood the charges against him.

The night before Andrew and Mallory's wedding, more than a hundred of their friends and family gathered for the rehearsal dinner, a celebration larger than many wedding receptions I had attended. The dinner was in a hall set off from a large restaurant, one with garden dining, an indoor fountain. Two of the walls had floor-to-ceiling bookcases, each lined with bottles of brown liquor, labeled and cataloged like a library—Jim Beam to Eagle Rare.

Andrew and Mallory had sprawling extended families, an array of aunts, uncles, and cousins filling the round tables. We—Andrew's friends from college—sat as a separate contingent, almost like we were envoys, Yankees from the Northeast.

Toasting, it became clear, was an important practice for both families. Some delivered their messages in well-metered rhyme. The string of toasts meant that glasses needed steady refilling, rotating bottles abetting my buzz while I listened to how Andrew and Mallory, who'd started dating when they were sophomores in high school, had grown up—from prom to marriage—together.

One of Andrew's aunts rose to give a toast. As many did before her, she gleefully recounted Andrew and Mallory's thirteen years of courtship. Most remarkable, she thought, was that even though the two had grown up on the same street, they had gone to separate colleges, many states away, and had lived apart for most of their adult lives. She returned to this idea, the absurdity of falling in love with your neighbor, moving nearly a thousand miles away, then marrying more than a decade later. This absurdity, she would repeat, was clear evidence that "God has a sense of humor."

Every time she returned to this refrain, eliciting laughs from the tables around her, I remembered that there had been four priests and a bishop on the altar during my mother's funeral.

I hated that she said it, *God has a sense of humor*. In that moment, I despised this flip turn of phrase. I hated this idea, that the divine was filled with whimsy, fate simply a frivolous matchmaker.

And I hated that I felt this way, how quickly an innocuous comment—a lighthearted line played for laughs—could pry me from happiness, even as I was surrounded by my closest friends, celebrating two people we loved.

To comfort myself, I tried to feel righteous in my anger, like I knew *the truth* and this woman didn't. But my smoldering anger, the way I bunched my napkin under the table, only made me feel alone, enveloped in laughter, in the ring of toasting champagne flutes.

In that hall, sprawling family surrounded me, scores of mothers and sons. I'm certain that this family had their complications, their sources of sadness, but to me, this family looked entirely unrecognizable from what my family had become. That woman, Andrew's aunt, clearly loved her nephew. She cried, overwhelmed that a day she had hoped for had finally come.

Then, more concretely than I had before, I started to visualize the future without my mother in it. She would never be with me at a gathering like this one, a family celebration, a wedding.

This feeling built during the next day, at the wedding reception, when Andrew danced with his mother while I stood on the periphery of the dance floor.

I don't remember the song Andrew and his mother danced to. I don't remember who was standing next to me, if my friends were looking toward me, if they were worried, if they whispered to each other, *Do you think Vince is okay?*

I never saw my mother dance. I can't think of a single time. Dancing does not remind me of my mother. Were I to get married, were she still alive, we might not have done this part, the mother-son dance. Or maybe we would have fumbled through it, my mother laughing, looking at her feet, watching them shuffle in ways I had never seen.

I can't know the answer to this question, *Would my mother have danced with me at my wedding?* And this, the certainty that I would never find out, that there would be nothing new between my mother and me, descended while I watched Andrew dance with his mother, a new pain, a way I hadn't hurt before.

Yes, I missed my mother in those difficult moments, the times when I recognized all that we would never get to share.

Mom, there's so much I want to tell you.

But it was hard for me to remember my mother then, and though I missed her, I struggled when I tried to imagine her, to hear the words I wanted her to speak to me.

Two months after my mother died, my aunt—my mother's sister—gave Chris, Lizzie, and me a gift.

The gift was in a white box, unwrapped but tied with a red bow. My aunt included a note explaining what the box held, *letters written by your mother to me from September 1971 to April 1972.* During that period, my aunt, two years older than my mother, had left for Smith College—the first time the two had been apart. My mother was fifteen years old.

The gift came at a particularly difficult time, in the week after Chris, Tim, and Lizzie's birthday, which falls three days before our mother's.

There had been a party the weekend before. My friend Frances baked a cake and I frosted HAPPY BDAY CHRIS + LIZZIE across the top, the first time I can remember writing their names as just a pair. Chris and Lizzie blew out the candles surrounded by friends in Chris's apartment. I remember there being some trouble with a neighbor, Chris's single bathroom ill equipped for the crowd, leading many to use the shared driveway instead.

Our aunt made it clear that her gift was not a belated birthday present, but something for the three of us to share. Both Chris and Lizzie said that they weren't ready for the letters, couldn't take the box. By default, the letters fell to me.

"Please please please," Lizzie said, "don't ever lose them."

I was terrified when I first opened the box, folded back the pink tissue paper cushioning the letters. I was terrified because my mother was nearly twelve years younger than me when she wrote these messages. She was still a girl.

What if she sounds childish? What if I don't like her?

But as soon as I started reading, I heard my mother's voice, not as a fifteen-year-old girl, but her, my mother, complete with all of her encouragement, her teenage hand underlining her love.

Remember that I love you very much. I may only be your little sister but if you have any problems you can confide in me. We have to stick together.

From the beginning, it was her, her exhortations, her affirmations—*You'll knock 'em dead*, a phrase she'd spoken to me before so many childhood challenges.

And of course, there were moments that revealed her age.

By the by (don't breathe a word of this) there is a boy in my physics class who is really good looking—TALL—dark hair.

These passages did not make my mother unrecognizable. They made me marvel, thinking of my mother as girl with a crush on a boy in her physics class.

But these moments didn't leave me smiling. My mother's relentless hope—for her sister, for her future—gutted me, made the two-page letter nearly impossible to finish.

> *Don't be discouraged if everything isn't running perfect on your schedule or daily life. You'll adjust or it will.*

I stopped reading because I knew how my mother's story ended.

While I was reading, I wanted to tell her, to scream through the crinkly paper, *You don't know this, you don't know this, but in forty-two years your son will kill you in the family room where you taught him how to walk.*

And yes, in those forty-two years much more would happen than just her death. She would become a doctor, meet my father, a man who would be, like her physics-class crush, *really good looking— TALL—dark hair.* She would have children, four of us, raise us with the relentless encouragement she gave her sister.

But then, reading that letter, all I could see was the end of her story. That girl who would become my mother had no idea how her life would end.

I folded the letter, placed it on top of the unread stack. With the tissue paper shroud in place, I sealed the box, pushed it to a corner of my desk.

I waited three years to open the box again.

When I finally returned to the letters, I learned how to transform what had been, on first read, unbearably painful reminders of my mother into cues I could use to reanimate her, remember how she spoke to me.

In so many of her letters, the girl who would become my mother drew cartoonish illustrations, jokes on the literal meanings of the phrases she used. Next to *I decided to skip my history homework*, she drew a stick figure skipping over a textbook. After *Well, time is marching on*, she sketched a marching man with a clock for a face. When she told her sister, *Make sure you eat plenty*, she included a woman, mouth agape, next to a box labeled PLENTY.

The sum of these moments, her groan-inducing cartoon gags, can hypnotize me. These mannerisms, figures of speech, thought patterns, are the DNA of the mother I knew. How many times, when I was a feverish sick child, did she joke, *Does your face hurt? Well, it's killing me*, before taking the thermometer out of my mouth, offering a popsicle in its place.

In her last letter to her sister, one my mother wrote shortly after learning she would join her at Smith College, my sixteen-year-old mother crafted a limerick (know before reading, their last name was Dinan):

There once was a young Smithy named Din Din
Who committed one hell of a Sin Sin
She went to a dance
Began to wildly prance,
Because she had drank some gin gin!

Beneath the limerick, my mother—somewhat sarcastically I think—imagined the wild times she would have with her sister.

I'll bring some "liquor" and juice—and you + I will have a party— JUST THE 2 of US! We'll get STIFF.

When I first read this letter, I laughed at her language, at *STIFF*, like I was reading a passage from a booze-drenched Hemmingway novel. Beneath this sentence, my mother had drawn a picture of the two of them, eyes comically wide—*You + I stiff!*

But then, reading their last letter for the first time, I saw my mother's closing, the only time in all of the letters she used this parting phrase.

Bye for now.

This would become her coda, the way she always said goodbye.

Bye for now at the end of the recording on our home answering machine. *Bye for now* at the end of the saved voicemail I keep on my phone. *Bye for now* at the end of the last email she sent me while I was working in the Dominican Republic.

Here, in this letter, was the first instance of the phrase that would punctuate the rest of her life.

But it wasn't just her that I saw in this *Bye for now.*

Sometimes, when Tim calls me, when he has time in the morning or in the afternoon when I'm not able to talk, he'll leave me voicemails, messages thanking me for a book or asking me to look up a pastor he knew in college. At the end of every message, he says, *Bye for now.*

I don't know if he recognizes the phrase's origin, if he realizes that he's repeating the words he heard so often from our mother.

I have never told him how I remember our mother—her voice, the way she said goodbye—every time I hear him tell me, *Bye for now.*

18

On January 2, a Friday, the same day my friend Andrew was married, the Milford Superior Court filed a report declaring Tim competent to stand trial.

Our mother had been dead for nearly six months.

Tim appeared in court the following week to have a judge confirm his competency.

During the months before, Tim had attended mandated court appearances, brief proceedings where the only agenda seemed to be setting his next court date. Nominally, I believe these monthly court dates were to monitor his restoration, but to me, this process of trotting Tim in front of a judge was only a reminder that he was still in the nascent stages of a long legal journey.

I attended these court appearances, taking mornings off from teaching to travel to Connecticut. I left early in the morning to accommodate my father—every clock he owns is fifteen minutes fast—who insisted on arriving at the courthouse well before proceedings began.

In the mornings, a line formed at the entrance of the building as people waited to pass through a metal detector. In a building that imposed divides—between attorney and client, plaintiff and defendant, state and citizen—the metal detector democratized. Lawyers in suits waited alongside men challenging speeding tickets, parole violators, the families of alleged criminals.

In the hallway beyond the metal detector, posted dockets announced which courtrooms hosted which cases. The layout of the dockets resembled those of the brackets I used to scan for Tim's name at wrestling tournaments. Every time we entered the courthouse we looked for Tim's name, our name, GRANATA.

When it was time to enter the courtroom, my father made sure we sat in the front row on Tim's side. Courtroom design demands that spectators do this, pick sides.

There was always other business before Tim arrived, a host of other offenses for the court's consideration. I got used to the snippets of crime passing through the Milford Superior Court. A man had violated a restraining order, lingered in the parking lot of the restaurant where his ex-girlfriend worked. There were occasional drug charges, a man violating his parole by failing a urine test. Some of these moments stayed with me, like one man, a repeat DUI offender, who was arrested when he drove over a grass median to exit a Burger King. I remember him because there was a woman crying when the judge ruled he had to serve ninety days. I remember assuming that the woman was his mother.

When the other business finished, the judge usually paused, said something like, *If there's nothing else*, before looking toward Tim's attorney, a veteran of this courtroom, waiting on the bench next to us. Usually there would be a brief break between the first string of hearings and my brother's appearance, the judge retreating offstage as if to freshen up or grab a coffee before considering my brother's sanity.

We were allowed to wait in the courtroom during these breaks. Over time, I became familiar with some of the marshals, the men providing security. One marshal, nearly a foot shorter than me but ballooning with muscle, introduced himself the first time we were in court.

"I'm Art," he said. I shook his hand and saw MARSHAL ART printed on a thin nameplate pinned to his chest.

When he turned back around, my father was smiling.

"Marshal Art," my father whispered. We laughed, waiting for Tim in court.

During the interlude before Tim's hearings, Art would answer my father's questions, tell him when Tim had arrived. Art explained that the vans that transported Tim and other inmates left early in the morning, made a circuit of various penitentiaries, drove routes that often took hours. Tim would corroborate this, how he had to wake up at 5 a.m. on the days he was due in court. He told me that he tried to stay awake in the van, in the early-morning light, so he could twist his body from where he was chained to his seat, strain to look out the window. His view, dark through tinted glass, was usually of little more than the breakdown lane of Connecticut highways. But he looked forward to that part, his chance to see the outside world, before he arrived for a brief public exposure, for a judge's eyes to fall on him in court.

Art was kind to us in that courtroom, let us wait on the benches during breaks. These were small gestures, simple kindnesses, but they made what was a terrifying space—the arena where my brother would answer for killing our mother—somehow more tolerable.

The marshal who often flanked Art was a much larger man, oblong, gut heavy, appearing like a former football player who had let years of lethargy cloak muscle in lard. They made an odd pair, odder still when accompanying Tim. The three of them shuffled into the courtroom in a line—compact Art; my broad, handcuffed brother; the bigger marshal—standing in ascending height order.

We saw Tim's face only when he entered the courtroom, walking the ten steps from a side door to the bench next to his attorney. He would wave, needing to bring both hands in the air, his wrists cuffed. My father and I waved back, speaking in stage whispers. *Hi, Tim.*

During the proceedings, Tim wasn't allowed to turn toward us. Only once did I see him try. Marshal Art, standing at his left shoulder, leaned forward to correct him, whispered, *Face forward*, like a teacher keeping a student in line.

At the hearing when Tim was declared competent, his evaluating psychiatrist presented to the court. He explained how Tim had sat for a twenty-five-minute evaluation.

"His thoughts were clear and organized," Tim's evaluator said. "There were no significant memory deficits."

No significant memory deficits.

I stared into the back of Tim's head and tried to fit Tim's competency—what he could now understand about our mother's death—with the way he had spoken to me at Whiting.

I don't know if he truly understood then, or if he had just grown used to repeating what his clinicians told him.

They say I killed my mom.

They said it. *They* told him. I wasn't sure yet if Tim truly remembered holding the knives.

When I saw him next, after he was declared competent, I tried to ask him about what he now—in the eyes of the law—understood.

"They told me about my crime," Tim said.

My crime. He could place a pronoun in front of the word, could possess the *crime*. But when I asked him for more, pressed him about what *they* had told him, he looked away from me.

"It might attract the wrong type of attention," he said.

I thought he was talking about the corrections officer who chaperoned the visiting room, but he told me that he meant the demons, the forces he believed still battled in his head.

"I don't want to be under their control," Tim said. "Not again."

"I don't have a chemical imbalance in my brain," Tim told me the next time I saw him. "I was targeted by demons. That's over now."

Tim's anosognosia, the neurological defect impairing his awareness, worked like a translator, took what could be described clinically—*mental illness, schizophrenia, psychosis*—and translated it into words that made sense in Tim's world—*spiritual warfare, the wrong path, demonic possession.*

My mother had been reading a book about anosognosia in the weeks before her death. After she died, I found that book next to the sink in her bathroom, *I Am Not Sick. I Don't Need Help! How to Help Someone with Mental Illness Accept Treatment.* A bookmark waited at the beginning of part 3, "Staying on Guard and Next Steps."

It took me almost a year to open that book, remove her bookmark, start from page one.

The author, Dr. Xavier Amador, is an expert in psychiatric anosognosia. The impetus for Dr. Amador's book, for his study of psychiatry, was his years of arguing with his brother, a man suffering with schizophrenia and crippling anosognosia, a man who would not comply with the treatment Dr. Amador tried to convince him was necessary. For years, Dr. Amador's brother cycled through hospitalizations, disappeared from his family, lived on the street.

Eventually, Dr. Amador's brother accepted medication. Eventually, Dr. Amador found a way to lead his brother to the tools he needed to reclaim his life.

Initially, I think it was this—Dr. Amador had helped his brother—that made the book so painful for me to read. This book showed me a way I could have helped Tim, a way I could've spoken to him, a way I could have listened to him instead of rejecting the terrifying experiences he described to me.

I've listened to Dr. Amador present his decades of research and clinical experience. In these presentations, he prompts the audience to repeat the villain's name, *anosognosia*, aloud.

Anis-og-no-zha

Anis-og-no-zha

Anis-og-no-zha

He repeats the obscure word, stressing every syllable. Some pronounce the word more phonetically, *uh-no-sog-no-zha*, a pronunciation I prefer if only for the repeated *no no*.

But even this, the competing pronunciations, reveals part of the problem. Everyone knows how to pronounce *pneumonia*.

To try to understand my brother's anosognosia, I've sought out other experts, researchers who have dedicated their lives to decoding all of schizophrenia's tricks. I've used my mother's arsenal of psychiatry textbooks to identify them. This is how I found Dr. E. Fuller Torrey, the author of *Surviving Schizophrenia: A Family Manual*.

When I asked Dr. Torrey about anosognosia, he told me about all the hurdles that block our comprehension of the symptom.

"Anosognosia is one of the most difficult things for people to understand," he explained. "You can understand paranoid delu-

sions. You can understand auditory hallucinations. But to understand anosognosia, we have no personal experience that we can use
to help comprehend that."

I've tried. I've imagined what this would feel like, to be told that
there was something wrong with me, something serious, something
compromised about my body. There's no evidence that I'm diabetic,
but what if someone insisted, *Vince, you're diabetic.* What if someone
told me, *Vince, you need to take this insulin shot.* I would refuse. I would
be scared of the shot, scared of going into an insulin coma, scared of
dying.

But my imagining can only take me so far.

I don't know what it feels like to have a psychotic disorder. I
don't know that pain, no matter how I hard I try. I've read dozens of
books, listened to lectures on abnormal psychology, stared at brain
diagrams until my own brain aches, taken hallucinogenic drugs that
made plane contrails sparkle, my skin look like shimmering lizard
scales. With headphones I've listened to "schizophrenia simulations,"
blurred my eyes and imagined hallucinating spiders crawling on my
bedsheets.

But I don't know—I can't know—what Tim and millions of others feel when waves of neurotransmitters run roughshod over their
brains. No book or interview or simulation can give me this experience, can make the specter of the disease real for me.

When researchers try to make anosognosia's invisible aura concrete, they map the brains of schizophrenia patients, tracking neurological deficits. To catch these brains in the active grip of anosognosia,
researchers ask subjects questions while scanning their brains.

Do you think you have any emotional or mental problems?

*Why would doctors admit you to a psychiatric hospital if you didn't
have any problems?*

Through an MRI's lens, researchers capture the brain from different angles. The scans show brain activity as splotches of color—red and orange blazes on black-and-white brains. In the scans of patients with high insight into their illnesses, chambers of the brain glow, the medial prefrontal cortex, the insula, the inferior parietal lobule. In patients who cannot name their disease, brain images show only embers, single red dots, the glimmers of tired coals on a dying campfire.

Despite growing research, anosognosia is not yet a fully accepted feature of schizophrenia. In the most recent *DSM*, the establishment hesitates.

"Unawareness of illness is typically a symptom of schizophrenia itself rather than a coping strategy. It is comparable to the lack of awareness of neurological deficits following brain damage, termed *anosognosia*."

Is comparable to, a half step from naming it as a symptom, from acknowledging the disease's full potential to damage the brain.

In spite of this reluctance to codify one of the disease's most insidious symptoms, many researchers believe that half of those who suffer from schizophrenia and schizophrenia-type illnesses have anosognosia.

That said, there's no shortage of psychiatrists who highlight inconsistencies or flaws in certain studies and classify anosognosia as only *conjecture*.

There are some mental health professionals—some rooted in Freudian theory—who deny that our brains can have structural blind spots. They believe that we all—healthy and sick—know what ails us, but sometimes bury the truth, *deny, deny, deny*, until rigorous psychoanalysis, a medical practice akin to church confessional, peels back our defenses, our shame.

When I type *anosognosia*, my computer questions the word with a red squiggly line. I need to highlight the word, click *ignore all*, to make the doubt go away. Researchers like Dr. Torrey know there is work to do before we can erase that red squiggly line.

"We funded a couple of the early studies on the biology of anosognosia," Dr. Torrey explained to me. "Ultimately, that's the way you're going to turn it around, with lots of articles in good journals showing the MRIs that demonstrate how that brain is different."

And the key, many researchers believe, is the similarities in the brains of schizophrenia patients to the brains of stroke victims. The key is in the studies that show the same structural damage, anosognosia's MRI signature, the proof that patients like Tim are not simply denying that they are sick. Through these studies we can see how the disease can impose a neurological blindfold, the greatest defense the illness mounts to prevent those afflicted from freeing their minds.

Some experts like Dr. Torrey see psychiatry's incomplete efforts as a sort of anosognosia itself, psychiatry's lack of insight, the field's inability to see the greatest challenge of treating schizophrenia.

When I told Dr. Torrey about Tim, about his struggle, about the gaps in his treatment, Dr. Torrey nodded, my family's story not unlike stories he has heard before.

"You are being a good brother and son," he said.

But we had this conversation too late. We had this conversation more than two years after my mother died.

In a way, Tim started writing this story before I did. Once, during a visit, Tim told me that he was working on a children's book.

"It's called *Dreamland*," Tim said.

He had prepared to explain this story to me, written plot notes on paper spread between us on the visiting room table.

He apologized for his handwriting. "The only pens they give us here are these small flexi-pens," Tim said. "Normal pens could be weapons, I guess."

He looked at me before he began his story, his hands flat on the table among his notes.

"In this world, candy is currency," Tim explained. "There are these wood elves that mine fairy crystals, and then they use the fairy crystals to make candy."

In Tim's fantasy world, three benevolent fairy princesses live in a fairy castle. Their names are Estella, Desdemona, and Abigail. In his notes he describes them.

Sisters. They have a great relationship, intimately loving, caring, respectful.

"In the first scene, the fairy princesses are baking a cake," Tim told me. "They're using all of the candy the wood elves helped harvest. They treat the wood elves well."

Later, after he gave me his notes to take home, I read the description of what Tim wanted for the first illustration.

The fairy castle at night. Somehow there are rainbows, shooting stars, and fluffy pink clouds even though it is evening—surreal.

Conflict arrives when another trio of sisters—*evil fairies*—shows up in the kingdom. Their names are Jezebel, Delilah, and Cleopatra—two fallen biblical women and a seductress of classical antiquity.

Jezebel and her evil sisters: dishonest, Machiavellian, cunning. They want to enslave the wood elves and drain them of their energy! They are physically "beautiful" but in a very dark and seductive way. They are extremely vain, egocentric, and narcissistic—they don't even care about one another. They are wolves in sheep's clothing.

"Because they're so evil," Tim explained, "they won't win in the end."

In the beginning of his story, the evil fairies wreak havoc. They cast a spell to make the wood elves "mindless slaves." The fairy princesses have to flee their castle and find a wise dwarf living in the mountains beyond their kingdom.

"He lives in a holy crystal cavern," Tim said, describing this savior dwarf.

There, among the shimmering candy crystals, the dwarf judges the three sisters.

They are altruistic and they love each other. This is why the high dwarf decides to help them.

"He has a special kind of candy," Tim told me. "I don't know what to call it yet, but they can use it to banish the evil fairies. I need to figure that part out."

His notes stopped there too, the moment when the fairies—armed with their special candy—need to drive out the evil invaders.

"What do you think?" Tim asked.

I hadn't interrupted as he told the story. He spoke quickly, rambled even, but I didn't feel threatened by these currents of electricity, this racing speech different than his psychosis-fueled rants.

I could tell that he had rehearsed this delivery, practicing his presentation like he was pitching me, trying to impress me with his narrative. I knew I needed to encourage him. Before I spoke, I imagined him, holding his flimsy pen, scratching on these ripped pages against the mattress in his cell. I could see some small holes in the paper, perforations from when—maybe in excitement—he had pressed too hard.

"It's really compelling, Tim," I said. "It's a full world."

I had read much more into his story than this, but I didn't know how to tell him what I had seen. I had interpreted this tale as allegory, bent this story into evidence that Tim was crafting a narrative about combating his illness.

This came easily to me, fitting his story to my hopes. The benevolent fairy princesses were Tim's healthy brain, the boy he had been. The three evil fairies were the invading disease, the one that made the residents of Dreamland *mindless slaves*. The wise dwarf's special candy was the medication Tim needed to banish the evil fairies: *I have to figure that part out.*

Of course, this was too easy, how I superimposed my hopes onto Tim's children's tale. I twisted his fantasy world into this useful allegory, a way he could achieve insight into his disease by proxy, even if he couldn't believe in the reality of his treatment.

Not knowing how he would respond, I told him what I thought.

"It sounds to me like an allegory," I said. "It really could be a highly symbolic story about battling mental illness."

"Do you think that's what people would think?" Tim said. He seemed worried, worried that this story was just another way for people to see him as "crazy."

Often when Tim grew uncomfortable, he would pivot the conversation. He asked me if I could get him a "candy encyclopedia."

"It would help with the story," he said, "help me add detail."

I told him I'd try to find one.

But I wasn't done with his story yet. I remained rapt in the world he had spun, fixating on what I wanted to believe about his writing, about what I hoped was his recognition—if only through analogy— that he needed help through treatment.

"How did you get this idea?" I asked.

"I wanted to write a story for kids, one where good deeds are rewarded," Tim said. "I want to show kids that evil doesn't have to win."

He emphasized this intended audience—*for kids, for kids*—as if he was trying to rebuff what I wanted to insist, that Tim was telling his story, a fantasy version of *his* story.

"It's powerful," I said.

"Do you think . . ." Tim paused. "If this ever got published, would people see it differently because it came from me?" Tim looked down at his pages. "Because it came from in here?"

When he said *from in here*, I think he meant Whiting, his psychiatric prison, but when I heard *from in here*, I wanted to believe that he meant his mind. I wanted him to think about what it meant that he was the one who wrote this story.

"I think that makes it more valuable," I said.

The visiting room was quiet. On that evening, we were the only pair. I looked at Tim, still across from me, at the faint scarring on his forehead, at the tufts of his dark beard.

"Can you send me a book on Buddhist meditation?" Tim said.

I was surprised, not by the abrupt shift in conversation, but by what he requested. This book would be a departure from his focus on Christian scripture. In the past, Tim had told me that while yoga had helped heal his back, he couldn't attend classes because the meditation components were heretical. He couldn't stomach even the suggestion of non-Christian spirituality.

"Of course," I said, agreeing to get him the book, "but why the interest in meditation?"

"I need to learn," Tim said, "how to think about nothing at all."

19

The winter of 2015 demolished Boston's snowfall records. On March 16—my twenty-eighth birthday—the season's accumulation cleared 108 inches, eclipsing a mark set twenty years earlier.

Clearing my apartment's four-car driveway became daily exercise for my roommates and me. Our driveway, a patch of concrete wedged between our house, our neighbor's house, and a rotting wooden fence, had few dumping grounds for snow. Eventually, we resorted to flinging snow against the back of our house. By February, I could have stepped out of my third-floor window and tumbled harmlessly onto a frozen cloud.

In fact, this practice—leaping from windows into snowbanks— became so ubiquitous that the mayor of Boston held a press conference to condemn the activity.

"I'm asking people to stop their nonsense right now," Mayor Martin Walsh said. "These are adults jumping out windows. This isn't Loon Mountain."

That winter, when I drove to work, I had to nose into each intersection to see beyond the growing snowbanks. In the gray winter sun—tires spinning, hands frozen to the wheel—every turn felt like an exposure, like I was seconds from collision. Sidewalks surrendered to cascades of snow, my favorite running paths socked in, impassable. My world grew smaller.

In February, in the shadow of head-high snowdrifts, I made my way through handles of Bulleit bourbon, bottles my roommate Brendan brought back from his weekends as a New Hampshire ski patrolman.

The day before Valentine's Day, I drove south to New York and spent a frigid weekend in an apartment with my friends Charlie and Lis. We flailed over each other trying to make a multiple-course Indian meal, a Valentine's Day dinner for me to third-wheel. After our tangy curry—we forgot to add yogurt—and after Charlie and Lis went to sleep, I drank alone into the night. At 4 a.m., I vomited curried cauliflower all over the bathroom.

At home one weekend, after meeting some friends for pizza in New Haven, I sat in the family room, in my chair, working my way through the mismatched bottles in the refrigerator, then pouring the dregs of assorted Italian liqueurs—sambuca, amaretto—when the beer gave out. I knocked an empty bottle onto the floor when I spread my feet over the coffee table. The rattling woke my father, who found me, facing a semicircle of empty bottles, staring at the spot on our family room floor. I don't remember much of what he said, but he looked close to tears. I know he said, at least twice, *Vince, this isn't you.*

Vince, this isn't you.

Later that night, upstairs, I lay flat on the carpet in my parents' bedroom, at eye level with the stacks of books still hidden under my mother's side of the bed. Then, as fast as I could stagger, I entered my mother's bathroom, dropped to my knees, and vomited into her toilet.

This problem, this drinking that led to my father's observation—*Vince, this isn't you*—was something I had settled into in the months after my mother's death. While I had certainly been a social drinker in the years before, something had shifted, changed drinking from a way to enjoy time with friends to a dark bingeing, something to do with abandon, something to do alone.

Alcohol, an emboldening agent, did not steel me, did not help me endure grief. But the binges did overwhelm a fear, the fear *of* my grief, a sadness I couldn't bear to look at when I was sober.

With the exception of the day she died, I cried sober three times in the nine months after my mother's death.

Once, three days after, when I helped my father find a picture for my mother's obituary. The picture had sat on the mantel in the living room, a picture of the two of them smiling on our porch, a few years earlier. When I saw him hold the picture, looking for only a second before he closed his eyes, I cried in front of him as we sat around our kitchen table, while a visiting funeral home director shuffled brochures for caskets.

Once, with Dr. Franklin, two months later, after she asked me if my mother used to read my writing.

And again, with Dr. Franklin, around that same time, when she asked about how I had called my mother, terrified, driving away from home the morning after Tim banged on my door. I told Dr. Franklin what I had said to my mother, how afraid I had grown of Tim, of his illness's potential for violence.

"Then," I told Dr. Franklin, "Mom convinced me that I was wrong."

I was drunk every other time I cried, too scared to sob when I was sober. And when I was drunk, when I was alone or with people I trusted, I cried in gasps, into pillows or the shoulders of my friends.

Drunk, dizzy with the fragmented thoughts Tim revealed at Whiting, I would lay myself at my friends' feet, try to explain what I felt when Tim asked me about our mother's funeral.

How can he know and not know? Will we talk this way forever, for the rest of our lives?

When I was sober, when my friends would asked me about my visits, my answers were terse—*his memory is in bad shape, he seemed happy to see me, he asked me to send him a book.*

I couldn't talk about what it felt like to listen to him remember, remember how we chased each other on bikes around our neighborhood, took turns clearing snow off the driveway. I tried to hold these memories, the fleeting pieces of our childhood, but I couldn't talk about how these memories made me feel, how I felt so distant from them, how they felt like part of a story that wasn't about me.

I have many ways to explain why I couldn't emote during the daylight, why my drunk body grieved because my sober body was too afraid.

Some of them return to the logic of that odd condolence message—*You showed such manly grief*—or the Shackleton quote: *By endurance we conquer.*

On one school afternoon, I lingered after a meeting with the head of the English department—the woman who had been leaving me weekly dinners.

"When I see you walking through the halls," she said, "I think, 'Yeah, there's Vince, somehow he's really doing okay.'"

Her words, I know, were intended as a compliment, a recognition of perceived steadfastness, endurance—another way of saying *manly grief.*

But this assessment made me feel like an imposter. I didn't feel brave or strong or resolute.

I felt afraid.

But this is too easy an explanation, fear as the only reason I drank until my body stopped me.

Part of the problem was that when my father said, *Vince, this isn't you*, I didn't know which Vince he meant. Was I more myself in the sober daylight or when I was drunk and sobbing?

When I was drunk, the intensity that I hid from found its way to the surface. I could realize how surreal it felt when Tim laughed when we spoke at Whiting. I could think about listening to Tim remember our childhood, how unrecognizable those memories seemed. When I was drunk I didn't try to normalize, didn't try to endure, to proceed like everything was fine.

I wasn't strong enough then to find another way, to unravel without overwhelming my mind with drink. For a long time, I could only face how meaningless my memories with my family seemed—only a prelude to catastrophe—when I faced a line of empty bottles.

Once, driving Lizzie home to her apartment in Jamaica Plain, she told me that she was concerned. She had noticed small things at first, teetering bottles in my recycling bin, the amount of bourbon I poured at Chris's apartment. She asked me about some long nights in her neighborhood, nights when I'd driven to meet up with her and her friends, then promised to leave my car overnight when I was drunk and hugging her goodbye.

"I'll take an Uber," I'd say, "and run here in the morning to get my car. We can have breakfast."

I lied, every time.

The next morning, I'd drive my car back to her neighborhood, then sprint hungover laps around Jamaica Pond until I was sweaty enough to convince Lizzie that I'd run all the way from my apartment.

"I'm worried about you," Lizzie said, the night she confronted me. "I'm scared."

As she spoke, I pulled into a small parking lot off of Memorial Drive. I hadn't been drinking that night.

"Chris and I are both worried," she said. I stopped the car, turned to face her in the passenger seat. It was dark, Lizzie's face in shadow, only clear when passing headlights illuminated her body.

"This is the last fucking thing I need right now," I said, then slammed the center console. "With all I'm trying to keep together, this is what you're bringing up?"

I slammed the console again and again, breathless, stopping only when I saw that Lizzie was shaking. Terrified, I tried to apologize while I caught my breath.

Lizzie waited until I was quiet.

"It's okay," she said. "I know it's not me you're angry at."

That should have slowed me down, my sister's concern, how quickly I had raised my voice, shouted. She had inverted what I'd believed were our roles—big brother, little sister—to shake me out of my frequent bingeing. At that time, I'd convinced myself that I was the one who needed to be concerned for her, that the sharp end of her grief might threaten her life. I had watched and feared Lizzie's pain, but remained too scared to examine my own.

It would be a long time until I could look at what pushed me to drink with abandon, to surrender to sadness that seemed impossible to feel while sober.

My mother was not a drinker. I can remember only one time when I saw her consume more than an occasional glass of wine. On that night, we were in Maine, staying in Chris's college town to watch one of his final swim meets. It was late February. Tim was in the hospital.

At dinner, she ordered a second drink. Under different circumstances, I would have smiled. Chris was a decorated college swimmer. Watching him race was a joy. Why wouldn't my mother celebrate in a way I hadn't seen before?

"I'm going through hell right now," my mother said during her second drink. "Vince, I don't know what to do."

She had never spoken this way to me about Tim.

I wish I could remember what I said. Maybe I tried to encourage her, give her hope, tell her what she had told me so many times, that we would be fine.

It's so hard for me to be angry with her now. It will always hurt to wish that she did something that she did not do.

But when I remember that night, her second drink—*I'm going through hell right now*—I wish she had spoken like this more often, told me how she struggled, how far everything was from fine.

But my mother and I shared this, this wish for things to be fine.

And that wish, delusional as it was, still followed me in the year after her death. I tried to make things fine when I gestured to Tim across a visiting table at Whiting, speaking about when he was a wrestler. I tried to make things fine when I went to concerts with Lizzie, avoided talking about our mother, avoided talking about Tim.

But the strain of these efforts left me feeling like an imposter, like a poor facsimile of my mother, the woman who had tried to protect us with *everything is fine*.

On that night my father found me, drunk, alone in the family room, when he said, *Vince, this isn't you*, I couldn't tell him how right he was. I couldn't tell him how exhausted I'd become hiding from pain.

But pain finds its way. We try, but we can't stop the pooling, how trauma saturates.

And I had tried, lived like a white-knuckled fist, clenched until my defenses dissolved in empty bottles.

There was no epiphanic moment that led me to set booze aside. There was no revelation—even my father's *Vince this isn't you*—that dried me out.

It wasn't as simple as learning how to cry sober, as practicing by listening to my mother's saved voicemail—over and over—while straining to make myself cry. Though this was something I tried.

Eventually I found ways to discard the certainty that one drink would lead to a dozen, would lead to sobbing, would lead to a cycle of stoic days and emotive nights. I found ways to slow the drinking like I had slowed my nightmares, learned to allow sadness in sober daylight, to loosen trauma's vise without alcohol.

But none of this happened until after my brother's trial, until after I came face-to-face with the story I'd tried to avoid.

20

It's difficult to describe the people I love most in the moments when they were mired in pain.

In the winter after our mother died, Lizzie grew feral with grief. I'd started to fear the ways she spoke, the resignation I'd heard when she'd wanted to leave that concert on Halloween, *I'm done with this.* As snow smothered Boston, I began to feel powerless in the face of her pain.

It's not for me to detail the private terrors that shrank Lizzie's world. She had her own nightmares, nightmares more vivid and unrelenting than my own.

But this is what I remember about my sister during the winter after our mother died.

I remember a car ride, my sister sitting to my right on the passenger side, her seat belt stretched to the end of its tether while she bent forward to clutch her legs.

"She was the only one I could trust," Lizzie sobbed.

I didn't take a hand off the wheel. I didn't reach for her back. The roads were slick and icy.

I remember sitting above Jamaica Pond, an unseasonably warm

day before the cascading snow. We watched a family toss a ball to a bounding puppy, a handful of canoes float on the pond below.

"Mom would have loved this," Lizzie said. She hooked her fingers in the heels of her sneakers, collapsed in the grass, eyes open, red-rimmed in the sun.

I remember convulsive tears, Lizzie shaking on her bed surrounded by the nested pictures of her and our mother.

Lizzie and our mother next to a drooping sunflower in our backyard.

Lizzie and our mother holding clubs at a mini-golf course featuring a giant spouting whale.

Lizzie and our mother on either side of a bowl of ice cream, each brandishing a spoon.

There were mornings when Lizzie would call me, when she felt bedridden, frozen in place. I'd tell her to stay home from work, to rest—*go back to bed*—like grief was something she could sleep off.

When my sister was paralyzed with pain, I tried to train our focus forward, insist that we play new board games, that we cook new meals. We learned new sets of rules, new recipes, new jogging paths in the arboretum.

But this sadness was not one we could outrun.

As months passed, I grew fearful of so many things. I feared the razor in Lizzie's shower. I feared her behind the wheel of a car. I feared the bottles of pills her roommates stored in the bathroom, the handles of liquor on top of the fridge.

I know I missed our mother most when Lizzie was in pain. I know I wanted our mother to explain—*explain, explain*—to fix us, convince us that we would survive.

When I was a child, when we were alone, my mother would tell me stories from when she was a doctor. I called them *hospital stories*, the thing I wanted most when she picked me up from school.

Many of the hospital stories came from an emergency room nearly a decade before I was born. I remember one, a story about a girl convulsing on a stretcher. My mother explained this—a seizure, what it means to convulse—and told me how she slid a blanket under the girl's shaking head.

"It was her eyes that told me," my mother said. "Her pupils. They'd dilated."

We might have been anywhere, in a drive-thru line at Wendy's, in a parking lot waiting for Lizzie to finish softball practice.

"What's dilated?" I said.

"Look at my eyes." She took off her glasses. "Look here, the dark dot." She pointed with her pinky, her finger hovering just below one of her eyelids. "That's the pupil, the middle of your eye."

I leaned across the center console, aimed both of my eyes at one of hers.

My mother's eyes were hazel.

She explained dilation, the expanding pupil, the dark eclipse swallowing slivers of light.

"I knew then that she had a brain hemorrhage," my mother said, "that she was bleeding in her brain."

"What did you do next?" I said.

And she explained, as best she could, how she kept the girl alive so a surgeon could operate.

This was what I wanted to hear most, how my mother stitched or stanched or bandaged, how she healed the girl convulsing on the stretcher. I wanted to believe that there was nothing my mother couldn't fix.

We needed her then—Lizzie and I—but Lizzie most of all. I knew I wasn't the person to make sure that Lizzie would survive.

And Lizzie knew this too.

Once, when Lizzie sobbed, when she gasped, *I need Mom, I need Mom*, I got angry—yes, angry at my grieving sister.

"Well, Mom's gone," I snapped.

I said this to Lizzie when she was snarled in pain.

"Mom would never," she moaned. "Mom would never."

I'll never forget how Lizzie looked at me then, hazel eyes trembling, like my words had singed her face.

I'd strayed so far from the wish I'd made more than a decade before, the morning when I'd dug her dog's grave, the morning when I told myself that I never wanted to see her sad again.

Tim would ask me about Chris and Lizzie. When he did, I gave bulleted updates of their lives—Lizzie's teaching, Chris's job. Sometimes Tim would remember them in these moments, and I'd listen while he'd talk about Chris, about how when they were kids they'd steal my Game Boy and have secret sleepovers in each other's rooms.

When I had started visiting Tim, when my goal was *help him remember*, I had convinced myself that this aim had a straightforward purpose—that helping him to remember was a necessary part of restoring him to competency.

But we had moved past that point, past competency.

Remembering took on a different purpose, became a kind of reconstructing we could do together, became how Tim and I found our way back to each other, back to home.

More than a year after my mother died, I stumbled on an old Toni Morrison interview, something I found after rereading *Beloved*. In the interview, Morrison dissects the word *remember*, breaks the word in two—*re-member*, the opposite of *dismember*. She speaks about remembering in this way, as an active reconstruction, memories the result of a piecing together, a *re-membering* of the past.

I don't know if I've ever heard a more beautiful reflection on a single word.

I would come to think this way when Tim and I shared memories, both of us *re-membering*, our past something that needed reconstruction.

But this process was difficult. Many obstacles hindered our re-membering. And when memories involved Lizzie, speaking about her with Tim became almost too painful to bear. When we spoke about how Lizzie had scaled the tree in our front yard, remembering her as a smiling child only intensified the ways I'd seen her struggle, the way she heaved with grief because Tim's illness had made him hold the knives.

Once, Tim asked me if I remembered the last time all six of us were together on Cape Cod. I did. I had just graduated from college, and Chris, Tim, and Lizzie were about to start their senior year of high school.

"Remember that last night on the beach," Tim said.

On that night, armed with a handle of Absolut vodka and a twelve-pack of beer, the four of us snuck out to a quiet beach. This was the only time I'd ever see Tim drink.

Over the course of a couple hours, the four of us grew less steady on the soft sand. After Tim had guzzled some vodka, I remember lunging at one of his legs, pinning him to the beach, declaring a rare physical victory.

"Remember how drunk Lizzie got?" Tim said.

Chris, Tim, and I hadn't realized at first. I'd only seen her sip a beer, cradle the vodka and take a few small swigs, but my judgment was clouded. Soon, she teetered between us, then lay flat on the beach, arms spread wide, laughing and rubbing her hair into the sand.

"We had to carry her back," Tim said.

When we carried her, Chris and I had each grabbed a leg, Tim supporting her from under her arms. We made slow progress until Tim took over, held her at the waist, and boosted her over one of his shoulders.

"Yes, Tim," I said. "I remember."

I remembered how Tim had held Lizzie, how he had clutched her legs, let her body rest on his shoulder. I remembered how he'd stopped when she lost one of her sandals, then lifted her higher, waited, until Chris slid the sandal back on her foot.

There's more to that memory, more to that night Lizzie got drunk on the beach. For a long time I couldn't finish that memory because what happened next involved our mother.

When we got back to our cottage, Tim waited with Lizzie while Chris and I tried to sneak in. We eased through the door but found our mother awake, sitting on the green couch, a book folded in her lap.

"Where's Lizzie?" she said, before I could speak.

We brought Lizzie inside, all three of us supporting her. In the doorway, our mother enveloped her, held Lizzie without our help. She brought Lizzie to the bathroom, guided her down to the tile floor.

"Bring me water," my mother said.

When I handed her a glass, she looked at me, hissed, *How could you let this happen*, then turned back to Lizzie.

While I kept a penitent vigil on the couch, our mother held

Lizzie, brushed her hair from her face while she vomited. I listened while our mother soothed her, the gentle *it's all right, you're okay,* just like when Lizzie was a sick child.

I'm not sure if I can truly show you how much our mother loved Lizzie and how much Lizzie loved our mother. They spoke every day. So much passed between them.

When Lizzie was an infant, I remember our mother singing while she cradled her, her most frequent song, an adapted Sinatra classic.

The Rockies may crumble, Gibraltar may tumble, but Mommy and Lizzie's love is always here to stay.

Lizzie gave our mother elaborate gifts, sprawling Mother's Day posters featuring Polaroid pictures of the two of them—next to each other against a shoulder-high snowbank, cocooned together in a knitted afghan. Lizzie's gifts remain on our mother's desk, an atlas of their love.

They were together during our mother's last summer, Lizzie at home after her college graduation. Most nights, after dinner, they circled the walking track bordering the town fairgrounds before talking over coffee at Dunkin' Donuts—my mother's favorite coffee throughout her life.

They had planned to be together on our mother's last day, planned to go shopping for clothes for Lizzie's new job. But Lizzie had gone alone.

Lizzie lost so much that day. Our mother had been Lizzie's guide, a lens she used to see the world. When our mother died, Lizzie lost her orbit's center, became untethered, listless.

For a long time, Lizzie would fight the trauma and grief that conspired to diminish her, that conspired to end her life. And that story, of how she struggled, how she fought, how she survived, is not mine to tell.

But I can tell you that my pain sharpened, twisted through my skull, when I thought I'd failed my sister. I know that I wounded her when I told her that our mother would have wanted her to visit Tim, when I yelled at her when she was concerned about my drinking, when I snapped, *Well, Mom's gone*, while she was enveloped in grief.

I know that the seeds of this pain are in the chalk message I scratched into our driveway after my siblings were born. I know that my mission that morning became my life's mission, to welcome them home.

But there's more to that pain, more than just my belief that I'd failed my mission as big brother.

After tragedy, we offer thoughts and prayers to families. We hold that unit up, *the family*, hope that families can heal together, that grief is easily shared, a burden made lighter by many hands.

I know we projected some version of this ideal after our tragedy.

When each of us spoke at our mother's funeral: *Our family wants to thank you all for the support.*

In brief statements to newspapers: *Our family is grateful for thoughts and prayers while we grieve.*

This felt so important to me then—*the family, our family*—our unity after catastrophe, how together we could appear strong.

Our tragedy was a family tragedy. Our tragedy struck the core of our family from within, violence ravaging the unit that had shaped my life. If we crumbled in the aftermath, would that mean that all our bonds had been lies, that we had never been a family at all? If I failed to be a big brother to Tim, if I failed to be a big brother to

Lizzie, would all of my history vanish, amount to nothing more than a prelude to tragedy?

Of course not. Of course not, but it took a long time for me to recognize how families in pain don't simply coalesce, don't easily march forward, hand in hand, a bulwark against trauma.

Now, when I think about my sister's pain, about all that my big brothering seemed powerless to assuage, I can remember more than how I tried to distract her with silly costumes and walks around the pond. I can forgive myself for the moments I lashed out, for the way I tried to muzzle my sister's cries.

I know my own pain was too knotted then—too bound, too buried—to allow myself to unravel next to her, to share her roiling tears.

Now, I can remember that even when trauma worked to wrench us apart, we never turned away from each other. I can remember how Lizzie, the little sister, the one I'd convinced myself I needed to look after, never stopped looking after me.

Two weeks after our mother died, Lizzie reminded me about an upcoming milestone in my life. When we were alone together, at home on a long August afternoon, she reminded me that we had joked about this occasion earlier that summer, the arrival of my ten thousandth day.

The next week, on my ten thousandth day, Lizzie brought me a chocolate cake. The cake, a product of the same bakery that had traced Spider-Man in blue and red onto my childhood birthday cakes, had green frosted flowers and Happy 10,000th Day traced in pink icing.

When we ate the cake, we sat on the couch in the family room. We scraped our forks against the bottoms of our plates, captured all the sticky frosting. With a mouthful of cake and crumbs in her lap, Lizzie turned her body away from the dark corner next to the dogs' crates, the space in front of the bookshelf where we stacked our photo albums.

She turned to look at me, smile, frosting on the corners of her mouth, the sister I'd welcomed home twenty-three years before.

21

During that long winter, Whiting grew more familiar. I had been making the trip for long enough to notice changes in the flyers in the waiting room, holiday toy drive announcements giving way to winter parking notices for staff.

During these visits, Tim asked for more books. In February, he asked me to bring him a copy of Marcus Aurelius's *Meditations*.

"I want to get back into stoic philosophy," he said, like he was rekindling an old hobby.

I saw this request for a foundational stoic text as Tim's wish for *endurance*, a wish for aphorisms to help him *conquer*.

Confine yourself to the present.

We spoke about the present during most of that winter's visits, the present easier ground than the past we still avoided.

In late February, I told Tim that I had stumbled into an entry for the Boston Marathon. Through a connection at my school, I'd been offered a loophole, a way to run the famous race without logging a qualifying time or raising a substantial sum of money.

I told Tim that I had two months to train for a race that I had long admired as a spectator.

"How's your back?" Tim asked.

Tim and I share a similar injury, lower disk damage that can cause shooting pain down our legs.

One of the exacerbating factors is a flaw in our skeletal schematic. Three of the men in our family—Tim, our father, me—have incongruous leg lengths. Mine is the least dramatic, but even a few millimeters' difference—my left is longer—means that my hips rotate almost imperceptibly when my feet strike the ground, torquing my lower back, grinding down my lowest vertebrae, squeezing the bottom disk in my spine.

This, the squeezing, had been the source of the pain Tim was trying to combat with the inversion table in our basement. By hanging upside down, the weight of his body literally pulled his vertebrae apart, gave his lower disks room to breathe.

"I've had orthotics for a while," I told Tim, explaining my way to extend my right leg, level my footing.

"Keep working on your core strength," Tim said.

We talked about our physical aches, the ways we trained to make those pains go away.

I updated Tim on my marathon training during my next visits, described my lengthening runs, my mile splits, how I planned track workouts, hill repeats. I didn't forswear drinking while I trained, but the binging slowed out of necessity. It would have been hard to hit my weekly mileage if I spent mornings crippled with hangovers.

Though a small step—one that didn't eradicate my father's *Vince, this isn't you*—training gave me a way to start recognizing myself again, a return to a way of being that had been part of my identity long before my mother's death, long before Tim became sick. In this way, I started to reenter my body, even if my mind still trailed far behind.

I remember visiting Tim in April, the weekend after the marathon, describing the race to him.

"I started with the last group," I told him. "More than thirty-two thousand people ran the race."

"So you didn't win," Tim said.

I wanted to stay with him—in that joke, in that glimpse of him—for the rest of the visit.

Tim listened while I told him about the race, about how during the congested first mile I'd run behind a man dressed as a Roman legionnaire—aluminum breastplate, foil sword—who blazed a path until the crowds thinned. I told him about the spectators lining the course, shoulder to shoulder, extending water, peeled bananas, high fives.

"I wrote 'Vince' on my shirt," I said. "Hundreds of people cheered my name."

Tim was quiet when I started to tell him what this felt like, this swell of anonymous support. I stopped, hesitated around explaining how a new experience had felt meaningful, a small victory.

I'm not certain how I would have explained this to Tim, how hearing my name made me feel—if only briefly—like the world had tilted subtly in my favor.

It didn't feel right to show this to Tim, Tim whose days looked so different from mine, whose days involved building a bird feeder in a supervised woodshop, ordering General Tso's chicken as a reward for attending groups, reading Marcus Aurelius between books of the Bible.

Confine yourself to the present.

When Tim heard me describe the marathon, he heard a new

story, realized that of course I would have new experiences in the years after our mother's death.

I'm not sure how this—my new experience, my new story—made him feel. I don't know if he realized how thoroughly illness had co-opted his own story, imposed a narrative he never would have chosen.

Instead, I told him that I hadn't run since the race.

"Are your legs still hurting?" Tim asked.

"Yeah," I told him. "They still hurt."

That spring, I started dating a woman who was studying psychology—forensic psychology. At the time, she was interning at a forensic inpatient unit, a facility in Boston serving the same purpose as Whiting.

I met Elise online, using a dating app one of my friends recommended. I knew from exchanging messages with her that she was pursuing a graduate degree in psychology. She had told me about her internship at the forensic facility, asked me if I knew the term *forensic psychology*.

"The intersection of the criminal justice system and psychology," I had responded, hoping my answer was detached enough not to suggest personal experience with the field.

Yes, when I learned that Elise worked with people like Tim I grew more interested. The odds that I'd meet someone who might understand—clinically, legally—what Tim faced seemed impossibly small. I was excited to meet her.

We met in person for the first time in April. Without noticing, I had walked into the bar a few steps behind her. On the stairs leading to the lounge below, I recognized her from the curls in her dark hair.

I said her name and she turned, smiled, the stairs accentuating our height difference. This created a bit of an awkward first encounter, her head level with my torso as we performed one of those introductory three-quarter hugs, somewhat arching our backs. On level ground this type of hug can be challenging. On the stairs the maneuver was comical.

But that asymmetrical hug was the only part of the night that felt off. Quite quickly, sitting across from her felt different than other first dates. In the past, during those first meetings, I had felt like I was playing a character named Vince Granata. Everything I said, all of the fun facts—stories accrued from years of teaching high school— were true, but I still would feel like I was speaking from some script, like the ground I covered was a memorized performance, a sketch of this person, me.

The ease I felt with Elise made me want to avoid, to some extent, talking about her current work. It didn't feel right to have a conversation about forensic psychology while I withheld that my brother awaited trial at a forensic facility. I didn't want to start on this foot, on inequitable ground, in case later—and I wanted there to be a later—Elise would feel uncomfortable about how she had spoken about her work without knowing why I was so interested.

And I had no intention of bringing up my family's story on a first date. I was ready to parry questions about my siblings while still mentioning them—all of them, triplets—as part of my biography. I mentioned Chris and Lizzie, named the jobs they had in Boston. With Tim, I said, *He's living in Connecticut, figuring things out.*

But after our first date, I started wondering about how I could possibly tell Elise about my family. I wanted, wishfully, for this conversation to happen on my terms. I wanted the conversation to be sober, private, after we had spent a handful of times together, built a framework for trust. I started imagining how this conversation would unfold, how, perhaps, we would be sitting in my bedroom while she looked at the pictures of my family on my bookcase.

This was important to me then, some means of control, a way to explain what had happened to my family nine months before. I thought of it this way then, as something that could be *explained*.

Now, I've had this conversation, this first conversation about my family's story, so many times. I've had this conversation so often that I know what I'm doing isn't *explaining*, isn't accounting for some inconsistency, a résumé gap during an interview. What I try to do in these conversations is remember, compile the weight of my experiences into a picture that I can point to, just like I point to the pictures in my bedroom, the picture of my family standing arm and arm in our driveway.

But then, when I was thinking about how I would "explain" my family to Elise, I wanted to see if she would be surprised. I wanted her to be surprised so that I could believe that I wasn't conspicuously broken, that I could appear to be fine.

On our second date, after dinner, Elise asked me if I wanted to go with her to join some of her friends who were celebrating a birthday.

There were eight people gathered around a table when we arrived. As the new face, I drew considerable attention, fielded questions from Elise's tipsy friends. One asked me if I felt uncomfortable dating a future psychologist.

I was having fun, enjoyed this good-natured prodding, until an innocuous comment shifted the tone of the evening.

"I used to google guys before I went on dates with them," one of her friends said. "Have you googled Vince?"

I knew it would be the third hit, visible on the screen without scrolling.

I knew I couldn't say, *No, don't google me.*

I stayed quiet, tried to force a smile, while Elise hesitated, looked toward me, phone in hand.

"Can I?" she asked, softly.

I nodded, resigned, knowing then that saying no would warrant suspicion.

I looked at her eyes when she finished tapping my name with her thumb—the first hit my Facebook page, the second my athlete profile, still floating on the Yale crew website.

I could tell when she saw the third hit, listened as she started to form "What's this about . . ." before stopping, forcing a smile. "Well, I'm not sure about *this* picture."

She showed her friends the picture from my athlete profile, one where my hair covers my forehead in swoops, a cut my mother used to refer to as my "Beatles hair."

While the image distracted her friends, Elise looked toward me, not bewildered, not confused, but somehow, for a second, like she was in real pain.

I mouthed, *I'll explain,* before we turned back to the table, to the conversation, to the jokes from her friends, *Oh, you went to Yale. You must be fancy.*

I don't know if I loved Elise. In ways, I think I may have. There were times—that googling was the first—when I felt that I could trust her, without question, like she had chosen my side, aligned completely with me.

I told Tim about Elise. We spoke about her across the Whiting visiting tables.

At first, I didn't tell him that she worked in a forensic setting, that the last internship of her graduate degree was in a place similar to the one where we sat.

"We met online," I told him.

"That's how it happens now," Tim said, half question, half statement.

I explained to him how the mechanism of online dating—scrolling through pictures, brief personal treatises—made me uncomfortable, reduced people to flat avatars on my phone that I struggled to communicate with.

"Weird," Tim said. "You always seemed pretty comfortable socially."

He had mentioned this before, his perception of my social ease, when he was on the precipice of psychosis and accused me of never teaching him how to make friends.

I don't describe myself as extroverted, as socially at ease, though others—aside from Tim—have described me this way. A close friend once compared me to a chameleon, always able to match my surroundings, backyard kegger to book club. Though intended as compliment, this assessment has sometimes made me feel like an imposter, a person who can easily blend and hide.

"Have Chris and Lizzie met her?" Tim asked.

I nodded, waited for his next question.

But Tim didn't say, *Will I get to meet her?* He didn't say, *Someday, will I meet the woman you marry? Someday, will I meet your kids?*

While Tim was quiet, I raced through these questions, imagined a future when I'd bring a family, my family, to Whiting.

This is Tim, your uncle.

There would be so much to explain.

With Elise, in part due to her training, Tim was easier to explain.

She understood, clinically, the challenges he faced, understood what it meant to be restored to competency, to plead not guilty by reason of insanity.

All this made it easier, later that night after she googled me, for her to understand the story I told, the story I tried to explain.

But after I finished "explaining" Tim, she asked me to tell her about my mother.

I had no idea where to start. As I hesitated, stumbled to find my way into the myriad memories I was sure I had with my mother, Elise started to cry. I remember this, how she cried into my shoulder, lying against me on her couch, our second date.

It was with Elise that I grew aware of a new way that loss had marked me. When Elise asked me about my mother, I started to recognize how trauma had made memories of her difficult to find.

A month later, I spent part of Mother's Day with Elise, joining her at her apartment after she left brunch with her family. I had convinced myself, in the weeks before Mother's Day, that the holiday wouldn't affect me, that trivial displays—streams of photographs on Facebook—would do nothing to trigger sadness. I had decided that this day was just another day to endure.

So when I felt alone on that day, I tried to cast those feelings as exhaustion—*I'm just tired, I haven't slept*—my way of making depression a physical phenomenon I could explain away.

When I met Elise at her apartment, she had brought a box of baked goods from her morning with her mother. I remember eating handfuls of chocolate babka, my full mouth a defense.

But Elise asked about my mother again that day, and I eventually found a memory, one of my last with my mother, from the previous year's Mother's Day.

On that day, I had been with my mother. That weekend, in 2014,

I had surprised her, made a secret trip home. I don't think I'd ever surprised her on a holiday or birthday before.

My father had planned to take her out to dinner, to Adriana's, one of her favorite Italian restaurants in New Haven. I made the trip from Boston, beat them to the restaurant, parked my car a few blocks away. I remember explaining the surprise to the hostess.

"Don't tell them I'm here," I said. "Just lead them to the table."

This was not an elaborate surprise, but when my mother saw me, she gasped—*Vince? Vince?*—her voice, one she rarely raised, loud enough to interrupt diners around the restaurant.

She had not expected to see any of her children—Chris and Lizzie weeks from graduation, Tim sealed behind his bedroom door.

When I told Elise about that Mother's Day, I couldn't remember past the surprise. I couldn't remember the evening with my parents, couldn't remember what we talked about during dinner.

I can go back there now, to that dinner, allow the feeling around those memories to fill in gaps. I remember my mother listening while I told her that I was practicing my Spanish, preparing for the Dominican Republic. I miss her when I remember how she asked me about my students' final impressions of *Jane Eyre*.

I miss her when I remember how we spoke about Tim—briefly, not long that night—when she said that he had mentioned taking a course at a local college, transferring credits so he could graduate. Even then, this is what she saw in him: hope, a future.

Now, I can miss the way she loved Tim, two months before her death.

But I couldn't remember her then, when I sat with Elise on Mother's Day, couldn't miss my mother without also summoning all the violence of her loss. That weight was something I still didn't allow myself to feel—not sober, not awake.

Elise never pushed me, never pressed when I balked around my mother, only showed me, in small moments, that I could start to have the beginnings of memories, the moments with my mother that trauma worked to conceal.

The last time I saw Elise, nearly a year after that Mother's Day, after both of us had moved away from Boston, from each other, another memory would shadow us.

I visited her after nine months apart, a trip to see if we could reanimate over distance what we had left in Boston. But at the end of the visit, I feared that we would wear each other out if we tried again, our connection stretching thin over phone calls and scattered visits.

I told her, stammering at first, that I thought a later loss would hurt more, that we would end up resenting each other for trying to make distance work.

"You can just tell me, Vince," Elise said. "Just tell me you don't want to try."

I noticed it then. I noticed it because I had to break eye contact, scared of the decision I had just made. I looked away from her, toward her bookshelf, saw it displayed, propped open, the colorful cover.

Oh, the Places You'll Go!

I cried, sitting in the daylight on Elise's couch. She put her hand on mine.

"I just noticed that book, the one I was reading."

"I know," Elise said. "I remember."

"But I'm crying about *this*," I said, squeezing her hand, "not *that*."

It felt important then to explain these tears—crying about *this*, not *that*, mourning our lost relationship, not my mother's death.

"It's okay if it's about *that*," Elise said.

I don't know how much was about *this* and how much was about *that*. I don't know why I thought I could partition this sadness, draw boundaries around tears, name their sources like countries on a map.

We were quiet then, holding each other on the couch, while I realized that I mourned two things simultaneously.

Days later I would recognize a small gift in that simultaneous sadness, a way I had let my mother into that room, a way that I had started to let her back into my life.

During that first year without my mother, I would have been too afraid to look at the cover of *Oh, the Places You'll Go!*, to let myself remember where I had been when she died.

But when I cried with Elise, when I tried, at first, to separate *this* from *that*, I was allowing the type of sadness I had fought so fervently, the sober tears I had shunned while I tried to *endure*, tried to *conquer*.

I try to welcome that sadness now, when I see my mother in Lizzie's handwriting, when I hear my mother every time Tim says, *Bye for now*.

Without allowing that sadness, I let loss dismember, eliminate my mother from my memories, the place I keep her now.

22

Now, I know that my mother is never out of view. I know that I remember her every day, Rocky Road ice cream in a grocery store, the stack of books next to my bed, a Guns N' Roses song on the radio—yes, my mother loved Axl Rose.

I remember her when I see nothing but the white wall behind my desk—she's rubbing sunscreen into Chris's shoulders, writing messages in the margins of my grade school stories.

I'm grateful to have her this way now, in my students' groans when I make a pun, in Lizzie's voice on the phone, in a woman's laugh when I imagine, *What would Mom think of her?*

This is loss. This is *Mom, there are so many things I want to tell you.*

For a long time, it was not this way. With the violence of her death alive in my imagination, in my nightmares, all my memories of her felt like memorials, painful attempts to remind myself that she had been so much more than her violent end. This is what I had done when I eulogized her, canonized her—*a superhuman mother*—in an attempt to drown out the horror of her last day. But this practice—memorializing through memory—made every time

I remembered my mother feel like I was writing her obituary, each line pointing to her death.

I had to learn a new way to remember my mother, to remember Tim before the terror of his illness. To learn, I had to look at pieces of my life that seemed impossibly at odds with each other. I had to understand that these pieces could be simultaneously true.

I love my brother—and—my brother killed our mother.

This pair, this impossible simultaneous truth, is what I learned to hold.

There are many more of these pairs, pairs not specific to my family's story.

The vast majority of people with serious mental illnesses are not violent—and—some people with untreated psychotic disorders can be.

Stigma around serious mental illness is based in exaggerated fears of violence—and—stigma around serious mental illness multiplies if we don't discuss the rare cases of violence in the clearest terms possible.

To be as clear as possible, I want to dissect what I mean when I look at this question: *Is there a link between untreated serious mental illness and violence against self or others?*

All of my language here needs to be clear, every word.

To start, *untreated*. I'm referring only to diseases that are not treated, cases when psychosis is allowed to accelerate without medication. When we fail to treat diseases with medication, illnesses metastasize, have disastrous consequences. Tim had been without medication for four months when he killed our mother.

I'm also not speaking about all mental illness, but about diseases in a specific category, *serious mental illness*. One of our greatest mistakes is painting all mental illness with one broad brush. One in four

Americans have a diagnosable mental illness. One in four Americans experience real pain from these illnesses, pain I don't intend to minimize with this distinction. But the daily challenges that many of these millions face do not constitute *serious mental illness*. These mental illnesses don't contort reality through the prism of psychosis.

And it's that word—*psychosis*—that is essential here. Psychosis is the world-mangling symptom, the deadly insurrectionist.

Psychosis transformed Tim, led him to sprinkle our parents with salt, flee a floating coin in the basement, splash family members with a cup of water. Psychosis built in Tim, twisted his perception of our mother, made her someone who'd neglected him, someone who'd abused him, someone who'd raped him.

This is psychosis, the sinister symptom of untreated serious mental illness.

Though Tim's specific psychosis led to violence, psychosis unwinds in myriad directions, can—much more commonly—lead to homelessness, substance abuse, petty crime.

When violence occurs, it is most commonly *violence against self*. Substantially more people with schizophrenia will die by suicide than will ever harm another person. For years, this was our fear for Tim.

And yes, sometimes there is *violence against others*. This is the rare violence, the violence extended outward, the violence Tim's psychosis brought to our mother.

Mental illness—far too often—gets wedged between a murderer and his heinous crime. Far too often, the media, or politicians, or lawyers, pair mental illness with clear-eyed murderers—most often white men, men who murder with guns, men whose worlds were their own hateful construction.

During the 2017 trial of the man who massacred nine people in a Charleston, South Carolina, church, attorneys argued that mental disorders rendered the murderer only partially responsible for his terror. They posited half-hearted diagnoses—social anxiety disorder, mixed substance abuse disorder. Even if these diagnoses are to be believed, they do not spawn psychosis. Rather, they describe broader disorders that surround social anxiety, isolative behaviors, failure to blunt rage.

These disorders did not incite murder. Hate did.

So yes, we need to be extremely careful when discussing the link between untreated serious mental illness and violence.

I know too that Tim participated in a sport that condoned violence, that wrestling is about physically dominating an opponent, battering another person until they submit. I know that Tim learned that his body could be a weapon long before psychosis arrived.

I can understand how this conditioning, this history of combat, might suggest that Tim was programmed for violence, that violence was the only way he knew to exorcise his rage.

And I can't say that this type of sport—a sport that sanctions violence—doesn't contribute to producing some violent men.

But until psychosis arrived, my brother had never attacked another person outside of a ring. He'd never put his fist through a wall or smashed a bottle on a counter. So yes, while his body had battered other bodies, to suggest that this background alone bred violence would be as negligent as claiming a house fire raged because of its wooden beams and not the match and gasoline that started the blaze.

I know that this story—my brother's story, my family's story—is only a single piece of evidence. I understand the danger of extrapolating from our story alone.

And though our story is rare, it is far from an isolated incident.

In 2013, a mother died at the hands of her son or daughter approximately three hundred times. I've scoured the sources that count these killings, FBI Supplementary Homicide Reports and other nationwide data on murder. Most suggest that this estimate, three hundred, is low.

I've read studies that have tracked these killings, that have analyzed the cause of these parricides, as the murder of one's parent is termed. I've found media surveys that identify when untreated serious mental illness accompanies these killings in news reports, examined work by parricide experts from California, New York, Canada, England. In their findings—reports with titles like *Raising Cain*—many conclude that people in the grip of psychotic illness are responsible for at least two-thirds of parricides.

In 2013, two-thirds of the three hundred mothers who died at her son's or daughter's hands died because two hundred of these children had illnesses that had spiraled out of control. In 2013, there were two hundred other stories, two hundred other Tims, two hundred other tragedies like our own.

These are ugly stories. All of these stories have their brutal details—their bloodstained white Bibles, their bodies sprinkled with coins, their sledgehammers. After filling newspaper headlines, these stories are largely abandoned, left to congeal in the dark.

We are conditioned to fear these two hundred Tims. We are conditioned to fear the horror of their taboo killings, the real stories behind our pop culture reference points—insane asylum haunted houses, Hitchcock's iconic *Psycho*.

We left these two hundred Tims *untreated*. By ignoring their stories, by ignoring their *untreated serious mental illnesses*, we let ourselves off the hook. If we ignore these worst-case scenarios, the rare unwinding of unmitigated psychosis into violence—violence almost always unleashed on loved ones—we are accessories to the disease's murders.

It's easier to set the Tims aside. It's easier to let monsters disappear—in prisons, in forensic facilities—than to contend with the source of their monstrosity.

We can ignore the Tims, the rare worst cases—and—live in a world that cloaks mental illness in fear.

But we only conquer terror when we drag what scares us into the light. We only understand horror when we think about what we know, when we look at all the pieces.

Here's what I know. Here's what I know from growing up beside my brother.

I watched him fall through ice in the stream behind our house, heard his gasp when he felt cold water rush into his boots. I dipped French fries into Wendy's Frosties next to him in our mother's back seat, our hands a sticky chocolate mess. I learned his favorite games when we hid in the long cupboards in the basement, leapt and flopped over stacked pillows on the guest bed, ran barefoot on Cape Cod beaches, flinging rose hips at each other's legs.

I listened to him when he played a flute that looked impossibly small in his massive hands, the same hands he used to paint tiny models of alien elves, the same hands he used to distribute Krispy Kreme donuts after school assemblies.

I know what he was afraid of, the dark trip out of the basement after flipping the switch at the bottom of the stairs, paddling our canoe into the deep waters of Lewis Bay, letting his older teammates down when he was a sophomore on the football team. He was scared of math tests that required a graphing calculator, of asking a girl to prom, of a college essay on David Hume.

And then he had new fears, shadows that chased him from his college campus to a forest outside of town. There, he stripped naked and hid among the trees, safe, convinced that the demons couldn't see him.

But his fears multiplied, spawned delusions that bent toward our mother, that pushed him to flush his pills down the toilet, seal himself behind his bedroom door, believe that he could use the Google search bar as a medium to reach his demons.

Tim never wanted to live with these demons, the consequences of leaving him *untreated*, of ignoring the spiraling paths of the two hundred Tims the year before.

Tim never wanted to bind our mother, to hold the serrated kitchen knives, to leave her on the floor next to where she used to read him The Chronicles of Narnia.

Tim never wanted to kill our mother—and—Tim's untreated disease convinced him, slowly, over accelerating bouts of psychosis, that killing our mother was an act of self-defense.

Tim's story is about serious untreated mental illness leading to violence—and—Tim's story is about a young man who struggled with the worst strain of a terrible disease.

When Tim was psychotic, his disease spawned terror—and—now, at Whiting, Tim is terrified that the world sees him as a monster.

I know Tim thinks about this, how other people see him. Once, after I hugged him at Whiting, he told me that he felt disgusting.

"All my clothes smell kind of mildewed," he said.

He wasn't wrong. When I hugged him during our visits, I could smell a subtle dampness, a light mold I attributed to sweat. He would often be walking laps in the courtyard before our visits, as was his habit after dinner.

I offered to send him some new sweats, in the black and gray colors he seemed to favor. In response, he made what was, at first, an odd request.

"How about baby blue?" he said. "Or maybe pink."

"You sure?"

"Yeah," Tim said. "Pink for breast cancer awareness."

The sweatshirts were easy to order. I called Tim while I scrolled through color options.

"We've got hot pink, wine, rose, peach, fuchsia," I said.

"Something paler," Tim said. "Something more pastel."

Tim chose rose.

I ran into trouble with the sweatpants, XXXL pink impossible to find without a drawstring. These cords were prohibited, possible weapons to wrap around another man's neck. Eventually, through a specialty website—Bob Barker, America's Leading Detention Supplier—I found XXXL sweatpants, no pockets, no drawstrings. But Bob Barker carried only three colors—gray, orange, navy. When I told Tim this, he sounded disappointed.

"Let's go with the gray," he said.

When I saw him next, he was wearing his new clothes, gray sweatpants, pale pink sweatshirt. When I walked into the visiting room, a female corrections officer said, "Real men wear pink."

Tim laughed before we hugged. The sweatshirt was the largest pink garment I had ever seen.

"I love it," I told him. "It's really a lot of pink."

Tim wasn't finished with his clothing requests. During the next week he asked me to send him something yellow, another pale shade. I found him a XXXL sweatshirt in "Daisy."

To complete his look, he told me—smiling—that he wanted a hat.

"Is that allowed?" I asked.

"This kind will be."

He described something he called a "cat hat." I told him that I was confused.

"You know, one with the little ears," he said, "like kids wear."

I could picture the hat, similar to winter hats that Lizzie used to wear, plush white and black with a panda's eyes, ears, and mouth resting above her forehead.

"It might be tough to find your size," I told him.

To find the "cat hat" I scrolled through pages of child-size novelty hats. Eventually, I stumbled onto a host of sites selling garments adults use for furry cosplay. Leaving those vendors aside, I discovered that some kids' departments sold matching hats in "parent sizes." I bought Tim a "Parent Knitted Cat Ear Beanie." The hat had circular cat eyes, a tiny sliver of a nose, and the ears that Tim had wanted. The insides of the ears were pink.

Tim called me when it arrived. "I love the cat hat," he said. "I can't wait for you to see it."

Tim never told me why he wanted to dress this way. He had broached the subject by telling me that his old clothes smelled. He had explained pink only with a passing reference, *to raise breast cancer awareness.*

But I was starting to understand his requests. As Tim grew more aware of where he was, of what he had done, he grew terrified of how people saw him. Even in his facility, he knew that his specific crime—matricide—cast him as inhuman, as a monster.

I wonder too if these new clothes were also a way to change how he saw himself. Though he was still avoidant in conversation, though we still danced around the day he killed our mother, his awareness that she'd died at his hands was growing as we inched toward his trial. As we approached the first anniversary of our mother's death, we knew Tim would be tried in the fall, though the official date had yet to be set.

On my next visit to Whiting, Tim was wearing his cat hat. It fit snugly over his black hair, its pink ears standing up like a cowlick. The goofy white eyes drew attention away from his dark eyebrows. He wore the hat with his pink sweatshirt.

When I entered the visiting room, he stood, smiled, bit his lower lip to stop himself from laughing.

When I hugged him, the felt on his cat hat brushed the side of my cheek.

When I hugged him, his hands—yes, the same hands that had held the knives—spread wide on my back, gathered me to his sweat-shirt.

23

I never doubted the outcome of Tim's trial.

Only one result seemed possible, that Tim would be declared not guilty by reason of mental disease or defect.

Defect. That's the word three judges would use in their verdict. *Defect,* like there was a flaw in Tim's design, an error buried in the schematic for his brain.

Tim was not tried by jury. In Connecticut, defendants who plead not guilty by reason of insanity are permitted to choose trial by a three-judge panel. Attorneys suggest choosing the panel, as experienced judges are more familiar with the nuances of mental illness than most juries.

During the trial, Tim's attorney would not challenge whether or not the crime occurred. Yet the prosecution still needed to prove beyond a reasonable doubt that Tim had killed our mother. To this end, the state would present a litany of evidence illustrating when, where, and how my brother had ended our mother's life.

After the prosecution rested, Tim's attorney would prove, *by a preponderance of the evidence,* that Tim suffered from a severe psychiatric disorder and was not able to comprehend the wrongfulness of his conduct. This burden—*by a preponderance of the evidence*—is substantially less stringent than *beyond a reasonable doubt*. Tim only needed a majority of the evidence for his psychosis to be indicted, for him to be ruled not guilty.

And I was confident that this is what the judges would rule—*not guilty*.

Aside from my own certainty—the unimpeachable fact that Tim had been in the grip of psychosis when he attacked our mother—there was the fact that the prosecutor had not ordered an independent evaluation of Tim. The only report assessing my brother's sanity was the one that Tim's attorney had arranged. After choosing not to seek a second evaluation, the state tacitly acknowledged that they would not challenge that a disease had overthrown Tim's brain.

So I didn't fear the judges' verdict, wasn't worried about my brother's legal guilt.

But I was terrified in the weeks before the trial.

At Tim's trial, I knew I would face my mother's broken body.

I knew that when the prosecutor presented evidence, I would see pictures of her body, the body I had imagined on our family room floor.

I had, for more than a year, held *blunt trauma, sharp trauma, head, neck, torso, extremities*. My mind filled in the details, created pictures to stand in for an actual image.

At the trial, I knew I would have a choice. When the prosecutor introduced the crime scene photography, directed attention to the courtroom screens, I could look away. I could leave.

But I knew, almost immediately—so suddenly that it scared me— that I would look. Somehow, I decided that having one image—the *real* image, a picture of what actually happened—would be easier to hold than what I had imagined.

Ultimately—though this took time—I was right. Yes, I couldn't have fully anticipated the shock and horror of seeing those images—*those images, my mother's body, Mom's body*—but I knew what it felt like to live in my imagination, to feel terror in my nightmares.

So, for the first time, I chose the pain of keeping my eyes open. For the first time, I let myself begin to hold the pieces, all the shattered pieces, even my mother's body—her real body—broken on our family room floor.

Tim's trial began on a Tuesday, the first week of November, sixteen months after our mother's death.

My father and I arrived an hour early. We waited in line at the courthouse doors, passed through the metal detector, found Tim's name on the docket. Chris and Lizzie would join us the next day. That first day was for the prosecution, for the state to prove that Tim had killed our mother, a detailed process that would be needlessly painful for Lizzie, who had already seen so much.

The opening choreography was familiar. Tim entered from the left, accompanied by Marshal Art and the other, broader marshal. Tim waved. We waved.

My father said, "Hi, Tim."

Then Tim turned. I wouldn't see his face again until the end of the day. He sat directly in front of me, facing forward like when he had sat in the bow of our childhood canoe.

The judges entered—three of them, a panel, a line of dark robes hovering over the court. We stood until they sat.

I don't remember either attorney's opening statement. I don't remember if the prosecutor outlined the crime, or if Tim's lawyer named the culprit, the disease. This memory gap might exist because

I was focused on what I knew would start the state's case. The first witness the prosecutor called was my father.

When he heard his name, my father rested his cane against our bench, walked alone to the witness stand. After having my father swear his oath—*the whole truth and nothing but the truth so help you God*—and state his name, Attilio Granata, the prosecutor asked him to identify his son.

"He's wearing a jumpsuit." My father pointed. "A prison uniform."

I sat behind where he pointed, toes clenched in my dress shoes, waiting for my father to describe how his youngest son had killed his wife.

My father's strength used to be difficult for me to understand.

As a child, I was never in awe of him physically. Though his three sons would become college athletes, he was not a physically impressive man. My father couldn't throw a football over the roof of our house, beat me in a forty-yard dash, split logs for our suburban fireplace. He was not the superhero some boys make of their fathers, not one who performed feats of physical strength.

But I can't remember a promise that he ever failed to keep.

For hours, he would sit with me in the family room, build elaborate Lego structures, cut balsa wood with an X-Acto knife, construct a model of the great pyramids we painted in glimmering gold. After every childhood basketball game, he took me to the diner, watched me eat pancakes topped with mounds of powdered sugar, showed me how to make a saltshaker balance on one of its edges, held magically by a few coarse grains. When I was a shy new student at high school—slow to make friends, alone on many Friday nights—we would watch reruns of *Iron Chef*, assemble our own modest culinary masterpieces—sandwiches layered with cold cuts and cheese.

My father didn't teach me how to bait a fishing hook, how to throw a strike, how to fix a leaking pipe. He didn't take me up mountains or show me how to carve my way down a ski slope.

No, his strength was not the kind that inspired me, that moved me through heroic awe. His strength was a kind I learned to take for granted, the quiet strength of everyday consistency, of never having to wait for a ride, of never missing a fan in the stands, of never wondering, *Will Dad show up?*

He showed up at Tim's trial for us, for his children.

But most of all, he stood, answered the prosecutor's questions, for his youngest son, for Tim.

My father gave detailed answers, described how Tim had receded into his illness, remembered Tim's early depression after his freshman year of college, remembered his plans to drive his car into the wall of the West Rock Tunnel, remembered the names of the therapists who treated him.

While he discussed this gradual descent—Tim's semesters away from school, the mandatory campus counseling—he spoke about Tim not as the man wearing the prison jumpsuit, but as his son.

"He tried very valiantly to finish his classes," my father said. "He was two credits shy of graduating on the dean's list."

I don't know how this must have sounded to others in the courtroom, my father praising his son.

There weren't many opportunities to humanize my brother on the first day of the trial. Most of the following testimony would come from police officers, from forensic specialists, from the coroner who studied the wounds on my mother's body.

But my father spoke about what the disease had enveloped, the boy he used to drive to wrestling meets around New England.

When they drove together—just the two of them—my father

would play "Oh Holy Night" from one of his Christmas CDs. The two of them listened to this song regardless of the time of year. That song was Tim's favorite, an unconventional means of inspiration, not the stereotypical choice for a teenager preparing to wrestle.

The version of the song they listened to features a cascading crescendo, a chorus that inspired Tim before his matches.

Fall on your knees
O hear the angels' voices
O night divine
O night when Christ was born

I think about this now, this Christmas hymn they shared, when I remember how my father testified about some of Tim's behaviors, the religious preoccupations his illness fostered. My father described how Tim had burned a box of "cursed" items he had taken from his college apartment. My father stood next to him while the box burned on the driveway.

"While it burned, we read some Psalms," my father explained. "Tim believed he was exorcising demons."

Eventually, the prosecutor's questions turned to the day my mother died. My father remembered the last words he spoke with her.

"Earlier that morning, Claudia called me. She was worried. I told her that I could come home." My father paused. "Claudia said to wait. She said there was no need."

I listened to him as he recited the last text message my mother sent him. He remembered every word.

"Tim said things are going to be fine. No mention of what he said before. He ate fruit."

The prosecutor asked my father if he had spoken to anyone else that morning.

"Yes," my father said.

He explained how he had been in touch with Dr. Robertson, the two speaking shortly after my father received my mother's last message.

"Dr. Robertson told me that Tim's words might be a prelude to suicide, and that we shouldn't leave him alone," my father said. "He told us to try to make Tim feel safe."

My father's testimony began the story, started the narrative of my mother's death. I don't know if there was strategy behind this decision, to call him before the police officers, forensic experts, coroner, but I'm grateful that my father got to have the first word. I'm grateful that before Tim became the man who held the knives, he was a boy my father drove to wrestling meets in his minivan, an impossibly ill young man who fought valiantly to finish his classes.

For much of that first day, testimony rendered my mother's death in lists—one roll of duct tape, two sledgehammers, two serrated kitchen knives, sixteen separate fractures and wounds.

I braced myself for the images. I knew they would arrive once the prosecutor called the forensic specialists, the ones who had photographed the crime scene, photographed my mother's body.

In the years before she died, my mother, whenever we were together, kept her camera close by. As we grew older, there were fewer opportunities for pictures, the six of us rarely in the same place. But when we were together, our mother tried to get pictures, not only of the six of us, but of each of us with her.

"Before I get too old," she said, "I want to be in pictures with you."

I have pictures of my mother and me. Some of them are recent, taken close to her death. My favorite is slightly older—from our last trip to Cape Cod. In that picture, her auburn hair is level with my shoulder. Our smiles push our cheeks, faint dimples appearing in identical spots off the corners of our mouths. We stand facing the sun. You can see Lizzie's shadow cast against my shirt, the silhouette of her bent arm aiming the camera.

We had been in the courtroom for nearly two hours before we saw pictures of my mother's body. I remember that the prosecutor paused before showing the images. I remember that he lingered after naming which "exhibits" he wanted the court clerk to project on the screen. He waited, I think, because he wanted to give my father and me a chance to remove ourselves, to leave the bench where we sat behind Tim.

We didn't move. Tim would have heard us if we got up behind him. He would have heard our father's cane click down the aisle as we fled the scene. I'm not sure what Tim would have felt if he heard us leave him to face those pictures alone.

Before the first image, I felt my father's palm cover my right hand. I felt his fingers curl into mine, resting flat on the bench between us.

I leaned forward in that moment, in the seconds between when my father's hand covered mine and the first image appeared. I felt my shoulders tense, clench toward my ears.

Here's what I remember.

I can't tell what I'm looking at. I'm looking at the screen. I know it shows our family room floor. I know my mother is in the center of the image. I know *what* I'm looking at—the floorboards, my mother's body—but I can't put it together. Sections of the photo are too dark—too dark, too dark, *too bloody*. These are pools of blood—pools, on both sides of her body, in the space above her head. I can't see her neck. I can't see what should separate her head from her body. I can't tell if she's lying on her stomach or her back. I can't see her face. But I see her hands, see how they're bound at the wrists, pinned to her lower back—this is her back, her hands are behind her back. She's lying on her stomach. I can't see her face. She's lying on her stomach. There's too much blood.

The next image is closer—her neck, the back of her neck. I can see her hair. I can tell the difference between the color of her hair and the dark color pooling around her. I see three colors—her hair, her blood, the floor. I can't see her skin. The darkest part is the back of her neck—the center of the frame, the focus—a dark line across the back of her neck. The dark line that Tim made. Tim's hands made this dark line. I'm looking at Tim now, away from the photo, and see his head tilted, his tilted head in his hands, the hands that made the dark line.

The third photo. The last I remember. The last time I looked.

Her face. It's her face. Her eyes are closed. Of course they're closed. I see the space around her eyes, the space around Mom's eyes—this is her, this is her. I see her brown eyebrows—yes, the same color, untouched, unstained. I try to keep my eyes there—the space above her eyes—not below, not below, but my aim is bad. I see her skin. I see her cheeks. But they aren't cheeks. They don't look like cheeks. They're blue, ink stained, bruised, bone bulging, stretching the skin, my mother's skin, Mom's skin. But the bulging, like her skin is elastic, her cheeks bloated, too large for her face, too large for her eyes, for her eyebrows, for the bit of hair stuck to her forehead. Her cheeks, it's her cheeks, her face somehow malleable—something, blows to the head? the sledgehammer? I'm looking at the whole frame now. I'm trying to see my mother's face. I can't stop looking at her cheeks, her cheeks, Mom's cheeks.

Later, I'll know the name of the fractured bone beneath her chin, the hyoid bone, a horseshoe buttressing the face. Later, I'll know the zygomatic bones, the bones holding up my mother's cheeks, the bones the sledgehammer shattered.

But not then. I don't know the bones then. Then, I'm looking at my mother's face and I can't recognize her cheeks.

I feel my father's hand squeeze. I look toward my lap.

I can't remember a time when I saw my mother in physical pain. I don't think I ever saw her bleed. I can't remember a time when she stubbed her toe, nicked her finger in the kitchen, slipped on ice on the driveway.

I've seen her cry. I can remember when she cried, and when I remember her crying, she's never wearing her glasses.

When I saw her in that last image, she wasn't wearing glasses. Of course she wasn't wearing glasses. They must have been knocked from her face. They might have shattered on the floor beneath her.

Her vision was terrible. She was legally blind. Without her glasses, her world blurred into amorphous shapes. Did Tim no longer look like Tim? Did she look at him and still see her son?

Sometimes we talk about images that are *seared into memory*, like the material is burned into the folds of our brains.

Yes, that image of my mother—the last image, her face, her cheeks—is seared into my memory. I can see the image on demand, without closing my eyes. I can look at a wall in my bedroom, the gray felt in a cubicle, the back of an empty seat on the bus, and project her there—not her, not her—but her broken face, those cheeks. The image is not one I can *unsee,* of course I can't, but when I summon that photo—like now, like right now—I don't dissolve. I don't crawl under my desk and shake.

I needed the certainty of those images. I needed to see exactly how my brother's illness marked my mother's body. In a way, this certainty saved me some pain, allowed me to learn to live with the reality of my mother's broken cheeks.

My pain on that courtroom bench—the pain in translating images from *evidence* to *Mom*—was my first honest step, my first literal accounting.

This is what happened. This is what happened.

After seeing those images—only once, never again—I could live in the reality of the horror. I could start to look elsewhere, at the other pieces of my family's story.

I could start to regain control.

The prosecution didn't rest after the images, after all the proof that our mother had died at Tim's hands. There was more story to build, what Tim had done after he left her body, how he was apprehended.

I knew that Tim had called 911, told the dispatcher, *You can do whatever you want to me. I am scared they are going to kill me now.* Snippets from this call had appeared in newspaper articles. The prosecutor played the full recording at the trial.

I knew that Tim had left the front steps after Lizzie and our father entered our house. I knew he started walking—still on the phone with the dispatcher—and made it as far as Blue Ridge Terrace, four houses down the road, the mouth of the second cul-de-sac. There, I knew police apprehended him. I knew he carried his cell phone, his white Bible.

I didn't know exactly what happened next. I knew a squad car took him to the Orange police station. What Tim experienced, what he felt in the hours after he left our mother's body, remained a mystery, a mystery I had approached from oblique angles with my questions at Whiting—*Do you miss Mom?*

I knew, to some extent, that testimony from the apprehending police officers would fill some of these gaps. And I listened, as a police officer described taking cover behind the open door of his cruiser, training his gun on Tim, ordering him to his knees, then recognizing that Tim was unarmed, prostrate at the bottom of the hill.

My father and I didn't know that one of the officers who arrested Tim wore a recording device. We didn't know that Tim was also captured on video in the back seat of the squad car. The state had spliced these recordings together. They presented a video, a film tracking my brother in the hours after he killed our mother.

When the prosecutor introduced this piece of evidence, described what the recording would show—*footage of after Mr. Granata was apprehended*—my father and I turned toward each other, both mouthed, *Did you know?*

There was no time to prepare. I was about to see Tim, see where he'd been while I was sitting at a classroom table in the Dominican Republic. I would see, for the first time—in real time, in moving images—how his illness separated him from reality.

The audio starts before Tim is visible. The police have cuffed him, pinning his hands behind his back, binding him the same way he bound our mother.

"It's hurting my shoulders," Tim says.

Tim enters the screen when police duck his head into the back seat. Strands of hair reach his eyebrows. Enough light passes through the tinted windows to show our mother's blood on his shirt.

"I killed her," Tim says. "I stabbed her."

He's matter-of-fact. He's direct. He's subject, verb, object.

"She told me today that she had fun raping me," Tim says.

The police car doesn't move right away. It sits at the intersection of Wild Rose Drive and Blue Ridge Terrace. There's some chatter from outside the car. It seems like the entire police department is racing toward our cul-de-sac.

Tim asks for some Neosporin.

"I have a little cut," he says.

Tim asks to have his cuffs adjusted. He wants his hands cuffed in front of him. His shoulders tilt forward, torqued away from his body against the back seat of the car.

"How old are you?" the police officer, Officer Petrucelli, asks.

Tim tells Officer Petrucelli that he looks older than he actually is. "I think it's the stress from the torture," Tim says. "I thought about plastic surgery to make me look younger."

In this moment, Tim seems genuinely worried about his appearance. He's covered in our mother's blood and he's worried that he looks old.

"I'm not creepy," Tim tells Officer Petrucelli. "I'm not creepy."

The car starts to move away from the intersection. Through the tinted window, midafternoon light bends through the trees, casting thin shadows on Tim's stained shirt. Sometimes, the light fills his face. He looks forward, doesn't gaze out the window at our familiar neighborhood.

In the courtroom, I watched Tim watch himself, this past Tim, Tim more than a year ago. Tim had to angle his head to see himself on the monitor. At times, I saw Tim support his left cheek in his hand, elbow on the table in front of him, holding his head as he watched himself in the back seat of the police car.

Officer Petrucelli asks him why people think he's creepy.

"I think . . ." Tim pauses. "I think I was supposed to develop normally. I think that I was supposed to be fine."

He's looking straight ahead, almost as if he's addressing the camera, addressing the court, addressing himself.

I wondered, watching him, if Tim knew he was in the back of a police car. Yes, I know he could feel the metal cuffs around his wrists, how they wrenched his shoulders, how they pinched his hairy skin, but did he know—could he know—that he would not be free for years, for decades.

But Tim hadn't been free for a long time. Tim had been a prisoner of his disease long before Officer Petrucelli ducked his head into that squad car.

"Wounds became invisible," Tim says. "The way I come across, it's hard to make friends."

Officer Petrucelli tells Tim that he doesn't think that he's creepy. He's turned onto Orange Center Road. His siren isn't on, and I can't tell if the lights flash on top of the car. I can't tell if the oscillating light is from the sun or red and blue flashes.

"I just want a hug from you," Tim says. "I just want a hug from people." His speech starts to feel more pressured, more urgent—*I just want, I just want*—but he's not raising his voice.

"I want to be with Jesus," Tim says.

His voice is softer now. His shoulders sink against the seat. There's a quiet moment. His eyes tilt down toward his shirt.

As a child, Tim had bunched his shirt collars in his mouth, clenched his teeth, chewed, a nervous habit. In laundry piles, our mother could always tell which shirts were his.

Tim's head is down for a moment. His chin doesn't touch his shirt. His collar doesn't enter his mouth.

I think he sees the blood. I think when he tucks his head he sees the blood covering his shirt. He sees our mother's blood as shadows move across him in the back seat of the police car.

He breathes. He breathes and looks back at the camera.

"I hope she isn't dead," Tim says. "I really hope she isn't dead."

Tim is motionless on the screen.

Tim was motionless in the courtroom, body still in front of me. I watched the two Tims, Tim in the police car—*I really hope she isn't dead*—Tim sitting in front of me, staring at himself on the screen.

I don't know if Tim remembered what was about to happen in the recording. I don't know if he remembered what happened after he said, *I really hope she isn't dead.*

But I think he did. I think he remembered, because I saw his shoulders start to shake, his torso tremble in the courtroom. He cried. He must have remembered sitting in the squad car, noticing her blood on his shirt.

Tim's head jolts back. His thick neck fills the screen. He wails in the back seat, chokes on tears, wheezes words.

"If you want to kill me, I have nothing left."

He's sobbing now, harder than when I hit him with a plastic brick in second grade, harder than when a sharp reed impaled his palm one Cape Cod summer, harder than on the phone, three years earlier, when he felt alone, like an imposter on his college campus.

Between sobs he tries to form words. "Destroy me," he pleads, writhing against the seat in the police car.

Destroy me. Destroy me. Destroy me.

For a moment, it's like he's stepped out from behind the dark curtain of his illness, like he can see the disease that seized control. In this horror, I imagine he sees where he left our mother. I imagine he sees her body, the broken body I had just seen, the body he broke, the body he knows he broke.

"Destroy me," he sobs, like he's something broken beyond repair.

Destroy me. Destroy me.

I cried then, watching Tim watch himself.

Destroy me.

In that moment, I felt that too, that same wish, to be destroyed, to vanish with Tim.

I could see Tim's back heave under his prison jumpsuit.

I could see Tim choke and sob on the screen.

I could feel my pulse in my palms, hands flat on the courtroom bench.

I couldn't see Tim's face. Only his face on the screen, only his mouth move *Destroy me. Destroy me.*

I wanted Tim to turn around. I wanted him to turn and look at me, to look away from himself sobbing on the screen, to look away from where he sat in the back seat of the police car, soaked in our mother's blood.

I wanted Tim to look at me so we didn't have to see him on the screen. I wanted Tim to look at me—only at me—so we could look at each other and try to disappear.

24

After the first day of Tim's trial, after the images, after the film of Tim in the police car, the judges listened to testimony that indicted his disease. The two doctors who evaluated Tim explained their reports, the details of his delusions—how his disease amplified the smell of our mother's perfume, how Tim tried to communicate with his demons through the Google search bar. In measured summary, the experts exposed Tim's psychosis.

The state's attorney offered little challenge in cross-examination. He asked the questions he needed to, briefly assessed whether there had been any malingering—if it was possible that Tim had faked it.

I know that the district attorney took no pleasure in prosecuting my brother, in building the story around my mother's death. For him, my brother's trial was not a righteous crusade to punish the guilty.

There were moments during the trial when I could detect this— the prosecutor's hesitance, how he was careful not to intensify my family's pain. When he questioned my father, asked him, *Can you describe your son in the years before the incident?* I heard his voice catch almost imperceptibly on *your son.*

I knew from listening to him talk with one of the bailiffs that he had a son too, a son who played hockey. I listened once while he described all the early mornings, all the rides to the rink he gave his son.

I don't know what this man, the prosecutor, felt while he questioned my father. But he never asked him to clarify an answer, to linger any longer than necessary on a detail about where he found my mother's body.

The prosecutor was merciful again on the second day. After Tim's attorney questioned Chris, the prosecutor only shook his head when the judge asked if he intended to cross-examine. He spared Chris from having to answer more questions about how he had lost his best friend.

Later, Chris would tell me that when he testified that day, he'd felt like he was answering for Tim.

"But I've been his witness before," Chris said. "I've been his witness my entire life."

After the trial, the judges deliberated for less than an hour.

Not guilty by reason of mental disease or defect.

With the acquittal, the judges committed Tim to the jurisdiction of the Connecticut Psychiatric Security Review Board. This board would determine the length of his incarcerated treatment, a period that would likely span decades, but could not exceed sixty years.

Legally, our mother's death was not Tim's fault.

I didn't hear Tim's voice until three weeks after the trial. I retreated, turned inward with all I had seen.

I came back to Tim before Thanksgiving. During my drive to

Whiting, I knew that I wanted to tell him that I had seen him cry. I wanted to tell him that while we watched that recording, I had cried too. And this—our crying, ten feet apart—had been the closest we had come to grieving together, to being terrified together, to following the same story.

There were two women in the waiting room when I arrived. I sat across from them, listened to them talk about their drives to Whiting.

"My daughter taught me to use my phone for directions," one woman said.

"I'm scared I'd never figure it out," the other said.

"Who are you visiting?"

"My grandson."

She looked too young to have a grandson, let alone an adult grandson, someone who could be at Whiting. She didn't look much older than my mother had been.

"You look young for a grandma," the first woman said, as if reading my mind.

"His teacher thought I was his mother," she said, "when I used to pick him up from school."

When I used to. This phrase echoed in waiting room conversations, something I heard when parents told me about their children.

I used to help my son make wooden bows and arrows in our garage. He'd help me shape the bows and we'd sand them down together. He would practice his archery in the backyard. He used to be a fantastic shot.

I used to watch him perform in high school. He had such a great voice. He got the male lead in Thoroughly Modern Millie. *He was so talented.*

He had, he had. He was, he was, like we were grieving the people we were about to visit.

Eventually, the other woman in the waiting room also identified herself as a grandma. I took this as my way into the conversation.

"For what it's worth," I said, "I didn't think either of you were old enough to be grandmothers."

They laughed. I was glad for this laughter, laughter like we were in a different kind of waiting room, a dentist's office, the DMV. I had been coming to Whiting for more than a year, no longer needed to show my driver's license to some of the corrections officers, so I took this—making newcomers comfortable—as a sort of job, something I would have wanted during my first visits when I often sat alone.

"Who are you here to see?" one of the grandmothers asked.

"My brother."

"Where are you from?"

"Boston," I lied. I didn't name our hometown, Orange, because Tim had been back in the news. Then, I still wanted some anonymity. I wasn't yet ready to speak.

"You're a good brother," one of the grandmothers said.

I said nothing.

"I'm sure he appreciates that you see him," she said, "in his way."

"Yes," I said. "I think Tim does."

But how could I have been sure? How could I have known that *in his way* Tim appreciated my visits? He hugged me, said he loved me, said he looked forward to seeing me next, but I was also a reminder—I had to be a reminder—of the life his disease had ravaged, of our mother.

And I had been complicit in his pain. All I had wanted was for him to remember. Tim had to remember, first, as a part of the process—his *restoration*, his ability to stand trial.

But he had moved past that stage, had been restored, had been tried, had been declared *not guilty*. He had cleared these hurdles without ever discussing that day with me, without addressing how he'd held the duct tape, held the sledgehammers, held the knives.

He had circled the perimeter, spoken around that day.

Was I in the news?

Do you think the house is haunted?

What did the neighbors say?

Eventually, there was the phrase *my crime.*

It's been a year since my crime.

The doctors ask me about my crime.

My life changed because of my crime.

But at his trial, all the details emerged. We saw the story—the story of "my crime"—each piece building on the next.

I don't know how often Tim thought about these details, about what I imagined would coalesce into memories. I had used code to try to figure out how these memories affected him—*Are you sleeping okay, are you having a hard time during groups?* Once, he told me that he had trouble when it was quiet, right before he fell asleep, that it was then, lying in his bunk, that he felt that he was haunted—he used that word, *haunted*—by "my crime."

"I look like I'm okay," he told me, "but I can't express what's inside."

And I should have recognized him then. I had been this way too. Of course I had.

By endurance we conquer.

This tactic had failed me too—my unconscious exploring fears in nightmares because my waking body couldn't, my drunk body sobbing because my sober body couldn't.

Yet here I was, trying to get Tim to do the work I had refused. I was trying to make him *remember, remember, remember,* when I also worked in avoidance, in diversion.

I had started, slowly, to realize how worn away these tactics had left me, how I'd tried to stay tethered to Tim, to our shared family, but hadn't held all the pieces of what had actually happened. I had so rarely weighed the actual story, had barely broached my history with anyone who didn't already know me. I chose to keep that burden sealed, secret, too terrified to drag it into the light.

But I was starting to believe that looking at the story might, somehow, let me make sense out of the senseless. At first, this wish, *to make sense out of the senseless*, felt fleeting, like a fantasy. But through reconstruction, through careful assembly, I could examine all the pieces that had left me terrified. I could hope for a new way forward.

I could start to believe that the past would lose its power over me.

When I saw Tim, this first time after his trial, there was a solemnity to our hug. I kept my hands over his shoulder blades for a bit longer, felt the reality of him, the same Tim I had seen writhe in the police car during the trial.

Destroy me.

When we sat together, shins pressed against the familiar table, we were quiet, both, I think, realizing that this visit would be different, that we would have to account for what we had seen at the trial.

"That must have been hard," I started. "It must have been hard to see all that in court."

"It's strange," Tim said. "I'm not sure what I remember because I actually remember it, or if I only remember because I saw it in court."

"I had no idea they had that video of you."

"I said a lot of crazy stuff."

I asked him what he meant by *crazy stuff*.

"I called the police officer 'Dad'," Tim said. "I said I wished he was Dad."

That part of the recording was not one that I remembered. I hadn't yet read the transcript, the record of all the *crazy stuff*.

"I cried during the video," I said. "I cried when you were crying."

I didn't realize how *I cried when you were crying* was ambiguous—when Tim in court cried, when Tim on the screen cried? But this distinction didn't matter. All three of us—Tim, Tim on the screen, me—cried at the same time.

I watched Tim's eyes narrow, clench. I didn't know if he was cringing or about to cry.

"It was only like five or ten minutes," Tim said. "There wasn't much time before they came home."

There wasn't much time. This was the first detail I heard from Tim.

"You let them walk in," I said, not thinking, reacting, stopping just short of saying, *Why didn't you attack them too?*

"They were almost in time," Tim said.

"What do you think would have happened?"

"Maybe," Tim said, "she would still be alive."

I said nothing then. I said nothing and let us sit with the reality of the conversation we had started, sixteen months after our mother's death.

"You know I would do anything," Tim said, "to change what happened."

This was the first time Tim used these words. Before this visit, he had said, *I think everything that happened had to happen.* He had said, *I was prideful. God punishes people for their pride.*

"I don't hold you responsible," I said. "You know I don't, right?"

But Tim looked away, toward the table separating us. His head stayed down when he spoke again. If I hadn't been leaning forward, I don't think I would have heard him.

"When you found out what I had done," Tim said, "were you surprised?"

"No," I said.

I saw him crumple, sink into his sweatshirt, chin tuck in to his chest. I wanted to take my *no* away.

"But what I mean, what I mean is that . . ."

But I couldn't explain my *no* away. I couldn't erase *no* because it was the truth.

But this was also an opportunity, a chance for something new. I had never told him where I was when our father called, when I heard, *No. Tim killed Mom.*

And I had never told him about what I remembered, about the weeks before her death, about the way I watched his illness spiral out of control.

So I told him. I told him for the first time what I had started to remember.

"Do you remember that I was in the Dominican Republic?" I said. "That I was working at that summer camp?"

Tim nodded.

"Do you remember the night before I left? You woke me up. You banged on my door."

"I kicked it," Tim said.

Not his fist. Not his fist. My memories were starting to change.

"It wasn't locked," I said.

I told him how I had been terrified. How I had left my room, how I had seen our mother in the hallway, how I had knocked on his sealed door.

"I asked if it was you," I said. "You told me to go back to sleep."

"I remember," Tim said.

I told him about the next morning, how I had fled the house, said goodbye to our mother in the driveway, drove away from home until fear overwhelmed me. I told him that I called our mother.

"It was the first time I thought you could be violent," I said. "It was the first time I thought you might hurt someone who wasn't you."

And I explained this, how until then my fear had been a death by suicide, a fear that had echoed for many years.

I told him about how I had ranted to our mother, pleaded with her—*he might become violent, he might turn against you.*

"Then," I told Tim, "she convinced me that I was wrong."

"What do you think she believed?" Tim said.

"I'm not sure. But I know she was afraid to leave you alone."

Tim was quiet then.

I told him where I was when I got the phone call.

"I was reading a Spanish version of *Oh, the Places You'll Go!*"

I told him how I heard our father's voice crackling over the phone, how I had to walk outside to hear him, how the call was dropped.

No. Tim killed Mom.

"I was in shock," I said. "But I wasn't surprised."

But I knew then, sitting across from him, that while I had sobbed and retched in the Dominican Republic, Tim was a thousand miles away, writhing in the back of a police car.

I hope she isn't dead. I really hope she isn't dead.

We had sobbed at the same time.

"Do you remember," Tim said, "when the prosecutor asked the police where they found Dunkin and Pepper?"

Dunkin and Pepper were our dogs.

"Yes," I said. "I remember."

"I didn't put them in the kitchen until after," Tim said.

Until after. Until after.

"I found them in the bathroom. They were hiding."

I looked at Tim. I saw him remembering for the first time.

"They looked so scared," Tim said.

EPILOGUE

Just before Tim's trial, I moved away from Boston, left Chris and Lizzie. I tried to remain in their lives, but know that distance worked against me, that the two of them held each other up in my absence.

Chris rose through the ranks at his e-commerce company, managed different categories of goods. He's been cited as an "expert in backyard recreation equipment" in several newspapers. For years after I moved away, he lived a mile from Lizzie, until recently leaving Boston for business school.

Lizzie worked in preschools and first-grade classrooms, then started a graduate degree. Now she's a licensed social worker, and many benefit from her empathy. She's also raised a yellow Lab, named her Pilot—Pilot, after Mr. Rochester's dog in *Jane Eyre*.

Chris and Lizzie both speak to Tim now. Though those relationships are their own, I know Tim is grateful to have them back in his life.

Our father remains at home, surrounded by memories, but he's helped teach me that these reminders are far more than just signposts on the way to tragedy. He's helped me remember, *Vince, there was a happy life here too.*

I don't see Tim as often as I used to. I live farther away now, farther from home. But when I make it back, I try to see him, walk across the familiar parking lot, sit in the same waiting room.

I want to say that Tim's treatment has been seamless. I want to say that progress is linear, a steady ascent.

In the years since his trial, Tim has lobbied to go off his medication twice. On both occasions he was allowed to stop the injections. On both occasions a judge ruled that he was not, at that moment, a danger to himself or others.

Tim tells me that he hates the medication's side effects. I believe him. I believe that some of the antipsychotics have held him down, left him exhausted, heavy with extra weight.

I've visited Tim in the months when he was off medication, recognized his pressured thoughts after his disease shakes free of its shackles.

I don't have schizophrenia, he's told me. *Look, look, here's ten pages of calculus. There's nothing wrong with my mind.*

These visits were painful. When I heard the disease rehash old delusions, I imagined Tim embalmed at Whiting, how I might return to this same visiting room for the rest of my life.

But these were temporary terrors. I learned not to implode when his illness lashed out. I learned to look at Tim's struggle as a longer story, a battle not easily won. I have a new kind of hope now, not clear-eyed naïve hope, but a hope born from small moments—when Tim tells me about playing chess with a new friend, when Tim tells me about exchanging letters with one of his old professors.

And I have bigger reasons for hope. Tim hasn't stayed off medication. After both hiatuses, clinicians convinced him to return. He's learned, I believe, that the only path through Whiting, the only path to an afterward, is to demonstrate insight, prove to the psychiatric review board that he understands that he has a terrible disease.

He's been medicated—voluntarily now—for nearly three years, his longest period yet.

I don't know if his decision to take medication is pragmatism or true insight. I don't know that his anosognosia has been defeated, that this neurological defect can be easily blunted, a sword beaten into a plowshare.

But he speaks differently now.

"Mom would want this," Tim once told me. "She would want me to get the shots, to get the treatment, to take responsibility."

I keep no secrets from Tim. He knows that I write about him, that I write about how he's struggled with an illness too slippery for him to hold. He's told me to write the story "as you see fit." He's told me, "Write whatever you want about me."

Once, when we were talking about my writing, he said, "Just promise me you aren't going to make me look more guilty than I already look."

"That's the last thing I want," I told him.

But of course this is complicated, my greatest challenge. To show you the terror of his disease, I've had to show you the horror it wrought.

And I explain this to Tim, why I have to tell the whole story. I tell him, like I've told him so many times.

You know I don't hold you responsible. You know that, right?

One May, nearly three years since our mother's death, Tim told me that some of the men in his unit had written Mother's Day letters.

"Was that hard?" I asked.

"My counselor said that I could write one too," Tim said.

"What are you going to write to Mom?"

"I'm going to start with what I'm thankful for," Tim said. "I'm thankful for you and Dad visiting, for people writing me letters, for my new counselor."

Tim had started working with this counselor on a journal. To help him out, she had given him an emotions wheel—*APPREHENSION, TERROR, JOY, SADNESS* printed among others on a circular spectrum.

"What else?"

"I'm going to tell Mom that she deserved a better son."

I wanted to take that sadness from him, his belief that it was simply a question of him being a better son.

But I stopped myself, didn't leap to blunt his pain, remind him that he had been captive, under forces beyond his control.

Real sadness can pass between us now. Tim wanted to speak to our mother through his letter, a wish we can share.

Mom, there's so much we want to tell you.

We have these moments, moments when we can share her.

Remember when she found out we canoed across the bay?

Remember how she traveled to watch you wrestle?

Remember how she held your tail?

We can also see her during those last months, see her living, see without remembering only her last day.

Remember how she played the piano, that one song, that same song?

Remember the notes she passed under your door?

These conversations are difficult, halting. Both of us struggle. But we're learning, Tim and I, to remember together, to look without blinking, without stopping each other from seeing her there.

Now, I see her more clearly too. She has returned to me, when I remember, when I dream.

Yes, she visits me there now, in dreams. Sometimes, when I wake up, I'm thinking about her, but I can't tell if I'm remembering her or remembering a dream.

But I can find her when I'm awake. I can remember her in scenes that I choose.

I'm eight years old. Chris, Tim, and Lizzie are three, and my mother is afraid I feel lost in their shuffle. She's afraid I'm feeling less loved.

She invents a game. She calls the game Getting Lost. To play the game, I sit next to her in her minivan. She pulls out of the driveway and we leave our familiar neighborhood. When we get to Orange Center Road, she stops, looks at me, hazel eyes narrowing behind her glasses, cheeks lifting while she smiles.

"Which way, Vince?"

I point. As we drive, as we approach intersections, I pick out the familiar names—Lambert Road, Old Tavern Road, Meetinghouse Lane. I point and tell my mother which way to turn.

We drive until she sees me hesitate, sees me struggle to find land-marks. She stops the car.

"Looks like we're lost," she says. Her hands are on the steering wheel. She looks at me, alone with her, the two of us lost together.

"Time to find our way back," she says.

I laugh. This is my favorite part of the game.

As the car starts to move, I look at her, look at how she feigns confusion, squints through the windshield, asks me at every turn, "Vince, are you sure?"

We played that game whenever we could get away. We played Getting Lost so often that eventually we had to drive deep into neighboring towns to lose our bearings.

We played that game for as long as we could, turning, searching, until we found our familiar driveway, the only way, home.

ACKNOWLEDGMENTS

While writing this book, I was immeasurably lucky to have the support of many. Even in the most difficult moments, I knew I was never alone.

First, Lizzie. Liz, you've loved me more than I could ever ask for. You are the strongest, bravest, most beautiful person I know.

Chris, you've been our rock, cared for all of us, and shown me how to live after tragedy. I'm proud to be your brother every day.

Dad, thank you for your love and guidance. Your faith in me has helped push me forward for thirty-three years.

I wrote a large portion of this book during my three years as a student at American University's MFA program. I cannot imagine a better community for completing this work.

Thank you to AU's creative writing faculty, especially my phenomenal advisor, Rachel Louise Snyder. Rachel, thank you for all your wisdom, for your steady hand in helping me shape this book, and for pushing me to deepen my voice.

While living in Washington, DC, I was lucky to have many writers by my side. I'm thankful for all of you:

For David Keplinger, for your friendship and support. You are as selfless as anyone I've ever met.

For Emily Moses. Emily, thank you for sitting next to me during that first bus ride to campus and on all the rides that followed. You were the first person I trusted with this project. I'm forever grateful for your insight, care, and friendship.

For my DC writing group: Matt Bukowski, Yohanca Delgado, Lauren Johnson, Karen Keating, Karan Madhok, and Bron Treanor. Thank you all for making lonely work feel a lot less lonely.

And for the late Henry Morgenthau III. For several years, I worked for Henry, an amazing man who published a collection of poetry at ninety-nine. Though seven decades separated us, Henry became a great friend. I miss him very much.

While writing this book, I was incredibly lucky to benefit from the support of a number of artist residencies and foundations. Many thanks to all these heroic organizations: the New York State Summer Writers' Institute, Ucross Foundation, I-Park Foundation, Brush Creek Foundation for the Arts, Virginia Center for the Creative Arts, Bread Loaf Writers' Conference, PLAYA, and MacDowell.

Thanks to Jim Miller, David Treuer, and Angela Pelster, and the workshops they led at the New York State Summer Writers' Institute, and the Bread Loaf Writers' Conference.

Thank you to Alex McElroy for a timely and affirming read of the most difficult section of this book. Your generous help and friendship gave me the confidence I needed to push this manuscript into the world.

Thank you to De'Shawn Charles Winslow. De'Shawn, you sent an email that changed my life, that led me to Chris Clemans, my incredible agent.

Chris, your boundless support and belief in this project made you the perfect champion for this book. I'm beyond lucky to work with you. Thank you.

And thank you to my editor, Peter Borland. Peter, it was clear from the beginning that you understood the heart of this book. I will always be grateful for your close attention and expertise. Many thanks as well to Sean Delone, and the entire team at Atria for their diligence and care.

While I leaned on many experts to learn about schizophrenia, I'm most in debt to Dr. E. Fuller Torrey, Dr. Xavier Amador, and the work of the Treatment Advocacy Center.

Thank you to "Dr. Franklin." For nearly six years, you've listened while I've unraveled knots that seemed impossibly tight. I'm grateful for all you've helped me discover.

For reasons I'll never understand, I've been lucky to have more close friends than I could possibly deserve. While some of you appear in this book, many of you do not. I love you all and will always be grateful for how you've helped hold me up.

I don't know how I would have written this book without Richard McCann. Richard, you showed me that there was something I could do with my loss and pain. Your fingerprints are all over these pages. Your voice is with me whenever I write.

Tim. You've suffered so much already. Your support of my writing and your faith in me is a towering act of love. You are and will be so much more than the tragedy that incited this book. I love you.

And Mom. You read the first words I ever wrote. You were the only one, for years, who knew how badly I wanted to be a writer. I want to tell you how this feels, how a dream has emerged from a nightmare. There's so much I want to tell you.